W9-BFW-281

ESCAPING EDEN

ESCAPING EDEN

New Feminist Perspectives on the Bible

Edited by

Harold C. Washington,
Susan Lochrie Graham and
Pamela Thimmes

BS
521.4
.E73
1999

NEW YORK UNIVERSITY PRESS
Washington Square, New York

Regis College Library
15 ST. MARY STREET
TORONTO, ONTARIO, CANADA
M4Y 2R5

First published in the U.S.A. by
NEW YORK UNIVERSITY PRESS
Washington Square, NY 10003

© 1999 by Sheffield Academic Press
All rights reserved

CIP data available from the Library of Congress
ISBN 1-8147-9352-5 (clothbound)
ISBN 1-8147-9353-3 (paperbound)

Printed in the UK

CONTENTS

Abbreviations 9

List of Contributors 11

Introduction 13

I
INTERPRETATIONS: FEMINIST READINGS OF BIBLICAL TEXTS

LYN M. BECHTEL
Boundary Issues in Genesis 19.1-38 22

CAROLYN PRESSLER
The *Shema'*: A Protestant Feminist Reading 41

JOSEPH VLCEK KOZAR
Reading the Opening Chapter of Luke from a Feminist
Perspective 53

JUDITH K. APPLEGATE
'And she wet his feet with her tears':
A Feminist Interpretation of Luke 7.36-50 69

TERESA J. HORNSBY
Why Is She Crying? A Feminist Interpretation of Luke 7.36-50 91

JEAN K. KIM
An Asian Interpretation of Philippians 2.6-11 104

II
INTERROGATIONS: METHODOLOGICAL ESSAYS

PHYLLIS A. BIRD
What Makes a Feminist Reading Feminist? A Qualified Answer 124

PAMELA THIMMES
What Makes a Feminist Reading Feminist? Another Perspective   132

MARY ANN TOLBERT
Reading the Bible with Authority: Feminist Interrogation
of the Canon   141

TINA PIPPIN
Translation Happens: A Feminist Perspective on Translation
Theories   163

BURTON H. THROCKMORTON, JR
Why *The New Testament and Psalms: An Inclusive Version*?   177

SUSANNE SCHOLZ
Was it Really Rape in Genesis 34? Biblical Scholarship
as a Reflection of Cultural Assumptions   182

ANGELA BAUER
Jeremiah as Female Impersonator: Roles of Difference
in Gender Perception and Gender Perceptivity   199

LUISE SCHOTTROFF
A Feminist Hermeneutic of 1 Corinthians   208

III

INNOVATIONS: EXPANDING THE BOUNDARIES
OF BIBLICAL SCHOLARSHIP

MARGARET D. ADAM
This Is *My* Story, This Is *My* Song... :
A Feminist Claim on Scripture, Ideology and Interpretation   218

J.A. CRAIG EDWARDS
'Creative Reverence': A Womanist Hermeneutics of Imagination
in Maude Irwin Owens's 'Bathesda of Sinners Run'   233

SUSAN LOCHRIE GRAHAM
Patriarchy's Middle Managers: Another Handmaid's Tale   244

CHERYL A. KIRK-DUGGAN
What Difference Does Difference Make in Feminist
Hermeneutics? A Personal Essay   266

EPILOGUE
PAMELA THIMMES
Marking Boundaries Inside and Outside: The Ongoing Tasks
of Feminist Hermeneutics   279

Index of References   283
Index of Authors   287

ABBREVIATIONS

AB	Anchor Bible
ANRW	Hildegard Temporini and Wolfgang Haase (eds.), *Aufstieg und Niedergang der römischen Welt: Geschichte und Kultur Roms im Spiegel der neueren Forschung* (Berlin: W. de Gruyter, 1972–)
BBR	*Bulletin for Biblical Research*
BDB	Francis Brown, S.R. Driver and Charles A. Briggs, *A Hebrew and English Lexicon of the Old Testament* (Oxford: Clarendon Press, 1907)
BibInt	*Biblical Interpretation: A Journal of Contemporary Approaches*
BJS	Brown Judaic Studies
BST	Basel Studies of Theology
BTB	*Biblical Theology Bulletin*
BZAW	Beihefte zur *ZAW*
CBQ	*Catholic Biblical Quarterly*
CR	*Critical Review of Books in Religion*
EAJT	*East Asia Journal of Theology*
HAT	Handbuch zum Alten Testament
HTR	*Harvard Theological Review*
ICC	International Critical Commentary
IDB	George Arthur Buttrick (ed.), *The Interpreter's Dictionary of the Bible* (4 vols.; Nashville: Abingdon Press, 1962)
Int	*Interpretation*
ITC	International Theological Commentary
JBL	*Journal of Biblical Literature*
JR	*Journal of Religion*
JSNT	*Journal for the Study of the New Testament*
JSOT	*Journal for the Study of the Old Testament*
JSOTSup	*Journal for the Study of the Old Testament*, Supplement Series
JTC	*Journal for Theology and the Church*
KAT	Kommentar zum Alten Testament
KEHAT	O.F. Fridelin (ed.), *Kurzgefasstes exegetisches Handbuch zum Alten Testament* (Leipzig: S. Hirzel, 1812–96)
KHAT	Kurzer Hand-Kommentar zum Alten Testament
NICOT	New International Commentary on the Old Testament
NTS	*New Testament Studies*
OBT	Overtures to Biblical Theology

OTL	Old Testament Library
SBL	Society of Biblical Literature
SBLDS	SBL Dissertation Series
SBLMS	SBL Monograph Series
SLJT	*Saint Luke's Journal of Theology*
SNTSMS	Society for New Testament Studies Monograph Series
TDNT	Gerhard Kittel and Gerhard Friedrich (eds.), *Theological Dictionary of the New Testament* (trans. Geoffrey W. Bromiley; 10 vols.; Grand Rapids: Eerdmans, 1964–)
TDOT	G.J. Botterweck and H. Ringgren (eds.), *Theological Dictionary of the Old Testament*
THAT	Ernst Jenni and Claus Westermann (eds.), *Theologisches Handwörterbuch zum Alten Testament* (Munich: Chr. Kaiser Verlag, 1971–76)
VT	*Vetus Testamentum*
WTJ	*Westminster Theological Journal*

CONTRIBUTORS

MARGARET B. ADAM is an independent scholar living in Princeton, NJ.

JUDITH K. APPLEGATE is an independent scholar living in Seattle, Washington.

ANGELA BAUER is Assistant Professor of Hebrew Bible, Episcopal Divinity School.

LYN M. BECHTEL is Visiting Associate Professor of Hebrew Bible, Drew Theological School.

PHYLLIS A. BIRD is Associate Professor of Old Testament Interpretation, Garrett-Evangelical Theological Seminary.

J.A. CRAIG EDWARDS is Assistant Professor of American Literature, Bartlesville Wesleyan College.

SUSAN LOCHRIE GRAHAM is Staff Tutor at the South West Ministry Training Course and part-time Lecturer in Theology for the Department of Continuing Adult Education, University of Exeter.

TERESA J. HORNSBY is a Doctoral Candidate in New Testament at Vanderbilt University.

JEAN K. KIM is a Doctoral Candidate in New Testament at Vanderbilt University.

CHERYL A. KIRK-DUGGAN is Director, Center for Women and Religion and Assistant Professor of Theology and Womanist Studies, Graduate Theological Union.

JOSEPH VLCEK KOZAR is Assistant Professor of Religious Studies, University of Dayton.

TINA PIPPIN is Associate Professor of Religious Studies, Agnes Scott College.

CAROLYN PRESSLER is Professor of Older Testament, United Theological Seminary of the Twin Cities.

SUSANNE SCHOLZ is Assistant Professor of Religious Studies, The College of Wooster, Ohio.

LUISE SCHOTTROFF is Professor of New Testament, University of Kassel.

PAMELA THIMMES is Assistant Professor of Religious Studies, University of Dayton.

BURTON H. THROCKMORTON, JR, is Hayes Professor of New Testament, Emeritus, Bangor Theological Seminary.

MARY ANN TOLBERT is the George H. Atkinson Professor of Biblical Studies, Pacific School of Religion.

HAROLD C. WASHINGTON is Associate Professor of Hebrew Bible, Saint Paul School of Theology.

INTRODUCTION

Susan Lochrie Graham and Harold C. Washington

In recent decades, feminist interpretation has brought about a revolution in biblical scholarship. No longer at the margins of the biblical disciplines, feminist criticism today poses questions that the field of biblical studies cannot ignore. This volume is the outcome of the research of the feminist theological hermeneutics group of the Society of Biblical Literature. Our aim in the SBL Group has been to provide a forum for research in feminist hermeneutics, combining feminist treatments of biblical texts with sustained methodological inquiry. The reader will notice that no single definition of the term 'feminist' governs this collection. Indeed, prevailing definitions of feminism are among the boundaries that we seek to mark, to test and in some instances to transgress in this volume. The contributors are clear in their own commitments to feminism and diverse in their pursuit of gender-critical concerns. Recognizing that interpretation is always done from a particular point of view and for particular interests, the authors of the following essays explore the meanings and effects of their own social positions as feminist biblical scholars. Consequently they give critical attention to other aspects of social location in addition to gender, such as ethnicity and national origin, social and economic class, cultural and religious background.

The designation 'theological' applies to these essays in equally diverse ways. Some of the authors are biblical theologians; many, but not all, pursue their scholarship in the service of religious communities. Out of the varied contexts that shape their work, the contributors share ethical concern for the social consequences of biblical interpretation, both within faith communities and in broader cultural contexts. Motivated by this concern, the contributors often challenge the presumed objectivity to which so much conventional historical and literary biblical criticism still pretends. This collection therefore problematizes the boundary in the scholarly guild between descriptive and prescriptive readings of biblical texts. We have arranged the book into three sections containing first, feminist inter-pretations of biblical texts; second, feminist methodological inquiries; and third, feminist essays that attempt to expand the boundaries of conventional academic discourse.

Part I, 'Interpretations: Feminist Readings of Biblical Texts', begins with an essay by Lyn Bechtel that explores boundary issues of com-munity, gender and sexuality in the narrative of Genesis 19. Homo-sexual practice is not the central issue here, Bechtel maintains, nor does she focus on the widely observed issue of 'hospitality toward men taking precedence over the protection of women'. Ambiguities such as the uncertain identity of the messengers, Lot's marginal status as a sojourner, and the unclear motives of the townsmen of Sodom, govern Bechtel's reading. Rather than offering a simplistic moral lesson, the narrative raises complex questions of ethical discernment: how do diverse members of a community, faced with uncertain threats from the outside, respond to the unexplained appearance of strangers at their gate?

In the second essay, Carolyn Pressler offers a Protestant feminist reading of the *Shema'* (Deut. 6.4-5), focusing on this key text's significance within the context of the book of Deuteronomy. Pressler notes that feminist scholars have criticized models of divine sovereignty that emphasize power as domination. Yet, she observes, the Deuteronomic conception of a uniquely sovereign God can serve to challenge hierarchical structures of domination within believing communities. Pressler urges caution in embracing Deuteronomy's call for absolute loyalty. The Deuteronomic 'oneness and effective power of God' can ground feminist hope for wholeness and freedom, but Deuteronomy's intolerance of dissent and its hostility toward those outside the covenant community pose ethical problems.

There follows a group of feminist readings of Lukan texts. Joseph Kozar reads the opening chapter of Luke's Gospel with emphasis on the characters of Elizabeth and Mary. Kozar notes repeatedly how the conventional commentators overlook elements of the text disclosed by his feminist critical interest. Elizabeth and Mary, while never fully transcending the patriarchal context in which they are portrayed, are nonetheless vivid models of faith and strength. For Kozar, a feminist reading of Luke ch. 1 needs both to celebrate the importance of its female characters and to resist the overarching patriarchal structures to which they are subjected.

Luke 7.36-50, the account of the 'sinful woman' who anoints Jesus in the house of a Pharisee, is the subject of the next two studies. Judith Applegate analyses three elements of the woman's interaction with Jesus: 'her transformation from the status of a sinner to one who has been forgiven, her role as a prostitute, and her capacity as servant'. Each of these three aspects of the woman's portrayal is shown by Applegate to have empowering as well as oppressive dimensions. Teresa Hornsby, on the other hand, challenges the dominant understanding of the 'sinful woman' as a prostitute. The critical consensus, she argues, relegates the woman to 'deviant' status because her physicality can only be seen as negative. But Hornsby rejects such a misogynist and erotophobic perspective, insisting that the anointing woman's sensuality discloses her as 'someone who understands that physicality may be the ultimate display of love and that passion may be given as a gift of God'.

Part I concludes with Jean K. Kim's interpretation of Phil. 2.6-11 from an Asian feminist Christian perspective. Jesus' lordship in this christological hymn, Kim argues, has been used to legitimate Western imperialism and patriarchal authority. Meanwhile, the 'image of Jesus as suffering slave has been imposed upon women to persuade them to accept their suffering'. Kim traces the history of the tradition to demonstrate the contingency and political motivations of the pre-existent Christology of Philippians 2. 'The irony of Christianity', she notes, 'is that what started as an anti-imperial movement became the imperial religion.' Reappropriating Phil. 2.6-11 in conversation with the Asian conceptions of *yin/yang* and the Korean heritage of *Dong-hak* thought (the precursor to Minjung theology), Kim's reading aims to free believers in Christ from oppressive self-identifications, liberating them to become transforming agents for the well-being of all creation.

We began this volume with a series of readings, exegetical exercises that demonstrate the variety of interpretative possibilities grouped under the feminist theological banner. It is a diverse group that gathers there, and their differences point to the ways in which feminist interpretation is culturally situated. We interpret our texts from our perspectives, and even when the texts are the 'same', they are different. But this observation is merely the first step in feminist analysis:

we constitute the field, as it were, drawing the boundaries and admiring the lilies that are growing here and there. Yet the differences lead us to take another step, this time backwards, to distance ourselves and to look for patterns.

Part II: 'Interrogations: Methodological Essays' is a collection of papers from panel discussions in which the contributors were asked to reflect on their critical activity. By what process do certain interpretations gain authority? What makes interpretations specifically feminist? What is the role of cultural assumptions about gender? How can translation be a feminist act? As with our interpretations, so with our theoretical reflections: a variety of voices reflects a variety of perspectives. Yet beyond this democratic impulse lurks a very political awareness: the voices that are heard here are often silenced, marginalized in academic discourse which still privileges the past over the present; the 'original meaning' or 'authorial intent' over the contemporary effect; the 'objective' over the 'personal'; and so on. Some of these writers have already had distinguished careers, some are just beginning; some struggle to find a place in the academy from which to write. Some write from a North American perspective; others from the very different world of German academic theology. But all, in one way or another, reflect on the necessity for reading differently, for opening up theological hermeneutics in ways that both admit contemporary cultural considerations and allow for, and even celebrate, diversity.

In two responses to the same theme which took place in 1993, Phyllis Bird and Pamela Thimmes take up the 'essential' debate over how best to characterize 'feminist' readings. For Bird, while feminism claims equality based on a gender-inclusive view of human nature, as a political movement it looks for structural changes which will benefit all people. Interpretations which work toward that goal are 'feminist', but Bird cautions us against a universal idea of feminism, one which is not grounded in specific social and political situations. The biblical text may not speak with a feminist voice, but Bird reminds us that readers have an obligation to try to enter into conversation and to listen to the 'distinct voice' of the text. She recognizes the importance of the question of authority, even as it may test the limits of feminist critiques of the biblical text.

Pamela Thimmes, on the other hand, describes a hermeneutical circle with four 'arcs'. One, and the most important, is an understanding of feminism as both a political movement and as a category of analysis which enables the critique of 'the oppressive structures of society'. But along with this, a feminist reading takes into consideration experience, cultural location and the problem of language. Experience is not something we 'have' but something that creates our subjectivity, as does 'culture'; all are constructions of language. Seen from a postmodern perspective, 'feminism' as a concept threatens to deconstruct, leaving actual feminists with no base for political action. Recognizing the 'methodological minefield' she must negotiate, Thimmes nonetheless argues for gender as a category of analysis and resistance as a praxis, both the category and the praxis energized by the 'life-force' of diversity.

The debate reflected in these two articles is still open, as it is on the questions raised by Mary Ann Tolbert. Tolbert explores the canon and raises the question of biblical authority, one with which feminist writers continue to struggle. From a 'disruptive' ideological stance that calls for a new social order rather than more egalitarian participation in present structures, she argues that doctrines of biblical authority 'serve primarily as masks for human drives to power', particularly in conservative Protestant circles. Interpretations rooted in the search for authorial intent continue to thrive as sources for the authority of both academic and ecclesial interpreters. Tolbert wonders whose interests such a situation serves. How are the limits of 'plausible' readings set and enforced? Finally, how might feminist and liberationist readers best challenge and change the rules of the game? And while this essay was first presented nearly a decade ago, it is sobering to realize that the questions and some of the arguments are with us still.

More recently, feminist theory has begun to look at questions of translation. The issue of inclusive language is not new, but we are far from reaching any conclusions. Tina Pippin explores the theoretical issues raised in translating the Bible. Given the fact of language, 'Translation Happens', inevitably, and her discussion alerts us to both the dangers and the possibilities. Postmodern theory has taught us to ask new questions about translation and translators, to explore 'the ideological grounding of how and why translation occurs'. Criticizing Walter Benjamin's notion of 'transparent translation', she raises the possibility of translation that is, in Carol Jacob's words, 'rehearing, retelling, rediscerning the Bible in highly (and proudly) subjective ways'. Such translation returns us to our earlier discussion of authority, especially the notion of a biblical 'authority' which is undermined by the ethical commitment to resist oppression and to work for change. 'You must translate as if your life depends on it,' she concludes, and indeed for her, it does.

Burton H. Throckmorton, Jr, who participated in the translation of *The New Testament and Psalms: An Inclusive Version*, discusses the decisions made concerning inclusive language. The translation caused a 'hullabaloo', as he puts it, and he is concerned in this essay with the reasons for that. He raises the theoretical issue of how literally it is possible to translate any text. Idiomatic expressions point up the difficulty at the level of the words of the text, but a more difficult problem is accurately translating meaning in different cultural contexts. He concludes with a discussion of the language used for God, arguing that since 'it is our God-language that validates our language about each other' only when it becomes possible to use inclusive language for God will there be changes in our androcentric culture.

Our interrogations then continue with other questions, related more closely to specific biblical texts. Susanne Scholz, in her analysis of readings of Genesis 34, the rape of Dinah, casts a critical eye on cultural assumptions reflected in biblical scholarship. Taking the position that reading is always a culturally situated act, she examines contemporary critical attitudes toward rape. Focusing on the act of rape rather than other elements in the biblical story, Scholz states, often 'evokes fear and fury' in the reader-critic, but it reveals and confronts 'the extent of rape-supportive scholarship and culture'. Critics often attempt to excuse the sexual violence of the text by appealing to various factors which might mitigate our understanding. Scholz calls into question the social and ethical values inherent in such scholarship.

Gender as a critical category is next interrogated by Angela Bauer in her article 'Jeremiah as Female Impersonator'. Acknowledging that gender is socially constructed, she points out that the gender constructions of Jeremiah's time were different from ours, 2500 years later. It is this 'banal observation' that leads her to examine the very complex problems of gendered readings. How do the constructions of twentieth-century gender shape our reading, and how does our reading shape our contemporary constructions of gender? Bauer reads two texts in light of these concerns: the first (Jer. 4.19-21), in which the prophet 'impersonates' a woman in labor, and the second (Jer. 20.7), which portrays the prophet as a woman who has been raped. Constructing a prophetic persona using these female images of childbirth and sexual violence, Bauer argues, 'constitutes a subversion of gender dualisms' which may enable future 'gender-fluid' readings.

The section then concludes with Luise Schottroff's essay, which raises the importance of rhetorical criticism in feminist hermeneutics. Interrogating the methods of her own commentary on 1 Corinthians, in this essay she focuses on the relationship between Paul and the Corinthian community. She argues that early Christian communities attempted to create dominance-free social structures, in which Paul's voice is just one among many. She contends that the view of absolute Pauline authority is later, and that Paul himself uses all the rhetorical tools at his disposal to fight for his own interpretations of Torah. Schottroff calls for a new and different reading of Pauline texts, a critical project that she recognizes is 'only at its beginning'.

Feminist writing has often experimented with other forms and styles, although rarely in biblical studies or theology. But the cultural awareness demonstrated in the theoretical essays here leads, as we have seen, to ethical questions, and the third section of the book, 'Innovations: Expanding the Boundaries of Biblical Scholarship', raises these questions in a variety of ways.

In 'This is *My* Story', Margaret B. Adam argues passionately for a feminist appropriation of the Bible in its entirety: 'texts don't have ideologies', she states, people do. She argues that the recognition that the locus of meaning lies outside the text can be a powerful tool for feminist readers. Thus we as readers are responsible for the oppressive patriarchal interpretations we find 'in' the text. And if that is the case, we can resist them. If the biblical text is to remain 'our story', then we must recognize that it is 'our' reading that counts. The authority for our interpretations lies in the various reading communities to which we are committed. She denies the necessity, often found in feminist biblical scholarship, to create a canon within the canon, and gives herself the freedom to postpone interpretation. Revelation is an ongoing process, and those texts which today may seem irremediably damaging to women may tomorrow be revealed in new and life-giving ways.

J.A. Craig Edwards reflects on new ways in which the Bible as the 'Talking Book' might be made to speak again. Noting that Elisabeth

Schüssler Fiorenza had called for a fourfold liberationist strategy of interpretation including a 'hermeneutics of imagination', he argues that black women have developed such a revisionist method for reading the Bible which incorporates Cheryl Townsend Gilkes's concept of 'creative reverence'. He analyzes Maude Irwin Owens's short story 'Bathesda of Sinners Run' as a 'brilliantly engendered and racialized example' of this hermeneutic.

The technical limitations and the ideological implications of historical criticism are exposed in Susan Lochrie Graham's satirical story, 'Patriarchy's Middle Managers', which uses fiction to suggest that all historical writing is both culturally bound and in some sense fictional. Like its best-known intertext, Margaret Atwood's *The Handmaid's Tale*, this story ends with another story, that of its interpretation. But the misinterpretation reminds us also that all our interpretations are misreadings, creative perhaps, but inevitable in a world in which 'truth' is elusive.

Cheryl Kirk-Duggan's 'personal essay' closes this section, with a response to the question of difference, an interrogation that is at the same time an innovation. In response to the question 'What difference does difference make?' she responds differently. Not, or not just, as a womanist biblical scholar working within an academic context, but as a reader and writer who is aware of her many different contexts and who attempts to give them voice. This essay is not a dialogue but a multifaceted conversation including the voices of a woman of prayer, an athlete, a poet and musician and others, a feminist's voice, an academic's voice, a cultural critic's voice and a preacher's voice. Her/their essay responds to still other voices, focusing on the texts of Isaiah 50 and Phil. 2.6-11, once more raising the ethical question of the possibility of a liberating praxis.

The volume closes with an Epilogue written by one of the early members of the Group, Pamela Thimmes. Her own reflections on these articles, as well as on the story of the Group, provide another perspective on feminist theological hermeneutics. We began at a time when both feminism and hermeneutics were unusual topics in the academy. The SBL group began at a time when feminist hermeneutics was a marginal enterprise in the academy. The group has now been reconstituted for the longer term as the SBL feminist hermeneutics of the bible section, where the agenda set in this volume will be carried forward.

I

INTERPRETATIONS: FEMINIST READINGS OF BIBLICAL TEXTS

BOUNDARY ISSUES IN GENESIS 19.1-38

Lyn M. Bechtel

In the traditional interpretation of Gen. 19.1-11 the main issues are the practice of homosexuality[1] and hospitality toward men taking precedence over the protection of women.[2] Many exegetes assumed that homosexuality is the cause of the destruction of Sodom, despite the fact that none of the biblical references to Sodom's destruction mention homosexuality as the cause. The destruction is mentioned numerous times in the Hebrew Scriptures as an example of God's judgment, yet the crime that is associated with the judgment varies. In Isa. 1.10 the crime is social oppression; in Jer. 23.14 it is adultery, lying and criminality; and in Ezek. 16.49 it is pride, excess of food and prosperous ease (see Westermann 1984, after W. Zimmerli and E.A. Speiser). The assumption of homosexuality overlooks many important dimensions of the text, particularly the fact that if sexual activity had taken place, the central issue would have been *rape*. The potential rape of Lot's daughters is largely overlooked because the focus is on the men of the story. But when this story is read from a group-oriented perspective, where boundary issues are determinative, the interpretation of the text can shift significantly.

Because of the importance of boundary issues, it is essential to

---

1. Scholars who focus on condemnation of homosexuality: e.g. Alter 1986: 30-38; Brueggemann 1982; Carmichael 1979; Westermann 1984.

2. Scholars who focus on hospitality over protection of women: e.g. Lasine 1984: 37-59; Carmichael 1979: 55-56; Westermann 1984: 301; Coats 1985: 113-32. For a discussion of the connection of hospitality and righteousness, see Alexander 1985: 289-91. Others decry the fact that hospitality protects only males: e.g. Block 1990: 325-41; Trible 1984: 65-91. Other exegetes question Lot's character as a way of making sense of Lot's outrageous offer: e.g. Jeansonne 1988: 123-29; 1990: 31-42; Turner 1990: 86-101.

establish the position or status of the characters in the story, so that their function can be determined. First, there are two *mal'ākîm*. Many exegetes assume that the *mal'ākîm* are 'angels', spiritual beings sent from the divine world, who should be easily recognizable to righteous folks (e.g. Gaster 1962: 129; von Rad 1961: 217; Speiser 1964: 138)[3]. But the concept of an angel as a non-human representative from the divine world enters Israel's tradition in the Hellenistic period, so it would be inappropriate for the interpretation of this story, particularly since it adds a degree of Christian spirituality. In ancient Israel *mal'ākîm* are human messengers who may represent either a king or God. In 19.1 there is nothing to indicate that the messengers are anything more than ordinary human messengers and nothing to suggest specifically who has sent these messengers.

But there are a variety of clues as to the identity of these messengers imbedded in previous texts. In 14.1-16 there is a coalition of powerful kings who have made war against Sodom, plundered the town and taken Lot captive. If they are messengers of a king, they would be recognizable as such through their dress. This guarantees that they are recognized and treated with the honor and respect due the king. But since messengers are commonly sent as spies, these messengers could also be spies for the coalition of powerful kings in preparation for another attack. In light of the previous attack, the presence of the messengers could definitely raise concern in the town. Lot and the men of the town would be keenly aware of the grave danger they pose to the continued welfare and existence of the community.

To heighten the ambiguity concerning their identity, in ch. 18 there are three men ('*ᵃnāšîm*) who are associated with an announcement that God *may* destroy the city of Sodom *if* the outcry against its injustice is corroborated (18.16-33).[4] So the messengers could simultaneously be spies for God. But Lot and the townsmen are not aware of this development. Are the two messengers in 19.1 related to the three men in ch. 18? If so, why the change in number? Are messengers of a king also recognizable as messengers of God? Did Abraham honor and give them

3. In contrast, Brueggemann would rather call them 'strange men' (Brueggemann 1982: 162).

4. The major catastrophe that hits Sodom is assumed to be an earthquake and eruptions of petroleum gases underground (e.g. Speiser 1964: 142). The possibility of military destruction with accompanying burning is seldom considered, which is strange in light of the coalition of powerful kings.

hospitality because he recognized them as messengers of a king or messengers of God? The text gives no answers.

So the messengers are clearly outsiders, who in a group-oriented
society, would be perceived as threatening once they cross the boundary of a group by entering a city gate. In group-oriented societies clear-
cut group boundaries must be well articulated and highly valued
because they define the limits of the group. Boundaries are powerful
because they protect the group, but dangerous because they can be violated, threatening the existence of the group. To protect a close-knit
community from incursion by outsiders, boundaries and entrances must
be carefully guarded (see Barth 1969; Lifton 1967), and the categories
of insiders, outsiders and marginal figures carefully observed. Insiders
are generally considered good, contributing to the life of the group, and
outsiders are generally considered threatening, contributing to the dissemination and possibly destruction of the group. Likewise, there is
protection, cooperation and mutual assistance inside the group and
threat or possible death outside the group.

Will Lot and the townsmen simply assume these men are recognizable messengers of a powerful and threatening king? Even the audience
only suspects that they *may* also be spies for God who are testing the
behaviour of the people of Sodom. Consequently, if the potentially
threatening messengers are treated well, they will not be able to verify
the outcry of injustice against the city, and God may not destroy
Sodom. Yet if they are well treated, they may be able to spy for the
coalition, and the coalition may destroy Sodom. But if they are ill-
treated, God may destroy Sodom. Yet if they are ill-treated, they might
not be able to spy, which could save Sodom. The issue of the treatment
of potentially threatening messengers is extremely complex, ambiguous
and ambivalent! It will require a great deal of discernment.

In contrast to the outsiders, there are the insiders, the men of the
town. There are specific roles and clear boundaries related to insiders
and marginal people, roles and boundaries that have to be carefully
observed. It is stressed that the townsmen are mature adults; they are
described as na'ar (young adult males) and zāqēn (old adult males), so
the maturity of the group is emphasized. As mature adults they should
have the capacity to discern 'good and bad'—a capacity that the situation clearly calls for (see Bechtel 1993: 77-117; 1994b: 152-73; 1995:
3-26). As adult insiders, they have the legal right to 'judge' at the gate
for the 'good' of the community. But since their town has recently been

plundered and Lot and others taken captive (14.10-16), these townsmen are, no doubt, extremely cautious and defensive of their community, families and property.

Finally, there are the marginal people, Lot and his two daughters. Because of the inside/outside differentiation in group-oriented societies, status is extremely important. The closer to the center of the group people are, the more secure they are; the closer to the boundaries people are, the more marginal and threatened they are (see Barber 1957; Lenski 1984; Mead 1937; 1953). This means that sojourners, who are marginal in status, are less secure and more threatened. The text stresses that Lot and his family are sojourners; they are outsiders who are allowed to dwell and have full protection, but limited political rights within the town. Since Lot might be able to recognize the messengers from his captivity, the audience would expect Lot to react to the messengers with extreme caution and defensiveness.

How will the potentially threatening outsiders be treated by the insiders, who are responsible for the welfare of the community, who are mature enough to discern 'good and bad' and who have the political right to 'judge' for the community? How will their reaction differ from the treatment by the less secure marginal character, who is mature enough to discern 'good and bad, but does not have the political right to 'judge' for the 'good' of the community (see Rowlett 1992: 15-23)?

Hospitality (19.1-3)

(19.1) Two messengers (*mal'ākîm*) come to Sodom. Lot is sitting in the gate of Sodom. Lot sees, arises to greet them and bows down to them with his nose ('*ap*) to the ground ('*ārᵉṣâ*). (19.2) He says, 'Now, my lords ('*ᵃdōnay*), turn aside please to the house of your servant, spend the night, wash your feet and start going on your way early in the morning.' They say, 'No, for we will spend the night in the square'. (19.3) But he strongly urges/presses (*pṣr*) them, so they turn to him and come to his house. He prepares for them a meal (*mišteh*), bakes unleavened bread and they eat.[5]

---

5.   Some scholars condemn Lot for his inferior meal (e.g. Alter 1996: 85). They assume that baking unleavened bread makes the meal less desirable. But although unleavened breads are quicker, they are definitely not inferior! From the perspective of some people, Middle Eastern unleavened breads are far superior to many commercial, leavened breads. And Lot's meal (*mišteh*) is a substantial one (see Est. 5.6; Dan. 1.5; Jer. 16.8; Job 1.5; etc.; see Turner 1990: 92).

Lot's marginal status is stressed by the fact that the only place that Lot functions in the story is on boundaries: at the *entrance gate* of the city and at the *entrance* of his house. An entrance gate to the city is a point of danger because of incursion from outside, so it is a place where there is general awareness of who comes and goes. It is also the location of the judicial system, so it is where the community (the insiders) make judgments during the day. But being of marginal status, it is *not* Lot's place to judge, despite the fact that the situation clearly calls for careful discernment of very complex issues.

Because of his marginality Lot would normally be expected to be more open to interaction with outsiders. Yet since his position in the community is less secure and since he has already been taken captive by the kings that these messengers *may* represent, the audience would expect Lot to be resistant to interaction with these particular outsiders. Consequently, his response is surprising. He honors them in a manner in which an ordinary person would act before a king: he humbly bows down with his nose (*'ap*) to the ground.[6] Does this point to his assuming that they are the messengers of a king? Shame and honor, which are part of the predominant social control system of group-oriented societies, are ways of maintaining and manipulating status.[7] Shaming decreases status and emphasizes inferiority and marginality, while honoring increases status and emphasizes superiority and centrality. Inferior and marginal people are expected to express their low status through shameful body positions, such as lying flat on the ground in an extremely vulnerable position. Thus Lot's bowing down demonstrates his marginality, vulnerability and need for protection in the presence of the superior messengers. Lot also honors the messengers by calling them, 'my lords', and offering them protective hospitality. But in light of his previous experience, his hospitality and openness contradict normal human defensiveness because it risks bringing threatening outsiders inside (see Malina 1985: 408-409).

In a shame/honor culture the messengers respond appropriately: they refuse the hospitality.[8] Hospitality involves the crossing of a household

---

6. Bowing down is the behaviour of courtiers before a superior, such as a king (Speiser 1964: 138).

7. See Bechtel 1991: 47-76. Cf. Abu-Lughod 1986; Ausubel 1955: 378-90; Dodds 1951; Horney 1950; Hsien-Chin 1956: 447-67; Isenberg 1950: 329-49; Lynd 1958; Piers and Singer 1953; Riezler 1943: 457-65. Scheff 1988: 402-34.

8. Most scholars do not understand the messenger's refusal as an element of a

boundary by an outsider, so appropriately they refuse. Then, typically, Lot strongly urges/presses (*pṣr*, v. 3) them to accept his hospitality. At this point it would be shameful if the messengers refused. So they accept. This pattern of behavior is part of the normal dynamics of a group-oriented shame/honor society (see Gen. 33.6-11; Judg. 19.7; 2 Kgs 2.17), and it shows that there is mutality in their interactions. In honoring the messengers and risking hospitality, Lot accepts the difference between himself and the outsiders and creates bonding with them. Accepting difference is one way of diminishing the threat that outsiders may pose. But is he protecting both himself and the community? Or is he protecting himself at the expense of the community? If these men are messengers of a coalition of kings, Lot's hospitality may in the long run benefit Lot, as did Rahab's (Josh. 2 and 6), but allow the violation of the boundary of the community so that the messengers can spy on the defenses of the community. His hospitality could contribute to the downfall of the town. But if the messengers are messengers of YHWH, then Lot's hospitality may in the long run benefit Lot as well as the community—providing the community responds in a similar way. But what if the messengers represent *both* the coalition and YHWH, what will the consequences of Lot's hospitality be? And how will Lot's hospitality be perceived by the men of the town? Will they view this boundary violation positively or negatively?

Inhospitality: Shaming (19.4-5)

(19.4) Before going to bed the men (*'ᵃnāšîm*) of the town, the adult men (*'ᵃnāšîm*) of Sodom surround the house, from the young adult men (*na'ar*) to the old adult men (*zāqēn*)—all of the people (*'am*) to the last. (19.5) They call to Lot and say to him, 'Where are the men (*'ᵃnāšîm*) who came to you tonight? Bring (*yṣ'*) them to us so that we may know (*yd'*) them.'

In light of the ambiguity about the messengers and the consequences of hospitality, is the mention of the time just before going to bed indicative of a period of increasing darkness and, therefore, lack of clarity? Next it is stressed that it is all the adult men (*'ᵃnāšîm*), the young men (*na'ar*) and the old men (*zāqēn*), that surround the house. The term *'ᵃnāšîm* (men) indicates adult men and this is emphasized by the terms

shame/honor etiquette (e.g. Turner 1990: 90; Speiser 1964: 138; Jeansonne 1988: 126).

na'ar (the young adult men) to the old men (*zāqēn*). As adult men they should have the maturity to discern 'good and bad' in all its complexity. They should normally be able to have some clarity. But this is a time of growing darkness, of increased lack of clarity, so that issues are obscured and 'good and bad' are harder to discern, although the audience is already privy to the complexity of the issues.

The townsmen want to 'know' (*yd'*) the messengers, which is intentionally *ambiguous*. 'Knowing' covers broad intellectual, experiential and sexual knowing. Do the men only have intellectual knowing in mind? Do they just want to 'know' who the messengers are and what they are doing in the town? Or do they have sexual knowing in mind? If *all* the adult men of the town want to 'know' the two men sexually, it would be aggressive homosexual *rape*.[9] But at this point there are *no* clues in the text about the intentions of the townsmen. The *ambiguity* of the men's *intention* is important to discern.

It is also important to distinguish between a desire for sexual pleasure and rape. Sexual pleasure is not a community activity; it is private and requires mutuality. But in this scene, 'all of the people (*'am*)' of Sodom are present and mutuality is absent, so the desire for sexual pleasure, homosexual or heterosexual, can be ruled out. In contrast, rape does not entail a desire for sexual pleasure. Both heterosexual and homosexual rape are forceful, non-consensual *boundary violations* (see Bechtel 1994b: 19-36). Heterosexual rape is rape of a woman and homosexual rape is rape of a man. Both are rape; one is not better or worse than the other. Is the boundary violation of rape an appropriate response to the messenger's boundary violation of the town? Rape of either males or females is deeply shameful, dehumanizing and status reducing, so it would strip the messengers of their dignity and honor and would have lasting harmful, psychological and physical effects. After being raped the messengers would probably be incapable of spying and certainly in their shamed condition they would be incapable of reporting their information to their community. The use of shame as an incapacitating device is seen in 2 Samuel 10 where the representatives of King David are shamed by Hanun, king of the Ammonites, because they are suspected of being spies. After having one side of their beards shaved off, their garments cut off at the hips and being paraded out of town,

9.   See Niditch 1982: 365-79. Some exegetes become preoccupied with the morality of homosexuality and miss the implications of rape (e.g. Coote and Ord 1989: 127-28).

they are too shamed to return to Jerusalem and must remain in isolation until their shame subsides. Compared to this shaming, the shame of rape is of a different magnitude; it is lifelong. So as immoral as it is, rape could have a protective function for the community of Sodom. And in a group-oriented society 'sin' is behavior on the part of an individual or a group that violates the well-being, social bonding or continued existence of the group. It is a failure to respond to social need or a failure to carry out mutually beneficial action. So the interpreter's focus needs to be on the ability of the act to respond to social need and be mutually beneficial.

And in this type of society sexual intercourse should create the kind of bonding of difference (male and female) that is essential in keeping the group together. Rape is the antithesis of bonding. It is a boundary violation that eliminates bonding and is the opposite of hospitality. Finally, rape creates the illusion of power, control and superiority for the perpetrator, so it could help silence the townsmen's feelings of vulnerability, inferiority and lack of control in the face of the threatening messengers/spies.[10] The townsmen may consider it an appropriate counter-boundary violation to the boundary violation of the messengers. Thus, it would be a way of protecting the community that the community might consider mutually beneficial. Homosexuality is not the issue. But of course, the intentions of the townsmen are ambiguous; rape of the messengers may not be their intention.

As the behavior of Lot and the townsmen is examined, it is seen that they are both trying to respond to social need by diminishing a threat to the community. Both the townsmen and Lot respond with boundary violations. Lot is open to outsiders and tries to secure favor through hospitality, but in doing so he risks the community by housing potentially threatening 'spies' within the community. The townsmen may be closed to outsiders and at worst they may be trying to protect their community from a boundary violation by a counter-boundary violation, which is intended to prevent the messengers from spying.

Lot's marginal status is again stressed by his functioning on a boundary—at the *entrance* of his house. Although the entrance is a point of danger, there is now a reversal. The threatening outsiders are inside being protected by Lot's hospitality and the insiders are outside

---

10. My definition of rape is a composite of the work of Beneke 1982; Bouque 1989; Brownmiller 1975; Griffin 1977: 26-35; Chappell, Geis and Geis (eds.) 1977; Horos 1974; Tomaselli and Porter (eds.) 1986; Sanday 1981b.

forming a threatening boundary around the house. The marginal figure
has moved to the entrance of his house to mediate between the insiders
and the outsiders.[11]

Rescue of the Messengers: Lot's Offer (19.6-8)

(19.6) Lot goes out to them at the entrance and he closes the door after
him. (19.7) He says to them, 'Please, my brothers, do not act badly (r").
(19.8) Since I have two daughters who have not known (yd') a man ('îš),
let me bring them forth (yṣ') to you. Do to them what is good (ṭôb) in
your eyes, only to these men ('ᵃnāšîm) do not do ('śh) anything for they
came for safety under my roof.'

Lot's hospitality and his honoring of the messengers by calling them
'my lords', has already bonded Lot to the outsiders (the messengers).
Now he calls the townsmen 'my brothers', which establishes bonding
between himself and the insiders (the townsmen). Again Lot accepts
difference, this time between himself and the insiders and creates bonding with them. Then in his role as mediator, the position of a 'judge',
Lot takes control of the situation and begins to discern good (ṭôb) and
bad (ra'). He asks his brothers 'not to act badly' (r"), but 'to do good
(ṭôb)' in their eyes.[12] Picking up on the word 'know' (yd'), he offers the
townsmen, who want to 'know' (yd') the two men ('ᵃnāšîm), his two
daughters, who have not 'known' (yd') a man ('îš). Does Lot assume
that the townsmen simply want to 'know' (yd') what the messengers
are doing in Sodom? If so, offering his daughters to be raped by the
townsmen would reflect the ambiguity of the word 'know', but would
be completely incongruent and inappropriate to their intentions. It
clearly would be rejected.

Or does Lot assume that the intentions of the men are sexual and that
the men want to rape? If so he offers his daughters. But the men are
attempting to rape two threatening male outsiders. In doing so they are
responding to a threat to their community, not trying to fulfill their
sexual needs. The homosexual rape of these potential spies would

---

11. Jeansonne (1988: 126-27) assumes that Lot goes outside and closes the door
in order to create secrecy because of his wicked and shameful proposal.

12. The expression 'every person does right in their own eyes' (Deut. 6.18;
12.28; Josh. 9.25; Judg. 17.6; 19.1, 24; 21.25) is a deuteronomistic expression for a
community in which there is virtual anarchy and no king to judge and control the
community (see Lasine 1984: 37).

deeply shame them and make them incapable of carrying out their mission. So as an attempt to protect the city from danger, this homosexual rape could be effective. But Lot's offer of two non-threatening, marginal women is startlingly incongruent and totally inappropriate under the circumstances; his offer does not address the situation and would clearly be rejected.

And as abhorrent as the homosexual rape of two threatening outsiders would be, the heterosexual rape of two non-threatening marginal women who are, no doubt, engaged to men of the town, is even more abhorrent in a group-oriented society. Although the homosexual rape of the threatening outsiders might qualify as 'good' for the community, the heterosexual rape of the daughters would be clearly 'bad' for the community. So his offer is as jarring as the fact that many modern commentators disregard the potential rape of the women and concentrate on the protection of the men and the issue of homosexuality.[13] But this disregard for and devaluing of women does not fit into the assumptions of a group-oriented society. In group-orientation the continuing process of birth, growth, decay, death and rebirth of nature is the pattern for the household and society. Each individual has a sense of continued existence through the biological continuation of life through children. This guarantees the continued existence of the household and, in turn, the society as a whole. So the production of children is essential. In addition, in small agrarian societies such as ancient Israel, children are essential to carry out the heavy work in the fields when parents become old. Physical survival and longevity depends on children. Thus sexual intercourse functions in two critical ways. First, it produces progeny. And second, it creates the kind of strong bonding, allegiance and obligation that is essential in keeping the community and the household together. It is a woman's sexual power of productivity that produces children in partnership with her husband and YHWH. Since women's sexual power leads to the continued existence of both the

13. See Alexander 1985: 291; Skinner 1930: 307. Other exegetes are sympathetic to Lot (Vawter 1977; von Rad 1961: 218-19) or see Lot's action as an act of despair and hopelessness, but suggest that today's standards should not be imposed (Westermann 1984), or suggest that the offer would not be shocking to the ancient sense of proprieties (Vawter 1977), or see Lot as a tragic buffoon (Coats 1985: 121). Jeansonne (1988: 128) considers Lot to be a cruel exploiter of his daughter's welfare, a procrastinating, ungrateful dweller in a sinful city, a self-centered, incompetent, disobedient, insincere and disrespectful man that God saved (cf. Turner 1990: 95).

household and society and functions in the realm of YHWH's creating and sustaining life, it must be used carefully and properly *inside* the household (see Foucault 1980; Goody 1983; Rosaldo and Lamphere [eds.] 1974; Sanday 1981a: 5-27; Whyte 1978; Meyers 1988; 1989: 265-78). Thus women in this type of society are central, not marginal, and the idea of women being disregarded or devalued is inconceivable (contrary to Lerner 1986). In the story Lot's two daughters have the potential of 'building' a household and thus the community as a whole. Since they are still under the protection of their father, Lot has an obligation to the community to protect them—particularly since they are engaged (v. 14), probably to men of the community (Alter 1986: 33). So Lot's offer seems strange. Lot makes the offer in order to protect the messengers who may 'destroy' the community, but in doing so the offer appears to violate his own community responsibility and the ideals of the community (see the prohibition against the violation of an engaged woman in Deut. 22.25-27). Lot's offer protects the 'potential community destroyers' (the messengers) and threatens the 'potential community builders' (his daughters).

In both cases, the offer is totally inappropriate and thoroughly offensive. It would be easy to judge what is 'good' and what is 'bad', so the offer would be *rejected*. And of course, that is the point. Lot's offer responds to the ambiguity of the townsmen's intentions by presenting something that contradicts both possible intentions. In such a tense situation the function of an incongruent, totally offensive offer is to defuse the tension, stop the action and prevent possible aggression. Lot's 'bad' offer crosses the boundary of decency in order to have a 'good' outcome. Lot says, 'Do what is *good* in your own eyes.' What is 'good' in their eyes is to reduce the threat to the community, *not* to rape two non-threatening women—that would threaten the community. So contrary to the opinion of some scholars, Lot does not offer his daughters as a way of being the perfect Near Eastern host (e.g. Alter 1986: 307), or as the desperate act of a wicked man (e.g. Lasine 1984),[14] or as a father doing what he has the right to do (e.g. Lerner 1986: 173; cf. Tapp 1989: 157-74). Lot presents an offer that protects both the messengers and his daughters.

14. Or Jeansonne (1988: 31-32) stresses the unjust treatment of his daughters; Lot is abnegating his responsibility. Skinner (1930: 307) feels it is abhorrent to Hebrew morality. Lot's offer is simply ignored by Speiser (1964) and Brueggemann (1982).

Rescue of Lot (19.9-11)

(19.9) They say, 'Present yourself (*ngš*)!' And they say, 'Now the one who came as a sojourner is definitely judging (*špṭ*). Now we will do more bad (*r''*) to you than to them.' Then they strongly press (*pṣr*) against the man (*'îš*) Lot and come near (*ngš*) to break down the door. (19.10) So the men (*'ᵃnāšîm*) send forth their hands and bring Lot to them into the house and close the door. (19.11) They strike (*nkh*) the men (*'ᵃnāšîm*) who are at the dor with blindness (*sanwērîm*) from the smallest to the largest and they stop finding the door.

So the reaction of the townsmen to Lot's offer is critical. The townsmen do *not* respond to Lot's sexual offer. This should indicate that their intention is *not* sexual pleasure or the rape of two non-threatening women. His offer does not accomplish their goal of protecting the town.

Instead the townsmen ask Lot to present himself (*ngš*). *Ngš* generally means to 'come near', and in some cases it is a judicial term meaning 'to present oneself before a court' for judgment (e.g. Deut. 25.1). Isaiah 50.8 states, 'Who contends with me? Let us stand (*'md*) together. Who is my adversary? Let him present himself (*ngš*) to me.' The context in Isa. 50.8 and Gen. 19.9 is that of judgment. The townsmen are taking Lot to court and they stress Lot's status as a sojourner, which implies that sojourners do not have the right to 'judge'. From the perspective of the townsmen this marginal sojourner is acting inappropriately and is violating the norms of the community.[15] Lot is definitely guilty of 'judging' (*špṭ*). He has been discerning what is 'good' and 'bad' for the community (see Trible 1984: 75). Having judged him, as punishment for his improper behavior they now intend 'to do more bad (*r''*) to him than they had intended to do to the threatening outsiders. Does this indicate that they did not intend to do anything more to the messengers than 'know' what they are doing in the town, but they intend to punish Lot for his violation? Or does it indicate that they intended to rape the messengers to protect the community and now they will do worse to Lot to protect the norms of the community? There is no way of knowing. Of course, the irony of the situation is that God is in the background judging both Lot's ability to discern and judge and the

15. In addition, as a marginal member of the community Lot has a responsibility to cooperate, be interdependent and offer mutual aid to the community. Instead, Lot is perceived as adding additional threat to the community.

townsmen's ability to discern and judge (18.25-26; see Alter 1986: 32).
Whose judgment is better: the townsmen's or Lot's? Who has the
ability to discern 'good' and 'bad'?

As Lot has strongly urged/pressed (*pṣr*) the messengers to cross a
boundary and accept his hospitality, now the townsmen strongly press
(*pṣr*) against Lot to break down his door and violate his boundary. The
verb *pṣr* (urge/press) is used to highlight the two kinds of boundary
violation, one that is potentially saving and one that is potentially
destroying. And as Lot has protected the messengers, now the
messengers protect Lot by pulling him into the house.

Then, at the entrance of the house the townsmen are struck (*nkh*)
with blindness (*sanwērîm*).[16] *Nkh* means 'to smite' or 'strike' and it is
often associated with legal punishment. The townsmen wanted to
punish Lot, but instead they are punished with blindness. But what are
the implications of this blindness? Since the townsmen wanted to
'know' the messengers, there may be a connection between 'knowing'
and 'seeing' (Coote and Ord 1989: 131; see Alter 1986: 30-38). The
connection is seen in the ironic statement in Isa. 6.9c, 'They hear, but
do not understand. They see (*r'h*), but do not know (*yd'*).' Furthermore,
in 2 Kgs 6.20 people are struck with blindness (*sanwērîm*) and 'their
eyes are no longer open'. For mature adults this blindness is the opposite of having the eyes opened after eating of the tree of discernment of
'good and bad' (Gen. 3.5; see Bechtel 1995). So if the townsmen
cannot 'see', they cannot 'know'. Their blindness is indicative of the
fact that they do not have the mature capacity to judge 'good and bad',
which in ancient Israel is part of the wisdom acquired in maturation
into adulthood (see Ackerman 1990: 41-60). The emphasis on the
townsmen being mature adults who should have this capacity is now
understandable.

Who does the striking? Is 'the blindness' of the townsmen something
that is imposed as punishment from outside, by God? If God imposes
their blindness as punishment, then the townsmen are not directly
responsible for the blindness; they become victims. But if blindness
symbolizes their immature attitudes, their inability to discern the complexity of 'good' and 'bad' and their lack of acceptance of difference,
then their blindness is something that they themselves have caused.
And they themselves are responsible for the consequences. Does God

16. Some scholars assume that *sanwērîm* is a blinding light that reveals the
messengers as 'angels' (e.g. Speiser 1964: 139-40).

punish humans or do they punish themselves by their attitudes and immature thinking?

This story illustrates that the discernment of good and bad is never easy or clear cut. The lack of clarity is emphasized by having the story take place at bedtime, when there is increasing darkness and vision is more hazy. Throughout the story good and bad have been ambiguous and ambivalent. What seems 'bad' may also be 'good': (1) Lot's risky hospitality (inclusion of outsiders); (2) Lot's incongruous, offensive offer of his daughters, which defuses a hostile situation and (3) the messengers, who probably represent threatening kings and may also represent God. What seems 'good', turns out to be 'bad': the townsmen's potentially aggressive behavior (exclusion of outsiders) which is supposed to protect the community. Because of their xenophobia, their lack of acceptance of difference, the townsmen are 'blind' to the danger they have created and 'blind' to the possibilities of mediation, cooperation and hospitality. The sin of the men of Sodom is *not* their practice of homosexuality, but their immaturity and inability to deal with difference and the complexity of discerning good and bad. Life is far too complex to establish fixed judgments of absolute good and bad. Each situation has to be evaluated and discerned on its own merits, because things are not always the way they appear on the surface.

The book of Deuteronomy advocates utterly destroying outsiders. Do the townsmen represent people who are obedient to this prescription, so they do not think critically about each situation or weigh the ramifications of all possibilities? Does the story challenge these xenophobic tendencies by projecting them onto the men of Sodom—whose fate is proverbial? Is this story set during the premonarchical period of Israel's origins because at that point in time the people of Israel are all outsiders or marginal people who include outsiders in order to grow as a nation? If inclusion of outsiders is part of Israel's coming into existence, does this imply that exclusion of outsiders may contribute to Israel's going out of existence—like Sodom?[17] Inclusion requires

---

17. The similarities between elements of Gen. 19 and Judg. 19 have been long observed. Some scholars assume that since the two stories share a similar foundation, both stories go in the same direction. But if the two stories are compared carefully, it is seen that there are radical differences in the direction of the two stories. They share a theme of hospitality, but in Judges 19 the main characters are all 'insiders' (tribal folks, though some are sojourning in other tribal areas), so the issue is hospitality among *insiders*, not with outsiders. The only outsiders are the

boundary crossing and violation, but some boundary crossing and violation may preserve rather than destroy. Accepting difference, though threatening, builds and expands.

BIBLIOGRAPHY

Abu-Lughod, L.
    1986   *Veiled Sentiments: Honor and Poetry in a Bedouin Society* (Berkeley: University of California).
Ackerman, J.S.
    1990   'Knowing Good and Evil: A Literary Analysis of the Court History in 2 Samuel 9–20 and 1 Kings 1–2', *JBL* 109: 41-60.
Alexander, T.D.
    1985   'Lot's Hospitality: A Clue to his Righteousness', *JBL* 104: 289-91.

Alter, R.
    1986   'Sodom as Nexus: The Web of Design in Biblical Narrative', *Tikkun* 1: 30-38.
    1996   *Genesis* (New York: W.W. Norton).
Ausubel, F.
    1955   'Relationship between Shame and Guilt in the Socializing Process', *Psychological Review* 62: 378-90.
Barber, B.
    1957   *Social Stratification* (New York: Harcourt Brace Jovanovich).
Barth, F.
    1969   *Ethnic Groups and Boundaries: The Social Organization of Culture Differences* (Oslo: Universitetsforlaget).
Beach, E.F.
    1993   'Feminist Interpretation of Genesis 38: An Iconographic Approach', paper given at the 1993 Annual AAR/SBL Meeting, Washington, DC.
Bechtel, L.
    1991   'Shame as a Sanction of Social Control in Biblical Israel: Judicial, Political and Social Shaming', *JSOT* 49: 47-76.
    1993   'Rethinking the Interpretation of Genesis 2.4b–3.24', in A. Brenner (ed.), *Feminist Companion to Genesis* (Sheffield: JSOT Press): 77-117.

Jebusites who are definitively identified as dangerous, supporting the xenophobic, exclusionary tendencies of deuteronomistic theology (compared to the inclusionary tendencies of the Genesis stories). In Judg. 19 '*rape*' (heterosexual) with all its characteristic motivations is actually carried out among the 'insiders'. The sojourning Levite does the 'judging' at a time when there is virtual anarchy with no king in Israel to 'judge'. 'Judging' without a deuteronomistic king or law leads to inter-tribal civil war. And the concubine is a woman who does not have full status in her husband's household, but returns to the protection of her father's household—thus incorporating a host of Northern/Southern relationship issues.

1994a   'The Adam and Eve: A Myth about Human Maturation', *The 1994 Annual of Hermeneutics and Social Concern* (New York: Continuum): 152-73.

1994b   'What if Dinah Is Not Raped? (Genesis 34)', *JSOT* 62: 19-36.

1995   'Genesis 2.4b–3.24: A Myth about Human Maturation', *JSOT* 67: 3-26.

Beneke, T.

1982   *Men on Rape* (New York: St Martins Press).

Berger, P., and T. Luckmann

1966   *The Social Construction of Reality: A Treatise in the Sociology of Knowledge* (New York: Doubleday).

Block, D.I.

1990   'Echo Narrative Technique in Hebrew Literature: A Study in Judges 19', *WTJ* 52: 325-41.

Bouque, L.B.

1989   *Defining Rape* (Durham: Duke University Press).

Brownmiller, S.

1975   *Against our Will: Men, Women and Rape* (New York: Simon & Schuster).

Brueggemann, W.

1982   *Genesis* (Atlanta, GA: John Knox Press).

Carmichael, C.M.

1979   *Women, Law and the Genesis Traditions* (Edinburgh: Edinburgh University Press).

Cassuto, U.

1961   *A Commentary on the Book of Genesis, Part One: From Adam to Noah* (Jerusalem: Hebrew University Press).

Chappell, D., R. Geis and G. Geis (eds.)

1977   *Forcible Rape: The Crime, the Victim and the Offender* (New York: Columbia University Press).

Coats, G.W.

1983   *Genesis with an Introduction to Narrative Literature* (Grand Rapids: Eerdmans).

1985   'Lot: A Foil in the Abraham Saga', in J.T. Butler *et al.* (eds.), *Understanding the Word: Essays in Honor of Bernhard Anderson* (Sheffield: JSOT Press): 113-32.

Coote, R.B., and D.R. Ord

1989   *The Bible's First History: From Eden to the Court of David with the Yahwist* (Philadelphia: Fortress Press).

Dodds, E.R.

1951   *The Greeks and the Irrational* (Berkeley: University of California Press).

Foucault, M.

1980   *The History of Sexuality*. I. *An Introduction* (New York: Vintage Books).

Gaster, T.H.

1962   'Angel', *IDB*, I: 129.

Goody, J.

1983   *The Development of Marriage and Family in Europe* (Cambridge: Cambridge University Press).

Griffin, S.
    1977   'Rape: The All-American Crime', in D. Chappell, R. Geis and G. Geis
                (eds.), *Forcible Rape: The Crime, the Victim and the Offender* (New
                York: Columbia University Press).
Harari, R.
    1989   'Abraham's Nephew Lot: A Biblical Portrait', *Tradition* 25: 31-41.
Helyer, L.R.
    1983   'The Separation of Abraham and Lot: Its Significance in the Patriarchal
                Narrative', *JSOT* 26: 77-88.
Horney, K.
    1950   *Neurosis and Human Growth* (New York: Norton).
Horos, C.V.
    1974   *Rape* (New Canaan, CT: Tobey).
Hsien-Chin, H.
    1956   'The Chinese Concept of Face', in D.G. Haring (ed.), *Personal Character
                and Cultural Milieu* (Syracuse: Syracuse University Press): 447-67.
Isenberg, A.
    1950   'Natural Pride and Natural Shame', *Philosophy and Phenomenology* 45:
                329-49.
Jeansonne, S.
    1988   'The Characterization of Lot in Genesis', *BTB* 18: 123-29.
    1990   *The Women of Genesis: From Sarah to Potiphar's Wife* (Minneapolis:
                Fortress Press): 31-42.
Lasine, S.
    1984   'Guest and Host in Judges 19: Lot's Hospitality in an Inverted World',
                JSOT 29: 37-59.
Lenski, G.E.
    1984   *Power and Privilege: A Theory of Social Stratification* (Chapel Hill: Uni-
                versity of North Carolina).
Lerner, G.
    1986   *The Creation of Patriarchy* (Oxford: Oxford University Press).
Lifton, R.J.
    1967   *Boundaries: Psychological Man in Revolution* (New York: Vintage
                Press).
Lynd, H.M.
    1958   *Shame and the Search for Identity* (New York: Harcourt Brace
                Jovanovich).
Malina, B.J.
    1985   'Hospitality', in P.J. Achtemeier (ed.), *Harper's Bible Dictionary* (San
                Francisco: Harper & Row): 408-409.
Martin, J.D.
    1989   *The World of Ancient Israel: Sociological, Anthropological and Political
                Perspectives* (Cambridge: Cambridge University Press).
Mead, M.
    1937   *Cooperation and Competition among Primitive Peoples* (New York:
                McGraw–Hill).
    1953   *Cultural Patterns and Technical Change* (Holland: UNESCO).

Meyers, C.

    1988   *Discovering Eve: Ancient Israelite Women in Context* (New York: Oxford University Press).

    1989   'Women and the Domestic Economy of Early Israel', in B.S. Lesko (ed.), *Women's Earliest Records: From Ancient Egypt and Western Asia* (BJS, 166; Atlanta: Scholars Press).

Niditch, S.

    1982   'The "Sodomite" Theme in Judges 19–20: Family, Community, and Social Disintegration', *CBQ* 32: 365-79.

Piers, G., and M. Singer

    1953   *Shame and Guilt* (New York: Norton).

Rad, G. von

    1961   *Genesis* (Philadelphia: Westminster Press).

Riezler, K.

    1943   'Comments on the Social Psychology of Shame', *American Journal of Sociology* 48: 457-65.

Rosaldo, M.Z., and L. Lamphere (eds.)

    1974   *Women, Culture and Society* (Stanford: Stanford University Press).

Rowlett, L.

    1992   'Inclusion, Exclusion, and Marginality in the Book of Joshua', *JSOT* 55: 15-23.

Sanday, P.R.

    1981a   *Female Power: Male Dominance: On the Origin of Sexual Inequality* (Cambridge: Cambridge University Press).

    1981b   'The Socio-Cultural Context or Rape: A Cross-Cultural Study', *The Journal of Social Issues* 37: 5-27.

Scheff, T.J.

    1988   'Shame and Conformity: The Deference–Emotion System', *American Sociological Review* 53: 402-34.

Skinner, J.

    1930   *A Critical and Exegetical Commentary on Genesis* (Edinburgh: T. & T. Clark).

Speiser, E.A.

    1964   *Genesis* (AB, 1 ; Garden City, NY; Doubleday).

Tapp, A.M.

    1989   'An Ideology of Expendability: Virgin Daughter Sacrifice', in Mieke Bal (ed.), *Anti Covenant: Counter-Reading Women's Lives in the Hebrew Bible* (Sheffield: Sheffield Academic Press): 157-74.

Tomaselli, S., and R. Porter (eds.)

    1986   *Rape* (Oxford: Basil Blackwell).

Trible, P.

    1984   'An Unnamed Woman: The Extravagance of Violence', in her *Texts of Terror: Literary–Feminist Readings of Biblical Narratives* (Philadelphia: Fortress Press): 65-91.

Turner, L.A.

    1990   'Lot as Jekyll and Hyde: A Reading of Genesis 18–19', in D.J.A. Clines *et al.* (eds.), *The Bible in Three Dimensions: Essays in Celebration of 40*

Years of Biblical Studies in the University of Sheffield (Sheffield: JSOT Press): 86-101.

Turner, V.
    1967   *The Forest of Symbols* (Ithaca, NY: Cornell University Press).
Vawter, B.
    1977   *On Genesis: A New Reading* (Garden City, NY: Doubleday).
Westermann, C.
    1984   *Genesis 12–36* (Minneapolis: Augsburg).
Whyte, M.K.
    1978   *The Status of Women in Preindustrial Societies* (Princeton, NJ: Princeton University Press).

THE *SHEMA'*: A PROTESTANT FEMINIST READING*

Carolyn Pressler

Introduction

Feminist interpreters of the Bible have for the most part focused attention on those texts which refer explicitly to women, which provide data for the feminist reconstruction of biblical history, or which use gender-specific imagery for God. Such texts shape imagination and determine the horizons of vision; the importance of critically examining and reappropriating them cannot be overstated.

Another task of feminist biblical interpretation has remained comparatively unexplored. That is, feminists have not often evaluated and appropriated biblical texts which do not explicitly refer to women, but which play a central role in biblical literature and tradition. Such texts can project assumptions about God, power and differences among peoples that profoundly impact the welfare of women.[1]

This essay examines the claims made about God in the *Shema'*, Deut. 6.4-5.[2] The heart of Deuteronomic theology is its insistent confession

---

* This essay was originally entitled: '*Shema'*: A Feminist Reading'. In response to it, Drorah O'Donnell Setel correctly challenged the assumption of a universal feminist perspective implicit in the title. Setel suggested that the essay would be more appropriately subtitled: '*A Christian Feminist Reading*', especially in light of the centrality of the *Shema'* in Judaism. I wish to express my indebtedness to Setel for this and many other insights incorporated in this revision.

1. Important feminist investigations of biblical passages that do not highlight gender include Sharon H. Ringe, 'Luke 9.28-36: the Beginning of an Exodus', *Semeia* 28 (1983), pp. 83-99, and Carol A. Newsom's discussion of the character of God portrayed in the book of Job in C.A. Newsom and S.H. Ringe (eds.), *The Women's Bible Commentary* (Louisville, KY: Westminster John Knox Press, 1992), pp. 130-36 (135-36).

2. The title *Shema'* can be used to designate Deut. 6.4-9, Deut 6.4 alone or Deut. 6.4-9; 11.13-21 and Num. 15.37-41 as well as Deut. 6.4-5. I have chosen to limit my discussion to Deut. 6.4-5 because of space constraints.

that Israel's God alone is sovereign, and its repeated command to render absolute allegiance to that sovereign God. The claim and command are negatively stated in the first commandment. They are positively expressed in the *Shema'*: 'Hear O Israel, YHWH[3] our God, YHWH is unique. You shall love YHWH your God with all of your heart, with all of your being, indeed with all of your capacity.'[4] I will explore both the potentially liberating and the potentially violent ways in which the insistence of the *Shema'* on God's radical sovereignty and related assumptions about power and difference function in the book of Deuteronomy.

Two caveats are in order. First, I wish to acknowledge the particularity of this interpretation. All readings of texts are shaped by what the interpreters bring to the task—including their religious identities, social locations, and previous experiences with the passages. This is especially evident in the case of the *Shema'*. The *Shema'* is an important text for Christians, both because it is pivotal for understanding the book of Deuteronomy, and especially because of its identification in the Synoptic Gospels as the 'great commandment'. The significance of the *Shema'* to Jewish life and thought is exponentially greater. For more than two millennia, Jews have included it in their daily prayers; Jewish martyrs have died with its words on their lips.[5] I am a Protestant who

---

3.   Translating the tetragrammaton poses a serious problem for feminist interpreters. 'Lord' and 'Adonai' are masculine terms. *Hashem*, a Hebrew term meaning 'the Name', which Jews have often substituted for YHWH, has the advantage of being gender neutral and of having ancient roots. It is incomprehensible to most Christians, however. The inclusive language lectionary committee's translation, 'Sovereign', may be the best choice in most cases. In the context of this paper, however, to translate YHWH as 'Sovereign' would be to predetermine the outcome of the discussion. I have therefore left the tetragrammaton untranslated.

4.   S. Dean McBride, Jr, 'The Yoke of the Kingdom: An Exposition of Deuteronomy 6.4-5', *Int* 27 (1973), pp. 273-306 (274 and 301-304), presents a convincing case for translating the last clause of Deut. 6.5 'indeed with all your capacity'.

5.   In response to an earlier version of this paper, Setel noted that she had been taught to regard the *Shema'* not as one of the key texts of her tradition, but as *the* central text, the distillation of Jewish monotheistic faith. Particularly helpful discussions of the role of the *Shema'* in Jewish life and thought are found in Arthur Marmorstein, *Studies in Jewish Theology* (ed. J. Rabbinowitz and M.S. Lew; London: Oxford University Press, 1950), pp. 72-105; Louis Jacobs, 'Shema, Reading of', in *Encyclopedia Judaica*, XIV (Jerusalem: Macmillan Press, 1971), cols. 1370-74; and McBride, 'Yoke', pp. 273-306.

teaches Hebrew Bible at a liberal Christian seminary. The *Shema'* is one of several key texts that shape my theology and my teaching. Nonetheless, I bring to the text a very different perspective than would a Jewish feminist interpreter. Moreover, in light of the role that these verses play as the central Jewish creed, it is important to state explicitly that my critique of Deut. 6:4-5 is not intended as a critique of either ancient or modern Judaism.

Secondly, my discussion of the *Shema'* is limited to its meaning and function within the book of Deuteronomy. It should not be taken as a critique of the meaning or function of the confession more generally. The language of the *Shema'* is general and multivalent. Its meaning comes into sharp focus only as it is examined against or interpreted from a particular background. Deuteronomy is not the only nor the most authoritative context against which to interpret these verses. As suggested above, the *Shema'* has a rich and varied history independent of its role in Deuteronomy and in a variety of contexts. Within Judaism, the *Shema'* is first of all a liturgical text, a prayer recited twice daily.[6] A feminist reconstruction of the text in the context of liturgy, drawing on layers of meaning that have been built over centuries of prayer, would encounter a different set of constraints and possibilities than an examination of the same words in Deuteronomy. The metamorphosis of the *Shema'* as the 'great commandment' in the Synoptic Gospels offers another context with another set of possible meanings. Both Jews and Christians have reinterpreted the *Shema'* in light of the needs and insights of their day. In S. Dean McBride's words, the verses are 'something of a palimpsest...upon which our various forebears...have left behind a succession of exegetical imprints'.[7]

The meanings which have accrued to the *Shema'* as it has been interpreted and reinterpreted in various contexts are resources for a feminist rereading of the verses. Such rereading is certainly possible. Indeed, I believe that the *Shema'* makes a claim about the uniqueness and unity of God and a command for the wholehearted love of God that is vitally important, especially for women. The confession that the power at the heart of reality is whole, not divided against itself, can provide hope of wholeness for women whose lives are fragmented, and whose minds and bodies are torn by the violence of sexism. Confessing the uniquely effective power of God can provide women with the

6. So Setel, in her response.
7. McBride, 'Yoke', pp. 304-305.

power to resist misogynist people and systems. The command to love God wholly can challenge the finality of human claims to allegiance that pressure women to remain in subordinate positions. Women can and will continue to leave our imprint on this palimpsest.

This essay is more narrowly focused. I have chosen to examine the meaning of the *Shema'* in Deuteronomy. Various interpreters including myself have lifted up the liberating impulses of the Deuteronomic call to reject all claims to allegiance except the claims of a God whose authority and identity were decisively established in the act of freeing slaves.[8] The purpose of this essay is to investigate Deut. 6.4-5 in its literary context, in order to ask if the *Shema'* can provide theological grounding for a feminist reappropriation of Deuteronomy and if Deuteronomy can provide content for a feminist reinterpretation of the *Shema'*. I will first sketch what I understand to be the basis of a feminist critique, and secondly discuss the meaning of the *Shema'* within its Deuteronomic context. I will then examine the potentially liberating function of the Deuteronomic confession of divine sovereignty within the covenantal community, and will finally look at the dangerous implications of those claims for the community's relationships with 'outsiders'.

Feminist Critiques of 'Sovereign' as a Metaphor for God

It is axiomatic among feminist theorists that patriarchy maintains itself by defining differences among people dualistically: male, female; white, black; Christian, Jew. As Mary Ann Tolbert writes, 'Such dualisms, always hierarchically ordered with one element in the superior position and one in the inferior, are the basic building blocks of patriarchal culture...they must be broken apart.'[9] The work of Tolbert and others suggests that valuing differences among peoples, fostering relationships which respect the 'integrity and specificity' of each party, and seeking ways to express power as creativity and empowerment rather than domination lie at the heart of an alternative feminist vision.

Constructive theologians such as Sallie McFague, Letty M. Russell,

---

8.   Carolyn Pressler, 'When Scriptures are Unholy' (An Occasional Paper published by United Theological Seminary of the Twin Cities, 1991); Patrick D. Miller, Jr, 'The Most Important Word: The Yoke of the Kingdom', *Iliff Review* 41 (1984), pp. 17-29 (20).

9.   Mary Ann Tolbert, 'Reading the Bible with Authority: Feminist Interrogation of the Canon', pp. 141-62 in this volume.

and Judith Plaskow have discussed at length how metaphors for God undergird or undercut hierarchical, dualistic social structures, and how understandings of divine power shape understandings of human power.[10]

They have raised serious questions about the adequacy of political metaphors such as 'Sovereign', 'Lord' or 'Ruler' for God. Plaskow, McFague and others argue that these images portray God exalted over creatures and ruling by coercion and benevolence.[11] Other feminists recognize the dangers inherent in using monarchical metaphors for God but cautiously suggest that images of divine sovereignty can function to abrogate human claims to domination.[12] The work of these constructive theologians suggests that one task for feminist biblical interpreters is to investigate exegetically the ways in which metaphors for God function to uphold or to challenge dualistic and hierarchical understandings of human relationships within concrete biblical texts.[13] This essay examines the claims of God's radical sovereignty made by the *Shema'* as those claims function in Deuteronomy.

The Deuteronomic Shema' as a Confession of Divine Sovereignty

The translation and interpretation of Deut. 6.4-5 have been rigorously

10. Sallie McFague, *Models of God: Theology for an Ecological, Nuclear Age* (Philadelphia: Fortress Press, 1987); Letty M. Russell, *Household of Freedom: Authority in Feminist Perspective* (Philadelphia: Westminster Press, 1987); Judith Plaskow, *Standing Again at Sinai: Judaism from a Feminist Perspective* (San Francisco: Harper, 1990).

11. Plaskow, *Standing Again*, pp. 132-33, writes that such images function as a 'fundamental and authorizing symbol in a whole system of hierarchical' relationships which 'fosters and mirrors the tendency to conceptualize all difference in terms of graded separations'.

12. For example, Rosemary Radford Ruether, *Sexism and God-Talk* (Boston: Beacon Press, 1983), p. 64, writes that the scriptural view of the divine Sovereign has functioned to break ties of bondage under human kings and fathers.

13. In her book *Jesus, Liberation, and the Biblical Jubilee: Images for Ethics and Christology* (Philadelphia: Fortress Press, 1985), pp. 95-97 and *passim*, feminist New Testament scholar Sharon H. Ringe has explored the metaphor of divine sovereignty as it functions within concrete texts. She suggests that the problem lies in our contemporary experience of sovereignty and of power rather than in the biblical use of the metaphor. *We* do not experience power as serving justice or liberation. She believes that feminists can and should reclaim the biblical view of God as the Sovereign who comes declaring liberation.

debated. Before examining how the claim that YHWH alone is sovereign functions in its biblical context, it is necessary to show that the *Shema'* as Deuteronomic Torah makes such a claim. During the past few decades Deuteronomic scholars have made a strong case that Deut. 6.4-5 consists of a confession of the sole sovereignty of Israel's God followed by a command that Israel respond with wholehearted loyalty.[14] This divine sovereignty is depicted using ancient Near Eastern suzerainty treaty language as a metaphor.

Deuteronomy 6.4 reads: 'YHWH our God, YHWH *'ehad'*. The meaning of the word *'ehad* in this context is ambiguous. It can mean 'unique' or 'one'; that is, it can refer either to the exclusiveness or to the unity of God. Both meanings have deep roots in the history of the *Shema'* as a living tradition.[15] Exegetes debate the meaning of the term within its Deuteronomic context. McBride and others present a number of compelling reasons for interpreting *'ehad* as primarily a reference to the uniqueness of Israel's God.[16] First, the word *'ehad* is found with the meaning 'unique' in a Deuteronomistic passage. In 2 Sam. 7.23, David's prayerful exclamation that there is no God like Israel's God is followed by the assertion that there is no people like Israel, a nation *'ehad*, that is, 'unique', in all the earth. Moreover, as McBride has shown, the meaning 'only, alone, unique', for *'ehad* and its cognates is clearly attested in Ugaritic and Akkadian.[17] Indeed, the title 'One', meaning 'Only One', is found ascribed to kings and deities in Egyptian, Akkadian and Ugaritic literature.[18] Finally, and most importantly, the translation 'unique' or 'alone' best fits the contexts. YHWH's exclusive claim to Israel's loyalty is *the* critical issue in the book of Deuteronomy.[19]

---

14. See especially McBride, 'Yoke'; Miller, 'Most Important Word'; W.L. Moran, 'The Ancient Near Eastern Background of the Love of God in Deuteronomy', *CBQ* 25 (1963), pp. 77-87; and Norbert Lohfink, *Great Themes from the Old Testament* (Edinburgh: T. & T. Clark, 1982), pp. 39-53.

15. McBride, 'Yoke', pp. 274-87, gives a helpful summary of the history of interpretation of the *Shema'* within Judaism and Christianity.

16. McBride, 'Yoke', pp. 291-93. So also Norbert Lohfink and Jan Bergman, *'ehad*, in *TDOT*, I, pp. 193-201; Miller, 'Most Important Word', pp. 21-23; and Moshe Weinfeld, *Deuteronomy 1–11* (AB, 5; Garden City, NY: Doubleday, 1991), pp. 349-51.

17. McBride, 'Yoke', p. 293.

18. Lohfink and Bergman, *'ehad*, pp. 194-95.

19. J. Gerald Janzen, 'On the Most Important Word in the Shema

Within the context of Deuteronomy, confession of the uniqueness of YHWH has to do with God's exclusive sovereignty understood in light of ancient Near Eastern suzerainty. This is suggested by an examination of the verb 'love' in Deuteronomy, by a consideration of Zech. 14.9, a verse that appears to be a midrash on Deut. 6.4-5, and especially by the widespread influence of the ancient Near Eastern treaty form on Deuteronomy.

The verb translated 'love' in Deut. 6.5, *'hb*, is not as ambiguous as the word translated 'unique' in Deut. 6.4. It is, however, such a general term that its meaning must be sharpened in light of its context. In Deuteronomy, the use of the verb 'love' in reference to Israel's response to God is parallel to the use of the verbs 'cleave to', 'serve', 'reverence' and 'obey'. The command to love God is consistently linked to prohibitions against following other gods or making and worshiping idols. It thus has to do with deliberate and heartfelt loyalty which can be commanded and which involves giving exclusive allegiance to the one loved. W.L. Moran has shown that 'love' belongs to the language of international diplomacy, where it is used in a similar way. In treaty language, love most often has to do with the exclusive fealty owed by a vassal to its suzerain.[20] Moreover, as Moshe Weinfeld has demonstrated, the following phrase, 'with all of your heart and with

(Deuteronomy VI 4-5)', *VT* 37 (1987), pp. 280-300, argues that *'ehad* in Deut. 6.4 means 'one' in the sense of 'integrity' or 'fidelity'. He brings together a number of texts from different parts of the Hebrew Bible to show that the integrity of God was a concern for biblical writers in general and the Deuteronomic compilers in particular. Deuteronomic concern about divine integrity is neither as well defined nor as prominent as Deuteronomic concern about YHWH's uniqueness, however. It is possible that Deut. 6.4 refers to 'oneness', that is, 'having integrity', as a secondary meaning. The primary meaning of the *'ehad* in this context appears to be 'unique'.

In the final analysis, the gap between these two ways of translating *'ehad* may not be as wide as it appears. Divine oneness (or integrity) implies divine sovereignty. That is, God's capacity to act with faithfulness presupposes God's sovereign power. Similarly, God's claim to exclusive allegiance is grounded in faithfulness to the promises made to the ancestors and in the deliverance from Egypt, and thus in divine integrity. In Deuteronomy, both nuances of the word are related to God's role in leading Israel out of Egypt and establishing covenant with Israel.

20. Moran, 'Ancient Near Eastern Background', pp. 77-87.

all of your soul', also corresponds to declarations of loyalty in ancient Near Eastern treaties.[21]

The connection between 'uniqueness' and 'sovereignty' is explicit in Zech. 14.9: 'And YHWH will become king over all the earth; on that day YHWH will be *'ehad* (unique) and his name *'ehad'*. This connection is further developed in the rabbinic traditions which define praying the *Shema'* as 'acceptance of the yoke of kingship'.

The influence of the form and language of ancient Near Eastern treaties on Deuteronomy has been well documented and need not be argued here. Deuteronomy 6.4-5 and the first commandment which it mirrors correspond to the basic demand in vassal treaties that the vassal refrain from serving or contracting treaties with any other lord.[22]

To summarize: within the Deuteronomic context, the *Shema'* confesses the exclusive claim on Israel's loyalty made by its sovereign God, and commands its wholehearted allegiance to that Sovereign.

The Sole Sovereignty of God and Those within the Community

An examination of the grounds and aims of divine sovereignty in Deuteronomy suggests that the metaphor of a uniquely sovereign God can serve to challenge hierarchical, dualistic relationships within the community of those who acknowledge that God's sovereignty. Deuteronomy explicitly bases YHWH's exclusive claims to sovereignty on the act of freeing Israel from Egypt. While God's claim to allegiance can be grounded in a series of God's salvific acts (Deut. 8.11-18), or in YHWH's nature as a God of impartiality and justice who cares for the widow, orphan and sojourner (Deut. 10.17-18), in a large majority of cases, the Deuteronomic call for wholehearted obedience is based on the Exodus (Deut. 4.20; 6.20-25; 7.8; 11.2-7; 29.24).

That act of liberation is also the criterion by which God's divinity is recognized. Israel knows that YHWH is God because that is the One who led them out of Egypt. 'To you it was shown, that you would acknowledge that YHWH is God; there is no other...' (Deut. 4.35).[23]

---

21. Weinfeld, *Deuteronomy*, p. 351-52.

22. See especially Moshe Weinfeld, *Deuteronomy and the Deuteronomic School* (Oxford: Clarendon Press, 1972); and Norbert Lohfink, *The Christian Meaning of the Old Testament* (Milwaukee: Bruce Publishing, 1968), pp. 87-102.

23. Except for translations of Deut. 6.4-5, which are the author's, Scripture references are taken from the *New Revised Standard Version* (ed. Bruce M. Metzger

There is some basis here for claiming that only that which liberates has revelatory authority within the community.

Having grounded God's claim to rule in the act of deliverance, Deuteronomy also insists that the aim of divine rule is the welfare of the people. 'YHWH commanded us to do all these statutes, to fear YHWH our God, for our lasting good so as to keep us alive, as is now the case' (Deut. 6.24). The gift of the law is portrayed as a continuation of the gift of deliverance from Egypt. Its purpose is to uphold the life of those whom God has freed. Moreover, a comparison of specific Deuteronomic laws with earlier versions of them found in the Book of the Covenant shows that the biblical authors felt quite free to reinterpret, add to or eliminate traditions which were no longer life-giving.

It is true that the exclusive claims to God's sovereignty do not always function in Deuteronomy to uphold life for women. The claim of divine sovereignty and command to love God serve as the impetus and rationale for obeying all of the particular instructions which make up Deuteronomic Torah. The Torah authorized by God's sovereignty includes a number of laws which presuppose the subordinate role of women and support the hierarchical structure of the family.[24] The texts reflect the patriarchal society out of which they emerged. The Deuteronomic recognition that the social practices of those who confess God's claims over them must manifest the will of a liberating God and exist to uphold life can serve as the basis of a critique of any customs or laws that subordinate a segment of the community. The metaphor of God's liberating sovereignty can function to challenge hierarchical structures within the community of those who acknowledge that Sovereign.

The Sole Sovereignty of God and the 'Other'

The picture is very different when one turns from relationships within the covenant community to relationships between the community and 'outsiders', that is, religious dissenters or other nations. Here, one encounters the dangerous dimension of the Deuteronomic insistence on the exclusive sovereignty of its God. That is, the Deuteronomic image of God the Suzerain is inseparable from the image of God the Warrior.

and Roland E. Murphy; New York: Oxford University Press, 1991).

24. See Carolyn Pressler, *The View of Women Found in the Deuteronomic Family Laws* (BZAW, 216; Berlin: W. de Gruyter, 1993).

The act of liberation which serves as the basis of God's claim to sovereignty is an act of war.

Moreover, the Deuteronomic Sovereign demands that the community's allegiance be totally pure, and threatens to punish severely any deviance from that pure allegiance. Deuteronomy views those who engage in other worship practices as enticers who threaten the purity of the community and therefore endanger Israel. They must be destroyed. Protecting God's sovereignty serves as a rationale for commanding Israel to annihilate the indigenous population of the land and to execute dissident local religious leaders (Deut. 13.2-6). The command 'love God' is made concrete in a violent demand: 'kill them...stone them to death' (cf. 23.1-6).[25] In these instances, the metaphor of God's sole sovereignty clearly implies a view of power as domination. Deuteronomy commands those who belong to its God to align themselves over and against those who do not. Differences among people are understood in hierarchical and dualistic ways that deny not only the 'integrity and specificity' of the other, but even the other's very right to exist.

The exclusivistic and militaristic cast of Deuteronomy is understandable in light of the historical periods during which the book was compiled and edited. Most biblical scholars agree that Deuteronomy provides not a realistic depiction of Israel's emergence in the land, but a theological and political interpretation of Israel's story compiled at the time of Josiah and edited during the exile. The martial character of the book served to support King Josiah's efforts to reassert Judah's national identity after generations of Assyrian domination. During the exile, the Deuteronomic insistence that ultimately the only sovereign power belongs to the God who fights for Israel and claims its total allegiance would have been a basis of hope of restoration for a power-less people. The concern of this paper is not to criticize ancient (or modern) Israel, but to investigate whether and how feminists in our time might appropriate the Deuteronomic assertion of the exclusive sovereignty of a liberating God.

---

25. 'Love' between God and Israel in the book of Deuteronomy is intertwined with violence. Divine destruction of the indigenous inhabitants of the land is cited as evidence of God's love for Israel (Deut. 4.37-38; 7.13, 16) and as the basis of Israel's love for God (Deut. 11.1, 4-6).

Conclusions

This essay has explored the dual questions: 'Can the *Shema'* provide theological grounding for a feminist reappropriation of Deuteronomy?' and 'Can Deuteronomy provide content for a feminist reinterpretation of the *Shema'*?' The answer to both questions must be: not without qualification. It is true that the image of the liberating warrior God who rules with absolute sovereignty has tremendous power to undergird the struggle of dominated peoples against their oppressors. The deity's exclusive sovereignty challenges any human claims to dominion over the community. Moreover, the image of an all-powerful warrior God fighting on 'our' side obviously has the capacity to engender confidence.

But Deuteronomy also highlights the dangers of the understanding of God as an exclusivistic warrior sovereign. When that image is united with the image of God as a judge who punishes lack of allegiance, and the view that others constitute a threat to the purity of faith, the danger is intensified.

Asserting the sole sovereignty of God need not be understood as asserting the exclusive rightness of a single image or understanding of the Holy. Nor does the confession of God's sovereign power necessarily lead to the assumption that God will use that power for 'our side'. Nevertheless, consideration of the *Shema'* as a Deuteronomic text demonstrates the dangerous ease with which these assertions can be confused. There is nothing in the Deuteronomic formulation of the sovereignty of its God which can serve as a critique of religious intolerance and violence against those outside the covenant community.

Other contexts may provide more useable insights for feminist reappropriation of the *Shema'*. For example, in her response to an earlier version of this essay, Setel noted that she responds to the *Shema'* from a liturgical context rather a biblical one. Her translation and interpretation of the verses are free from the constraints imposed by taking the *Shema'* as a Deuteronomic text. Setel lifted up 'one all together', or 'unity' rather than 'one all alone' as a possible translation of the word *'ehad*. As Setel implied, to affirm that God is 'unity' or 'one all together' suggests a view of reality that leaves room for respecting both the 'integrity and specificity' and the essential relatedness of differing beings. Another intriguing context for a Christian feminist appropriation of the *Shema'* is the Gospel of Luke. There, the command to love God with all of one's heart (etc.) is irrevocably linked to the command to love one's neighbor, while the adjoining parable, 'the Good Samaritan', establishes that love of 'neighbor' transcends ethnic barriers.

I would like to end this essay by repeating the theological affirmation with which it began. That is, I believe that the radical centralization of divine power affirmed by the *Shema'* is vital for women. The oneness and effective power of God is the basis of hope for wholeness and freedom. The *Shema'* can be interpreted from a positive feminist perspective.

Deuteronomy does provide some tantalizing ways to think about God's effective, unfragmented power as feminists set about that interpretation. The metaphors for divine sovereignty and power suggested by Deuteronomy cannot be adopted unreservedly, however. Feminist critique of dualistic thought and feminist commitment to respect the 'integrity and specificity' of those who differ from one another call for a non-hierarchical, non-violent, inclusive understanding of divine sovereignty and power.

READING THE OPENING CHAPTER OF LUKE
FROM A FEMINIST PERSPECTIVE

Joseph Vlcek Kozar

Introduction

My purpose here is not to give 'the' feminist reading of the opening scenes of Luke's Gospel, but 'a' feminist reading of them. My mandate is to read a particular text, Lk. 1.5-80, from a feminist perspective and, at the same time, reflect on the elements that constitute this reading. I follow a definition of feminism that Mary Ann Tolbert articulates as an agreed minimum: 'Feminism, like other liberation movements, attempts a critique of the oppressive structures of society.'[1] Such radical analysis identifies feminist criticism as coming out of a sensitivity to social location.[2] A feminist reading looks at gender, culture, class, politics and oppression as experiences which control one's reading and understanding of a text. Feminist reading readily acknowledges its subjectivity and argues that, in fact, no reading is ever objective and without its own agenda. 'Objective scholarship' masks interests in the status quo.

One task of the feminist reading of a biblical text consists of uncovering what have been termed 'counter-cultural impulses' within a text.[3] A second consists of reading against the text,[4] analyzing liberated

---

1. Mary Ann Tolbert, 'Defining the Problem: The Bible and Feminist Hermeneutics', *Semeia* 28 (1983), pp. 113-26 (113). Tolbert goes on to say that this radical critique, the possibility of male feminists, and the ensuing feminist praxis open up areas of wide difference of opinion.

2. Janice Capel Anderson, 'Mapping Feminist Biblical Criticism: The American Scene, 1983–1990', *Critical Review of Books and Religion* (1991), pp. 21-44 (24), asks, 'What difference does the gender (male and female), social location, and ideology of a reader make?' 'Social location' may serve as an inclusive term.

3. Anderson, 'Mapping Feminist Biblical Criticism', p. 24.

4. On feminist models of reading, see Patrocinio P. Schweickart, 'Reading Ourselves: Toward a Feminist Theory of Reading', in Elizabeth A. Flynn and

substructures which the final text may have pacified with a view to exposing them once again.[5]

The Gospel of Luke

Luke's Gospel has been rightly identified as a dangerous text for feminists since in the New Testament canon it contains much unique information about women. Some have regarded the Lukan evangelist as a special 'friend' of women. Yet incrementally Luke's Gospel narrative places women in a position of subordinate service under the headship of legitimate male leadership.[6] It is all the more surprising, then, that women in the opening chapter appear in roles far more powerful than in the rest of the Gospel.[7]

Setting Up the Reading

In order to facilitate a self-conscious reading of Luke's first chapter, four commentaries form a backdrop for my feminist reading: Frederick W. Danker (*Jesus and the New Age: A Commentary on St. Luke's Gospel*),[8] Joseph A. Fitzmyer (*The Gospel According to Luke I-IX*),[9] I. Howard Marshall (*The Gospel of Luke*),[10] and Robert C. Tannehill (*The Narrative Unity of Luke–Acts: A Literary Interpretation*, I).[11] Danker pays close attention to the Greco-Roman cultural environment.

Patrocinio P. Schweickart (eds.), *Gender and Reading: Essays on Readers, Texts and Contexts* (Baltimore: The Johns Hopkins University Press, 1986), pp. 31-62.

5.   See Judith Fetterley, *The Resisting Reader: A Feminist Approach to American Fiction* (Bloomington: Indiana University Press, 1978); Judith Fetterley, 'Reading about Reading: *A Jury of her Peers, The Murders in the Rue Morgue*, and *The Yellow Wallpaper*', in Elizabeth A. Flynn and Patrocinio P. Schweickart (eds.), *Gender and Reading: Essays on Readers, Texts, and Contests* (Baltimore: The Johns Hopkins University Press, 1986), pp. 147-64.

6.   For a critique of the female role models which the Gospel of Luke offers, see Jane Schaberg, 'Luke', in Carol A. Newsom and Sharon H. Ringe (eds.), *The Women's Bible Commentary* (Louisville, KY: Westminster/John Knox Press, 1992), pp. 275-92.

7.   Schaberg, 'Luke', p. 282. Schaberg notes that it may be because the women here inhabit the traditional woman's role of bearing and raising children.

8.   (Philadelphia: Fortress Press, rev. edn, 1988).

9.   (AB, 28; Garden City, NY: Doubleday, 1981).

10.   (Grand Rapids; Eerdmans, 1978).

11.   (2 vols.; Philadelphia: Fortress Press, 1986).

Fitzmyer offers a Catholic commentary. Marshall writes from a Protestant evangelical perspective. Tannehill writes one of the first literary interpretations of the Gospel of Luke. After presenting my own reading of a section, I summarize how my selected commentaries have read the text.

A Feminist Reading of Luke 1

A feminist reading of Luke's opening chapter focuses on the interplay between the chapter's two female characters, Mary and Elizabeth. It considers as well how both women contrast with the male character Zechariah. In the first chapter the angel Gabriel's appearance to both Zechariah and Mary invites comparison. Elizabeth's articulate response to events contrasts with her husband's forced mute reaction. In the chapter each of these characters speaks but Zechariah's speech (out of chronological order) closes the chapter.

The character of Elizabeth serves as a bridge linking the chapter's four scenes: (1) Gabriel's annunciation of John's conception and birth to Zechariah (and its fulfillment with Elizabeth's conception), (2) Gabriel's annunciation to Mary of Jesus' conception and birth (and the disclosure that Mary's kinswoman Elizabeth has conceived), (3) Mary's visit to Elizabeth, and (4) Elizabeth's argument with relatives over naming her child John. Since Elizabeth's character is the linchpin, I will focus on her narrative role in the chapter as the basis for this feminist reading.

Patriarchal Structure

Patriarchal structure dominates the chapter. King Herod's reign serves as the time-frame reference for the story (1.5, following the prologue 1.1-4). The male, Zechariah, is a priest (of the order of Abijah) and his wife Elizabeth is identified as a female descendant in the male line of Aaron (1.5). In a similar manner Mary is identified as the one betrothed to Joseph of the house of David (1.27). Zechariah travels to the sanctuary (1.9); Elizabeth remains at home in the hill country. Both promised children are males (1.13; 1.31). At the end of the chapter, kinsfolk attempt to overturn Elizabeth's bestowing the name 'John' to the child with an appeal to the father Zechariah (1.62). In the end, only Zechariah's naming of the child counts (1.63) and only the father prophesies about his son's future. The promises involved in the story trace their origins to the patriarchs Abraham and Jacob, and to King David. None of my reference commentaries explicitly notes the patriarchal bias of Luke's opening chapter.

A Childless Couple

The dilemma which opens the story consists of the fact that Zechariah and Elizabeth remain childless (1.7). Two reasons are offered by the narrator. First, the reader is told that Elizabeth is barren and, only afterwards, that both are advanced in years (1.7b). Clearly the blame rests with the barren woman.

Danker explains that this comment emphasizes that any hope for a child has faded away. He compares Zechariah and Elizabeth to Abraham and Sarah (Gen. 17–18); Isaac and Rebekah (Gen. 25.21); Jacob and Rachel (Gen. 30.1); the parents of Samson, Manoah and his wife (Judg. 13); and Samuel's parents, Elkanah and Hannah (1 Sam. 1).[12] The circumstance of Elizabeth's being infertile, Fitzmyer argues, informs the reader that she belongs to the class of barren women who are the mothers of famous Old Testament patriarchs or leaders.[13] Marshall notes that to be childless was considered a reproach and perhaps a sign of God's punishment.[14] Tannehill also emphasizes Elizabeth's resemblance to the barren Hannah, mother of Samuel (1 Sam 1.10-11) but does not comment on the blame assigned Elizabeth.[15] Reference to past instances when biblical scenes place blame for infertility on women enable commentators to minimize Elizabeth's plight.

The Angel's Appearance to Zechariah

An angel appears to Zechariah in the opening scene of the story while he ministers at the altar of incense. After announcing that Zechariah's prayer has been answered, the angel proceeds in predictive narration to describe events which have not yet occurred.[16] Since the angel is God's

---

12. *Jesus and the New Age*, p. 28.

13. *The Gospel According to Luke I–IX*, p. 323.

14. *The Gospel of Luke*, pp. 53. Marshall cites Gen. 1.28; Pss. 127–128.

15. *The Narrative Unity of Luke–Acts*, p. 18. Tannehill sees the barren motif as representative of a biblical type-scene.

16. On predictive narration, see Shlomith Rimmon-Kennan, *Narrative Fiction: Contemporary Poetics* (New York: Methuen, 1983), pp. 3-4. Rimmon-Kennan observes that narration, which is an event like any other in narrative, can hold various temporal relations with events of the story. In this instance the situation is

agent in the story, the angel's predictions deserve the reader's careful attention.

First of all, the angel announces an end to the couple's childless condition (1.13c), God's messenger offers a correlative role for Zechariah, he will name the child John (1.13d). The angel, moreover, describes the future. When these things occur, Zechariah will experience joy and gladness (1.14a). Many will rejoice with him at the child's birth (1.14b). This child will be great in the eyes of the Lord and he will be filled with the Holy Spirit even from the womb of his mother (1.15). The angel also reveals that God has given the child a mission. He will turn many of the 'sons' of Israel to the Lord their God (1.16). In the spirit of Elijah, the promised child will go before the Lord to turn the hearts of fathers to the children and the disobedient to the wisdom of the just, to prepare for the Lord a people prepared (1.17).

The angel's prophecy contains strong male imagery. A male, Zechariah, receives the promise of a son. The man will name the child. The father will experience joy and gladness and many will rejoice with him. The male child will be filled with the Holy Spirit from the womb. He will turn many sons of Israel to God, and in the spirit of the male prophet Elijah turn the hearts of fathers to the children.

Danker does not privilege the angel's prediction. He likens the promise of a son to the same promise given by God to Abraham concerning Sarah (Gen. 17.19). Without comment on the gender-specific nature of the promise, Danker points out a similarity to Sir. 48.10 and comments that the promise in Lk. 1.17 may mean 'that the fathers would recognize their children as God's righteous people and would rejoice that they were following the ways of the Lord'.[17]

Fitzmyer reads 1.13-17 in light of a five-element pattern of Old Testament birth announcements. He also notes the comparison between the promise to Abraham and the one given Zechariah. Fitzmyer holds that 1.15-17 defines the role of the Baptist as great in God's sight, a Spirit-filled Nazarite who is sent like Elijah for Israel's conversion.[18]

Marshall does not comment on the promise of a son but observes that Zechariah's joy will be occasioned by his son's preparing the people for the coming of the Lord. Previewing his reading of 1.41, Marshall

complicated by the fact that the predictive narration comes from a character whose actions are already the object of the narrator; see pp. 91-92.

17. *Jesus and the New Age*, p. 31.

18. *The Gospel According to Luke I–IX*, p. 318.

says the promise of the Holy Spirit from the womb implies a prenatal sanctification for John. Based on the Malachi text (4.5-6 RSV), Marshall interprets the promised task of turning the hearts of fathers to their sons to mean that fathers and sons are reconciled to one another.[19]

Tannehill views 1.13-17 as an interpretative preview of what will happen later in the story. The angel's promise of joy for Zechariah (and many with him) achieves fulfillment within the birth narrative itself. This is true of the promise that the child will be filled with the Holy Spirit in the womb.[20]

Only Tannehill reads the angel's opening statement as a preview. None of the commentators speak of necessity for the reader to observe how (and whether) the angel's predictive narration actually occurs. Zechariah's unexpected negative response to the predictive narration, which immediately follows, demonstrates that the angel's prophecy cannot be viewed as a straightforward outline of upcoming story events.

Zechariah questions the angel because he and his wife are advanced in years (1.18). Zechariah's objection comes as no surprise to the reader who judges the truth of what has been said from previous expositional material (1.7). Given Zechariah's seemingly justified misgivings, the angel's reply astonishes the reader. Explicitly identified as Gabriel who stands in God's presence, the angel pronounces judgment by silencing Zechariah (1.20).

The heavenly communicator breaks off all possibility of communication as a punishment for Zechariah's lack of faith. The reader knows that 'what' Zechariah says is true (1.7). But the reader could not know that Zechariah's words give expression to his unbelief, aside from the angel's verdict. Gabriel, who earlier identified Zechariah's hidden fear (1.13a), is able to detect the underlying lack of faith which sparks Zechariah's demand for a sign. Gabriel's response is not only punitive, it again contains predictive narration. The angel directs both Zechariah and the reader to a future moment in the story when the predictions will find fulfillment. The reader is left in a quandary. How shall the predicted future come about?

Since demands for signs typically identify unbelievers in Luke's story, Danker explains the angel's action as a direct result of the request. Danker also highlights the literary function of Zechariah's

---

19. *The Gospel of Luke*, pp. 55-60.
20. *The Narrative Unity of Luke–Acts*, p. 23.

request. This query allows for the chapter's final scene and the elaborate scenario which surrounds the naming of the child (1.57-80). Danker holds that Zechariah's muteness was a prophetic sign betokening rebellion and judgment.[21]

For Fitzmyer, Gabriel's exchange with Zechariah constitutes the fourth and fifth elements of the Old Testament birth-announcement pattern. Zechariah echoes Abraham's objection (Gen. 15.8). Fitzmyer calls Gabriel's stricture a punitive miracle.[22]

Marshall also likens Zechariah's request to that of Abraham. Based on Old Testament patterns, Marshall says that we should not regard Zechariah's request simply as a sign of lack of faith or his being mute as punishment for unbelief. Marshall identifies the punishment as a sign that conceals the wonder of what will happen at the appointed time.[23]

Tannehill also identifies Zechariah's punishment as a sign.[24] Again, the male's action is justified by reference to what other males have done in the Hebrew Bible. The identification of Zechariah's muteness as a sign originates in the interpreter's attempt to discover exact parallel structures between the annunciation scenes involving Zechariah and Mary.

None of the commentators are willing to see Zechariah's punishment as a punishment. His 'lack' of faith becomes a positive sign. It is a punitive miracle or a concealing wonder. Whereas the plight of Elizabeth's being barren receives slight sympathy, Zechariah's actually becomes a positive sign linked to Abraham's questioning of God's promise of Isaac.

The piling up of male imagery in the predictive narration of the opening scene demands careful examination in a feminist reading. Furthermore, given the punishment meted out to Zechariah, can the reader simply conclude that the male character will play the role which Gabriel's prophecy seems to promise him? A silenced husband (the male character) means that only the wife (the female character) remains in play.

Mary Visits Elizabeth
Mary's encounter with Elizabeth (1.39-56) marks the place in the story

21. *Jesus and the New Age*, p. 33.
22. *The Gospel According to Luke I–IX*, pp. 320, 328.
23. *The Gospel of Luke*, p. 60.
24. *The Narrative Unity of Luke–Acts*, p. 15.

where Gabriel's predictive narration to Zechariah first plays itself out in the story. The narrator reports: 'And when Elizabeth heard the greeting of Mary, the babe leapt in her womb; and Elizabeth was filled with the Holy Spirit' (1.41). These words fulfill Gabriel's prophecy that John would be 'filled with the Holy Spirit from his mother's womb' (1.15b). But where Gabriel emphasized the child John, the narration of the fulfillment highlights the character Elizabeth (1.41).

The reader must conclude that Elizabeth's being filled with the Holy Spirit (1.41c) means that her son John receives the Spirit as well. Clearly there is a change of focus. Responding to Mary, Elizabeth recapitulates and comments on the moment of her encounter with Mary. Commenting on the moment when she was filled with the Holy Spirit (reported by the narrator at 1.41), Elizabeth adds the additional information that the child leaped 'for joy' (*en agalliasei*, 1.44). Elizabeth, therefore, and not Zechariah first experiences the 'joy' (*agalliasis*), promised in Gabriel's predictive narration.

None of my reference commentaries detects this twist. Danker interprets the scene in terms of the male embryo in Elizabeth's womb. He notes that the movement in the womb is one of the portents which fix attention on the divine purpose which underlies the story. Elizabeth's words express the significance of John's activity. The unborn John relates to the unborn Jesus. Elizabeth is filled with the Holy Spirit but her son has already displayed the truth of Gabriel's words (1.15). When Elizabeth speaks at 1.44 she is merely echoing John's own understanding while he was yet unborn. John jumped for joy upon hearing Mary's voice.[25]

Fitzmyer has a similar reading of the verses. As Mary greets Elizabeth, the child in Elizabeth's womb leaps prophetically, and from that, Elizabeth, filled with the Holy Spirit, concludes that Mary is to give birth to the 'Lord' (1.43).[26]

Marshall explains that even before Elizabeth could respond to Mary's words, the child did. While the (male) foetus can do no more than jump for joy, his mother Elizabeth gives verbal expression to the significance of the scene.[27]

Tannehill also interprets the scene in light of the male child. While

---

25. *Jesus and the New Age*, pp. 40-41.
26. *The Gospel According to Luke I–IX*, pp. 357-58.
27. *The Gospel of Luke*, p. 80.

still in the womb, the unborn John provides a prophetic sign to his mother.[28]

It would seem that for these commentators an unborn male child must take precedence over his mother when it comes to reception of the Spirit. Rather than accept Elizabeth's explanation at 1.44 of the unexplained event of the child's movement in her womb (1.41), the text is understood in terms of the male embryo. Ignoring Elizabeth's words, commentators find a strict fulfillment of Gabriel's predictive narration (1.15).

Naming the Child

Three verses of summary (1.57-59) establish the background for the chapter's final scene, the naming of the child (1.57-80). The narrator's reference to the completion of Elizabeth's time and the fact that she gave birth to a son (1.57) refers back to Gabriel's predictive narration. This literally fulfills the promise given to Zechariah, 'Your wife will bear you a son' (1.13b). Secondly, Gabriel sets the time of Elizabeth's delivery as the *terminus ad quem* for the spell he cast on Zechariah (1.20a). The reader fully expects Zechariah to name the child 'John' (1.13b).

In describing the birth, the narrator gives a positive role to the neighbors and kinsfolk who are identified with Elizabeth (use of possessive 'her' at 1.58). This crowd rejoices with Elizabeth (*kai sunechairon autē*, 1.58b). Gabriel promised that 'many will rejoice (*charēsontai*, 1.14) at the child's birth. This joyous celebration occurs first with Elizabeth, the one who first expressed parental joy (1.44) and not Zechariah.

In the actual scene (1.59-66), the crowd switches roles and becomes a foil to Elizabeth. Taking the initiative on the day of circumcision, the relatives want to name (call) the child 'Zechariah' after his father (1.59b). Elizabeth rejects this counsel saying, 'Not so; he shall be called John' (1.60).

The obvious surprise is that Elizabeth usurps the place of Zechariah whom the reader expects to utter these words. She repeats Gabriel's predictive narration (1.13b; 1.60). The narrator intends just this surprise. Elizabeth has been the narrator's reliable vehicle throughout the story. In contrast to Zechariah, she believes that God has acted in her pregnancy (1.25a). Her pregnancy becomes the sign gratuitously

---

28. *The Narrative Unity of Luke–Acts*, p. 23.

offered to Mary by Gabriel as an indicator of God's power (1.36). Filled with the Holy Spirit, Elizabeth informs the reader that Mary's conception has taken place (1.43).

Limits Imposed by the Story
But the story's patriarchal bias cannot be overcome in the end. The crowd launches a final appeal of the matter to the silent Zechariah (1.61-62). Zechariah officially names the child (1.63b), fulfilling Gabriel's promise. While the points raised in Gabriel's predictive narration find surprising fulfillment in female characters, this recognition in a feminist reading is frustrated by the fact that they occur off the record and in the final analysis don't count.

Danker comments on Elizabeth's insistence that the child be called John in spite of the clamor to name him after the father. He explains that it is beyond the formal requirements of Luke's narrative to inquire whether Zechariah had already communicated the proper name to his wife.[29]

Fitzmyer sees no contradiction in the scene with what Gabriel predicted. 'With the birth of John', Fitzmyer says, 'the promise to Zechariah is fulfilled. This child, born to barren parents, becomes the source of joy to neighbors and relatives, as the angel predicted.' In his commentary, Fitzmyer ignores the controversy between Elizabeth and the crowd. In the notes Fitzmyer argues that for the sake of the story it must be supposed that the name 'John' was somehow communicated to Elizabeth.[30]

Marshall observes that Elizabeth's neighbors share her joy but simply draws a parallel to the shepherds' joy at the birth of Jesus. While acknowledging Elizabeth's strong 'no' to a family name, Marshall quotes other commentators who attribute Elizabeth's knowledge to the fact that Zechariah probably informed his wife a hundred times over the correct name.[31]

Tannehill ignores the character Elizabeth. He comments on the fact that Zechariah's promise of joy begins to be fulfilled in the birth narrative.[32]

29. *Jesus and the New Age*, p. 46.
30. *The Gospel According to Luke I–IX*, pp. 372, 381.
31. *The Gospel of Luke*, pp. 88-89. Marshall seems to think that the crowd may not have figured out that Zechariah consulted with his wife as to the proper name.
32. *The Narrative Unity of Luke–Acts*, p. 23.

Commentators subordinate Elizabeth as a character to Zechariah. Her words don't count, Elizabeth's naming of the child carries no weight until validated by the male Zechariah. The joy explicitly shared with Elizabeth is interpreted (wrongly) as a strict fulfillment of the promise of joy to Zechariah.

Elizabeth and Mary

Elizabeth and Mary are intertwined characters in Luke's opening chapter. Their experience moves the story forward. Indeed, Elizabeth's reliable commentary provides the reader with a proper understanding of Mary's role.

After the opening scene of the angel's appearance to Zechariah (1.5-23), the narrator documents the first fulfillment of Gabriel's predictive narration by reporting that Elizabeth conceives (1.24b; 1.13c). The narrator's description of Elizabeth's action in consequence of her pregnancy is surprising: 'And for five months she hid herself' (1.24c). Breaking away from summary,[33] the narrator next allows Elizabeth to speak: 'Thus the Lord has done to me in the days when he looked on me, to take away my reproach from among men' (1.25). Elizabeth speaks to the reader (at the level of discourse) but remains silent at the story level. Without benefit of angelic messenger, Elizabeth acknowledges the truth which the reader, privy to the prior annunciation scene, recognizes. In contrast to Zechariah, Elizabeth believes. By her words Elizabeth establishes herself as a reliable character. Her seclusion, however, remains a mystery.

In the chapter's second scene the angel appears to Mary. This scene invites comparison with the just-prior annunciation to Zechariah. As in the first scene, in predictive narration, the angel sketches out a future for Mary and her child (1.30-33). As before, male imagery predominates. A male child will be given the throne of David his father and rule over the house of Jacob, establishing an everlasting kingdom.

Mary's response, 'How shall this be since I have no husband (1.34)?', takes the reader back to Zechariah's questioning of the angel at just this juncture in his apparition scene. Unlike Zechariah, Mary receives no reprimand from Gabriel. The angel straightforwardly

33. R. Alter, *The Art of Biblical Narrative* (New York: Basic Books, 1981), pp. 67-68, notes, 'The biblical preference for direct discourse is so pronounced that thought is almost invariably rendered as actual speech, that is, as quoted monologue'.

answers her question and points Mary and the reader to the future
(1.35). But having answered completely Mary's question, the angel
freely grants the sign of Elizabeth's pregnancy (1.36a), the very thing
refused Zechariah.

Gabriel's revelation that this is Elizabeth's sixth month (1.36b) deci-
phers Elizabeth's period of hiding (1.24) for the reader. Elizabeth's
pregnancy is revealed at the story level as a sign for her kinswoman,
Mary. In fact, God waits to send the angel based on the progress of
Elizabeth's pregnancy (1.26a). A delayed report of the blood kinship
between Mary and Elizabeth further unifies the chapter and prepares the
way for Mary's visit of Elizabeth.

Danker interprets John's conception as Zechariah's keeping faith
with the angel's word. He suggests that Elizabeth's explanation of her
hiding contains a motif of judgment. She does not want to provoke further divine wrath in addition to Zechariah's muteness. The fact that
Elizabeth views the pregnancy as a result of God's agency remains
subordinate to the frightening method by which God accomplished this.
Danker does not comment on the male imagery of Gabriel's prophecy.
He notes that Mary's question seems irrelevant since, though she has
not had intimate relations with a man, she looks forward to a normal
marriage. Danker observes that, literarily, Mary's question provides
Gabriel an opportunity to relate the circumstances surrounding Jesus'
conception.[34]

Marshall says without comment that Jewish women regarded baren-
ness as a severe reproach (Gen. 30.23). Elizabeth's motive for hiding
may have been to avoid further reproach from incredulous neighbors or
an attempt to follow her husband's example in not spreading the news.
But Marshall identifies the delay primarily as a literary device. He does
not comment on the male imagery of the promises. Marshall lists as one
alternative that Mary may be asking how she can conceive since she
has not begun to menstruate. Finally, Marshall explains Mary's question as part of Luke's retelling of the event.[35]

Tannehill speaks of the imbalance between the description of
Elizabeth's conception and the visitation scene. Zechariah has been
silenced and cannot give his canticle till later. Elizabeth cannot serve as
a replacement songster for her husband since she has not received the
angel's message which forecasts the baby's role. Mary's canticle comes

34. *Jesus and the New Age*, pp. 33-38.
35. *The Gospel of Luke*, pp. 62-70.

first in the story even though Zechariah's would have taken first place had he believed. Tannehill draws out the implications between predictions made for John and Jesus. He notes, but does not comment on, the male imagery of the predictive narration (1.30-33). In Tannehill's reading, Mary's question fits the same pattern as Zechariah's— although Tannehill notes that Zechariah incurred punishment for disbelief.[36]

Commentators do not take seriously Elizabeth's recognition that God has caused her pregnancy. Her statement contrasts strongly with Zechariah's failure to believe Gabriel's message. Similarly, Gabriel's gratuitous gift of the sign of Elizabeth's pregnancy loses its uniqueness since commentators frequently construe Zechariah's punishment as the corresponding first sign.

Mary Visits Elizabeth

Mary takes the role of traveler and greeter that prior to this point Gabriel held in the story when she visits Elizabeth (1.39-40). Filled with the Holy Spirit, Elizabeth pronounces the first pair of blessings recorded in the Gospel: 'Blessed are you among women, and blessed is the fruit of your womb' (1.42). Her second blessing informs the reader that the promised overshadowing (1.35) has taken place. Mary is obviously blessed among women because she carries the blessed child.

Elizabeth concludes her speech by proclaiming the first macarism of the Gospel: 'And blessed (*makaria*) is she who believed there would be a fulfillment of what was spoken to her from the Lord' (1.45). What was spoken can only refer to Mary's assent to Gabriel's words (1.26-35). Spirit-filled Elizabeth, who is established by her belief from the start as a reliable vessel[37] for the narrator (1.25), proclaims Mary blessed for faith not simply for physical maternity. However, this dynamic portrayal of Mary has no lasting consequence. By ch. 2 Mary is transformed (deformed) into a passive, meditative character, devoid of initiative.

Mary responds to Elizabeth's blessings with a canticle (1.46-55). She speaks of God as her 'savior' and herself as God's slave (1.47-48; see

---

36. *The Narrative Unity of Luke–Acts*, p. 17.

37. 'The author is present in every speech given by any character who has conferred upon him [*sic*], in whatever manner, the badge of reliability.' Wayne Booth, *The Rhetoric of Fiction* (Chicago: University of Chicago Press, 2nd edn, 1983), p. 18.

1.38). Mary acknowledges the blessings that Elizabeth has given her
predicting that successor generations will do what Elizabeth has done
(1.48). Like Elizabeth (1.48) Mary speaks of God's power to reverse
oppressive circumstances. God puts down the mighty from their
thrones and exalts those of low degree (1.51-52). If such activity characterizes God in Luke's Gospel, Elizabeth and Mary serve as exemplars
of God's liberating activity. For all its hope, however, no chorus of
women take up Mary's song in the rest of Luke's Gospel story. Women
join the ranks of the exorcized and healed, they are servers, but never
leaders, apostles, or decision makers.

Danker observes that Elizabeth's double blessing is found also in
Gen. 14.19-20. He explains that the main focus is not Mary but, as is
customary in the East, a praise of remarkable offspring. Shifting the
focus, Danker argues that Elizabeth recites the Magnificat.[38]

Fitzmyer sees a double blessing for Mary: first for her motherhood of
the Lord and, above all, for her faith. Yet when Fitzmyer explains
Mary's humility in 1.48, he places emphasis on the former by saying
that all generations will call Mary blessed, not because of inherent personal holiness or merit, but because of him whom she is bearing.[39]

Marshall relates the remark of another commentator that Mary's high
evaluation relies solely on her Son. Mary is blessed in that she believes
that God will fulfill his word, since God will fulfill it.[40]

Tannehill likens the Magnificat to an aria in an opera, the action
stops and it should be sweetly savored. Elizabeth's neighbors hear that
the Lord magnified his mercy towards her (1.58). Mary proclaims that
her soul magnifies the Lord (1.46). Elizabeth explains that the Lord
looked upon her to remove her reproach before people (1.25). Mary
speaks of God's looking upon the humble state of his servant (1.48).
Tannehill sees that Mary's prediction that all generations will call her
blessed corresponds to what Elizabeth has just done.[41]

Commentators do not notice that Mary acts in the place of Gabriel,
that the first blessing in the Gospel is from a woman to a woman, or
that Elizabeth announces Jesus' conception. Mary is recognized as a
believer but too often physical maternity replaces active faith as Mary's
distinctive attribute. Literary critics pick out connections between

38. *Jesus and the New Age*, pp. 40-45.
39. *The Gospel According to Luke I–IX*, pp. 356-62.
40. *The Gospel of Luke*, p. 81.
41. *The Narrative Unity of Luke–Acts*, pp. 31-32.

Elizabeth and Mary as well as their role of exemplifying the reversal of circumstance which will characterize Jesus' ministry.

Conclusions

A feminist reading of Luke's opening chapter focuses on the surprising way in which Elizabeth and Mary fulfill a predictive narration which is almost completely overshadowed by male imagery. It listens to the women characters and respects their explanations of their experience. A feminist reading sympathetically follows and recognizes what may be a subversive substructure to the story Luke tells. In this substratum, Elizabeth and Mary clearly vocalize the deeper significance of story events.

A feminist reading of Luke's opening chapter esteems Elizabeth's primal faith and her decision to seclude herself in service of God's plan. It appreciates the strength of Mary's 'yes' to God in contrast to Zechariah's doubt. It recognizes Mary as the 'female Gabriel', bringing powerful greetings to her kinswoman Elizabeth. It values Elizabeth's role as Spirit-filled herald who proclaims Jesus' conception while, at the same time, she underscores the efficacy of Mary's faith. It celebrates the bonding between kinswomen.

At the same time, a feminist reading of Luke's opening chapter recognizes that the overarching patriarchal structure of the narrative cannot be finessed away. A feminist reading recognizes that at one level the forced postponement of Zechariah's speech opens narrative space for the characters of Elizabeth and Mary. Yet even this creative fissure can be seen as a reinforcement of patriarchal values. This pause becomes a punitive miracle in which the argumentative Zechariah imitates Abraham at Mamre. All the while, Zechariah retains the power to name. He claims his prerogative at the conclusion of the chapter when he names the child John and recites a canticle. Zechariah has the last word. Despite its seeming potential for affirmative feminist reading, Luke's opening chapter remains a text of terror which, in the end, reimposes patriarchal perspectives upon the unwary reader.

A feminist reading of Luke's opening chapter does not sanitize it or tame its horrors. Elizabeth never publicly speaks in the story world. Her naming of John doesn't count. Mary's canticle is sung only to a female audience of one. Mary never parlays her blessedness into recognized leadership. In the end a feminist reading of Luke's opening chapter must be recognized as a vigilant adventure, an experience of resistance, and a resolution more to subvert the text than to claim it.

'AND SHE WET HIS FEET WITH HER TEARS':
A FEMINIST INTERPRETATION OF LUKE 7.36-50*

Judith K. Applegate

Feminist Literary Method:
For the Marginalized and Not against Them

Because of the pernicious tendency of conservative religious and political groups to use the Bible against women, people of color, homosexuals and others who differ from privileged groups, I search for methods of biblical interpretation that take the text seriously, that proclaim liberation, and that cannot be coopted by oppressors to be used against the marginalized.

The two most popular methods used for liberation, imaginative historical reconstruction and neo-orthodox types of interpretations, have been inadequate.[1] Both allow the reader to use as authoritative those texts and reconstructions that coincide with the reader's value system.[2]

* I am grateful for the questions and comments I received from students, faculty and colleagues at the Faculty Forum at Earlham School of Religion and in the Feminist Theological Hermeneutics of the Bible Group at the 1990 Annual SBL Meetings in New Orleans (especially, Kathleen Corley, Jane Schaberg and Mary Ann Tolbert).

1. For feminist, African, *mujerista* and womanist liberation critiques of the latter method see Elisabeth Schüssler Fiorenza, *In Memory of Her* (New York: Crossroad, 1983), pp. 14-17; Itumeleng J. Mosala, 'The Use of the Bible in Black Theology' (who argues that the understanding of the Bible as God's word has been oppressive to black Africans); and Elsa Tamez, 'Women's Rereading of the Bible', both in R.S. Sugirtharajah (ed.), *Voices from the Margins: Interpreting the Bible in the Third World* (Maryknoll, NY: Orbis Books: 1991), pp. 50-71; and Clarice J. Martin, 'The Haustafeln (Household Codes) in African American Biblical Interpretation: "Free Slaves" and "Subordinate Women"', in Cain Hope Felder (ed.), *Stony the Road We Trod: African American Biblical Interpretation* (Minneapolis: Fortress Press, 1991), pp. 206-31.

2. While feminist historical reconstructions are extremely important to allow

For instance, in the nineteenth-century debate about slavery, slave owners amassed Bible passages to 'show' that slavery, practised by the patriarchs, condoned by Jesus and supported by Paul, was divinely ordained. On the other hand, abolitionists focused on those texts that speak of the liberation of the Israelite slaves from Egypt and those that affirmed the dignity of all creation. Both these positions used the Bible as authoritative, each using selected portions for support. In this way the Bible functioned to empower both groups. It empowered abolitionists to fight for the freedom of slaves and authorized slave-holders to continue in 'good conscience' oppressing them.[3] The same methods of biblical interpretation have brought to a stalemate the discussion of the role of women in the family and church and debates about homosexuality. All these debates are about power: preserving the power of the privileged and mainstream versus empowering the disenfranchised and marginalized.

The use of the Bible for empowerment should not be lost. However, a method adequate for supporting the liberation of oppressed groups must supplement the empowering potential of the text with a critical corrective. It must acknowledge and expose the biases of the Bible in the social, political and economic contexts of both the text and the society in which it is being interpreted. In the case of women's liberation, it must acknowledge the patriarchal ideology influencing both the biblical text and contemporary readers. No method will be adequate that does not recognize the human process of writing, canonizing and

for new interpretations to be considered, they are more concerned with discovering the 'reality' behind the text, than with making meaning from the text, itself. See Mary Ann Tolbert, 'Protestant Feminists and the Bible: On the Horns of a Dilemma', in Alice Bach (ed.), *The Pleasure of her Text: Feminist Readings of Biblical and Historical Texts* (Philadelphia: Trinity Press, 1990), pp. 5-23. However, Jane Schaberg ('Luke', in Carol A. Newsom and Sharon H. Ringe [eds.], *The Women's Bible Commentary* [Louisville, KY: Westminster/John Knox Press, 1992], pp. 275-92) does a good job of combining historical-critical methods and feminist analysis to critique Luke's 'extremely dangerous text'. She uses a method similar to mine acknowledging both liberating and oppressive potential in the Lukan writings.

3.   See Willard M. Swartley, *Slavery, Sabbath, War and Women: Case Issues in Biblical Interpretation* (Scottsdale, PA: Herald Press, 1983), pp. 31-67, for a good discussion of how the Bible was used in the slavery debate in the nineteenth century.

interpreting the Bible and the controversies over the role and function of women in the church.

Limited and restricted views of women were common in the patriarchal societies of the Second Testament world. The writers of the Second Testament inadvertently and intentionally incorporated these views into their writings. Therefore, when the ideology and value system of the Second Testament is uncritically accepted as an authoritative model for contemporary living, women's potential for full personhood and participation in family, church and society becomes impossible.[4]

On the other hand, some segments of the first-century society disregarded patriarchal norms and experimented with egalitarian visions. Certain philosophical groups included women in their company and argued for gender equality.[5] Worshipers of Isis and some segments of Hellenistic Judaism and Christianity offered women leadership opportunities in temple worship, synagogues and house churches.[6] This egalitarian impulse is also found in the Second Testament and non-canonical Christian texts. Therefore, Second Testament portrayals of Jesus' treatment of women can no longer be considered unique and remarkable for its era. Nor can the entire Bible be seen as the singular authoritative word of God. Different messages and world-views coexist in the same Bible. Therefore, close attention must be focused on determining

4. For a discussion of the Bible as a human product affected by patriarchal assumptions see Schüssler Fiorenza, *Memory*, pp. 7-14, 43-56.

5. For discussions of women in the Greek and Roman culture, see Sarah B. Pomeroy, *Goddesses, Whores, Wives and Slaves: Women in Classical Antiquity* (New York: Schocken, 1975); David M. Schaps, *Economic Rights of Women in Ancient Greece* (Edinburgh: University of Edinburgh Press, 1979); and Mary R. Lefkowitz and Maureen B. Fant, *Women's Life in Greece and Rome: A Source Book in Translation* (Baltimore: The Johns Hopkins University Press, 1982).

6. See Sharon Kelly Heyob, *The Cult of Isis among Women in the Graeco-Roman World* (Leiden: E. J. Brill, 1975), pp. 81-110, for women's participation and leadership in the Isis religion. On Hellenistic Judaism, see Shaye D. Cohen, 'Women in the Synagogues of Antiquity', *Conservative Judaism* 54 (1980), pp. 23-29; and Bernadette Brooten, *Women Leaders in the Ancient Synagogue* (Chico, CA: Scholars Press, 1982). Both provide a corrective to the famous appendix on women in first-century Judaism in Joachim Jeremias, *Jerusalem in the Time of Jesus* (Philadelphia: Fortress Press, 1969). Also see, A.-J. Levine (ed.), *Women Like This: New Perspectives on Jewish Women in the Greco-Roman World* (Atlanta: Scholars Press, 1991). Schüssler Fiorenza (*Memory*, pp. 105-334) discusses women's participation in first-century religions, including Christianity and Judaism.

the messages of each author and the variety of meanings possible within each writing, before application is made to contemporary life.

My interpretation of Lk. 7.36-50 will combine a close examination of the details of the story with a feminist critique in order to clarify the rhetorical potential of the passage.[7] Most studies of this passage have focused on form-critical issues. These have worked at discovering the historical sources of the story, rather than at discerning meanings of the text in its literary context.[8] By contrast, my feminist literary approach recognizes readers as cocreators with the text in the making of meaning. My reading of the story focuses sequentially on its literary context and its internal structure. I will use textual patterns to determine what is emphasized, what is implied and how terms, concepts and characters are defined.[9]

The Anointing of Jesus by a Sinful Woman, Luke 7.36-50[10]

[36]A certain one of the Pharisees asked him [Jesus][11] if he would eat with him, and when he had gone into the Pharisee's house he reclined at the table. [37]**And behold, [there was] a woman who was a sinner in the city, and when she discovered that he [Jesus] was in the house of the**

7.   I use a reader-response literary method informed by Jane P. Tompkins (ed.), *Reader-Response Criticism: From Formalism to Post-Structuralism* (Baltimore: The Johns Hopkins University Press, 1980), Susan R. Suleiman and Inge Crosman (eds.), *The Reader in the Text: Essays on Audience and Interpretation* (Princeton, NJ: Princeton University Press, 1980); and Wolfgang Iser, *The Act of Reading: A Theory of Aesthetic Response* (Baltimore: The Johns Hopkins University Press, 1978). For a feminist critique of reader-response criticism see Patrocinio P. Schweickart, 'Reading Ourselves: Toward a Feminist Theory of Reading', in Elizabeth A. Flynn and Patrocinio P. Schweickart (eds.), *Gender and Reading: Essays on Readers, Texts and Contexts* (Baltimore: The Johns Hopkins University Press, 1986), pp. 31-62.

8.   For an example, see Robert Holst, 'The One Anointing of Jesus: Another Application of the Form-Critical Method', *JBL* 95.3 (1976), pp. 435-46, who gives a fine summary of the issue and the literature.

9.   See Luke T. Johnson, *The Literary Function of Possessions in Luke–Acts* (*JBL* Dissertation Series, 39, Missoula, MT: Scholars Press, 1977), pp. 19-28, for a discussion of Luke as a literary text and the importance of a sequential reading for this Gospel.

10.   The following translation is mine.

11.   The brackets in this translation indicate a word or phrase that appears in the text only by implication.

Pharisee, she took an alabaster jar of ointment, [38]and being[12] behind him at his feet, while she was weeping, she began to wet his feet with her tears, and she was wiping [them] with the hair of her head, and she was kissing his feet and she was anointing [them] with oint-ment.[13] [39]And when the Pharisee who had invited him saw [this], he said within himself, 'If this man were a prophet, he would know who and what kind of woman is touching him, that she is a sinner.' [40]And Jesus answered and said to him, 'Simon, I have something to say to you.' [Simon replied] 'Teacher, speak.' And Jesus spoke forth, [41]'A certain creditor had two debtors. One owed five hundred denarii, and the other fifty. [42]When they did not have the money to repay the creditor, he forgave both of them. Therefore, which of them will love him more?' [43]Simon answered and said to him, 'I suppose the one to whom he for-gave most.' And he [Jesus] said to him, 'You have judged correctly.' [44]And turning to the woman, he spoke to Simon, 'Do you see this woman? I entered into your house, and no water did you give me for my feet, but she has wet my feet with tears and wiped them with her hair. [45]No kiss did you give me, but she, from the time she entered has not ceased kissing my feet. [46]With olive oil you did not anoint my head, but she, with perfume, has anointed my feet. [47]Because of this, I say to you, her many sins have been forgiven, because she loved much; but the one to whom little was forgiven, he would love little. [48]And he [Jesus] said to her, 'Your sins are forgiven.' [49]And those men reclining at the table with him began to say among them-selves, 'Who is this who even forgives sins?' [50]And he [Jesus] said to the woman, 'Your faith has saved you. Go in peace'.

While Jesus is the main character in the entire Lukan narrative, and while he and the Pharisee are the main speaking characters in this pas-sage, the structure of the story allows us to focus on the woman as a key character in the story. After the scene is set (7.36), the actions of the woman become the center of attention.[14] They are repeated before

12. The word is *stasa*, second aorist active participle of *histēmi*. While most translations render it as '*stood* at his feet', W.F. Arndt and F.W. Gingrich (*A Greek–English Lexicon of the New Testament and Other Early Christian Literature*, [Chicago: University of Chicago Press, 1957], p. 383) say that 'very often the emphasis is less on 'standing' than on being, existing, especially with adverbs of place'. See *opisō* (behind) for such a usage in this verse. This rendering makes it possible for the woman to be in a position which would allow her tears to fall on Jesus' feet.

13. I am using the continuous past forms of these last three verbs to reflect the imperfect tense in Greek.

14. On the other hand, the history of interpretation has been focused on Jesus. Again, see Holst, 'One Anointing' for a summary of the research. For a literary

and after the Pharisee's judgment of Jesus and Jesus' response to the Pharisee, thereby encasing those interactions. The woman's actions are further designated as central by being positively compared to the actions of the Pharisee (7.45). While not surpassing Jesus' role as the main character in the story, the woman may be seen as a secondary character of importance.[15] I will discuss three aspects of the woman's interaction with Jesus: her transformation from the status of a sinner to one who has been forgiven,[16] her role as a prostitute and her capacity as servant. In all three cases, I will show both empowering and oppressive tendencies by exploring a variety of interpretative signals found in the text.

The Sinful Woman

The story of the unnamed woman opens with the narrator establishing her as a sinner (7.37). This label is then repeated by the Pharisee and Jesus (7.39, 7.47), thereby emphasizing her sinful condition. To deny or diminish this character as a sinner would be to distort the storyline.[17] In Luke–Acts, while Jesus is repeatedly accused by Pharisees and Scribes of eating and drinking with tax collectors and sinners,[18] only Jesus' opponents are offended by sinners. In fact, Jesus has among his apostles both tax collectors and sinners, giving both groups a special, positive signification.

Luke depicts Peter as the first sinner in the Gospel. In ch. 5, after Peter witnesses a miraculous catch of fish, he realizes who Jesus is, falls at his knees, and declares, 'Depart from me, for I am a sinful man (*anēr hamartōlos*, 5.8)'.[19] Jesus responds to this confession, neither by ostracizing nor forgiving Peter, but by promising him he will be a fisher

approach focusing on the woman, see Robert C. Tannehill, *The Narrative Unity of Luke–Acts: A Literary Interpretation*, I (Philadelphia: Fortress Press, 1986), esp. p. 116.

15. See Johnson, *Possessions*, pp. 2-24, for a discussion of primary characters (Jesus and the apostles) and secondary characters who move the plot forward.

16. See Tannehill, *Narrative Unity*, pp. 111-19, for a discussion of Quest stories.

17. This is why I disagree with Rachel Conrad Wahlberg (*Jesus According to a Woman* [New York: Paulist Press, 1975], p. 59) when she wants to 'separate her sinner label from her act of ministry'.

18. Luke 5.30; 7.34; 15.2; 19.7.

19. While I am using my translation for Lk. 7.36-50, the Revised Standard Version will be used for quotations outside the passage.

of men and by inviting Peter to follow him. Levi, the tax collector (5.27), is the next character Jesus calls to follow him. Levi and Peter are both shown responding to Jesus' call by leaving everything to follow him. Jesus says, 'I have not come to call the righteous, but sinners to repentance' (5.31). As Luke progresses, Peter, the sinner, becomes the first among Jesus' apostles (5.10-11; 6.13-16), and Levi, the tax collector, is also numbered as one of the apostles.

Two chapters later, immediately before the anointing scene, the issue of tax collectors and sinners is raised again, reminding the reader that the ministries of both Jesus and John the Baptist have been focused on calling sinners to repentance.[20] In 1.13 John was introduced as the one through whom people would know of salvation and the forgiveness of sin. John is also depicted as one who will prepare the way for Jesus' ministry (3.2-17). In 7.29-30 the narrator says the people and tax collectors justified God, because they had been baptized by John (a baptism of repentance), but the Pharisees and lawyers who had not experienced John's baptism, rejected the purposes of God. Jesus compares 'the men of this generation' to children sitting in the marketplace calling to each other, 'we wailed, but you did not weep' (7.32), suggesting that weeping was an expected part of repentance. He also repeats the accusations the Pharisees and others directed at Jesus, 'Behold a glutton and a drunkard, a friend of tax collectors and sinners.' Jesus counters the accusation with, 'Yet Sophia (Wisdom) is justified by all her children', associating God with Sophia, and referring back to those sinners who had been baptized by John and who then justified God.

Therefore, in Lk. 7.37, when a weeping sinner enters the house of a Pharisee, the reader is prepared for that sinner to accept Jesus, and for the Pharisee, who is not weeping, to misunderstand or reject Jesus. The story of the sinner and the Pharisee functions as an illustration of Luke 7.24-35 regarding those who accept and those who reject God's

---

20. See Lk. 1.77 and 3.2-17. I am indebted to Johnson, *Possessions*, pp. 19, 102, and to John J. Kilgallen, 'John the Baptist, the Sinful Woman, and the Pharisee' (*JBL* 104.4 [1985], pp. 675-79) for many helpful insights about the relationship of this text to the John the Baptist material which precedes it. Schaberg ('Luke', p. 285) suggests the passage could also have been a description of the kind of women who followed Jesus, described in Lk. 8.1-3. However, as I show below, this woman is sent away by Jesus, rather than being invited to join his traveling companions.

messengers.[21] The woman's tears stand in contrast to God's adversaries
who refuse to weep. Here, it is clear the tears indicate sorrow and
repentance, rather than gratitude, as some scholars suggest.[22] Weeping
is associated with John the Baptist and his message of sin and repentance. The weeping of those in verse 7.32 depicts a funeral wake, and
the woman obviously illustrates those who weep in that verse, in contrast to the Pharisee who is not weeping. The woman enters with
mourning and repentance for her sins (which in Jesus' words 'are
many', 7.47), with love for Jesus, and with faith in Jesus' connection to
the One who forgives.[23] Her actions result in her transformation: she
finds salvation from her sins, and she is blessed with peace.

Her story of transformation offers acceptance, honor and dignity for
women,[24] especially in a world where women are shamed just for being
women. This sense of shame is often subtly, but forcefully communicated to women from childhood on, through the preference of boy
babies, the pervasive use of masculine language to describe human
experience, the passive and secondary roles in which women are

---

21. Johnson (*Possessions*, pp. 19, 102) develops the acceptance/rejection motif
illustrated by the sinner and Pharisee. However, he fails to account for the woman's
tears.

22. Joseph A. Fitzmyer (*The Gospel According to Luke I–IX* [AB, 28; Garden
City, NY: Doubleday, 1981], pp. 686-87) includes a good summary of the dispute
over whether the woman's tears represent repentance or gratitude. While the
woman's tears suggest she is repentant, after she anoints Jesus she is likened to a
debtor who loved out of gratitude, in response to having been already forgiven.

Kilgallen ('John', p. 677) argues Luke's use of the perfect tense for 'forgive'
(*apheōntai*, 7.47-48) proves the woman was forgiven before coming to the
Pharisee's dinner party. However, the perfect tense is used to emphasize the
fulfillment of an action, rather than its time (H.E. Dana and Julius R. Mantey, *A
Manual of Grammar of the Greek New Testament* [Toronto: Macmillan, 1927,
1955], p. 202). I will work with the tension in the story as a source of various interpretative possibilities. See John Martin Creed, *The Gospel According to St. Luke*
(London: Macmillan, 1960), p. 110 and Tannehill (*Narrative Unity*, p. 118) who
also accept and work with the tension in the text, rather than trying to resolve it.

23. While Jesus declares her sins forgiven, he does not take credit for forgiving
them. His response to the table guest's question, 'Who is this who even forgives
sins', is to say to the woman, 'Your faith has saved you. Go in peace' (7.49-50.)

24. This is the most common feminist interpretation of this passage. See
Leonard Swidler, *Biblical Affirmations of Women* (Philadelphia: Westminster Press,
1970), p. 272; Evelyn and Frank Stagg, *Women in the World of Jesus* (Philadelphia:
Westminster Press, 1979), p. 101; and Conrad Wahlberg, *Jesus*, pp. 51, 59 for
examples.

depicted in literature, and in many, many other ways.[25] By contrast, this story suggests that Sophia, a feminine image of God, represented by Jesus as a friend of sinners, will receive them and forgive their sins. When they repent with tears, Jesus will commend them for their part in their own salvation and send them on their way with a blessing of peace (Lk. 7.48, 50). Jesus' actions might be likened to Marilyn Frye's concept of the 'loving eye' which Frye argues women need in order to escape from patriarchal oppression.[26] In order to be empowered, women need to experience being

> ...under the gaze of a loving eye, the eye which presupposes our independence. The loving eye does not prohibit a woman's experiencing the world directly, does not force her to experience it by way of the interested interpretations of the seer in whose visual field she moves.[27]

The 'loving eye' accepts women as valuable individuals and expects them to be all they can be.

On the other hand, while in this story Jesus is the agent of the woman's transformation, because he is a male representative of God, he may also be seen to represent what Frye calls the 'arrogant eye'. The 'arrogant eye' of patriarchy views women as deficient without a man.[28] Frye argues that for all women in patriarchal societies a process of disintegration and 're(mis)integration' happens largely from living in a system which constantly imposes debilitating definitions and expectations on women. Frye calls this process of definition the 'arrogant eye', because it powerfully molds women into people with such a distorted sense of self and such a lack of self-respect that they focus their energy, not toward their own self interest, but toward the interest of others, often without even considering what is in their own best interest. This arrogant eye sees men as primary and dominant and sees women as secondary to men. It operates with a pervasiveness that cannot be underestimated. As Frye puts it, the 'arrogant eye' is made up of

> ...the stereotypes, the rules, the common expectations for us [which] surround us all in a steady barrage of verbal and visual images in popular, elite, religious and underground vehicles of culture. Virtually every individual is immersed most of the time in a cultural medium which

25. See Marilyn Frye, *The Politics of Reality: Essays in Feminist Theory* (Freedom, CA: Crossing Press, 1983), pp. 41-52, for a powerful analysis.

26. Frye, *Politics*, pp. 52-82.

27. Frye, *Politics*, p. 82.

28. Frye, *Politics*, pp. 66-76.

provides sexist and misogynist images of what we are and what we think
we are doing.[29]

While this passage may offer a redemptive message for women, it may
also be interpreted to reinforce the 'arrogant eye' described above. The
passage shows that the woman is not only forgiven through Jesus, but
that he assumes her guilt is real and valid.

The woman in this story is likened to a debtor who owes something
to Jesus. After telling the parable of the debtors in 7.41-42, Jesus compares the woman with the debtor who owes the most, saying, 'Because
of this, I say to you, her many sins have been forgiven, because she
loved much...And he said to her, "Your sins are forgiven"' (7.47-48).
Here, Jesus, the male divine figure, affirms that the woman's sins are
many and presupposes she owes him a large debt.

In a world where women are taught they have no right to exist outside their function as lovers and supporters of men, and that they need
men in order to be safe in the world,[30] close identification with the
woman in this story may serve to reinforce the stranglehold of the
'arrogant eye'. In order to escape the 'arrogant eye', women need personal transformation that frees them not only from guilt, but also from
the shame and sense of obligation to men they have been taught. In this
story, the woman is shown receiving forgiveness through a man who
calls her a sinner, after she shows sorrow and repentance for her sins.
This story thereby reinforces the 'arrogant' message women receive in
patriarchal society that we are guilty of many sins and that our salvation comes through faith in men.

The Prostitute
The woman in this story is not only named a sinner, but a 'sinner in the
city', a prostitute. While the text does not use the word 'prostitute' to
describe her, it is clear this is implied. She is shown in three ways to be
a prostitute who touches Jesus.[31] First, she is called a 'sinner in the

29. Frye, *Politics*, p. xiii.
30. See Frye, *Politics*, pp. 1-72 for an excellent discussion of the forces which
deliver this message to women and the dread women live with when they try to
break out of this system.
31. Schaberg ('Luke', pp. 276, 286) agrees Luke implies she is a prostitute. For
the need to pay careful attention to what is implied in the text, see Susan S. Lanser,
'(Feminist) Criticism in the Garden: Inferring Genesis 2–3', in *Semeia: Speech Act
Theory and Biblical Criticism* (Decatur, GA: Scholars Press, 1988), pp. 67-82.

city'. Next, she is found at a formal meal. And finally, she is shown publicly touching Jesus at this meal. I will deal with each of these in reverse order.

While many in Luke are touched by Jesus and healed,[32] the only two individual characters in Luke who touch Jesus are unnamed women: the sinful woman in this passage and the woman with the issue of blood in 8.44-47. Both are commended for their faith and told to 'Go in peace'. In addition to these women, three people are healed in Luke by Jesus touching them. In two of these instances, the motifs of tears, feet and/or forgiveness of sins recur: the leper (5.13) and the weeping widow's son (7.14).[33] Jesus tells the widow not to weep, because he is about to raise her son from the dead.[34] Luke depicts touch as a healing, forgiving agent and specifies this in particular ways with reference to women.[35]

However, the sinful woman's touch is different from those looking for healing. In this scene, while the emphasis is on touching of Jesus' feet, the position at his feet might have suggested a posture of humility, repentance, request or gratitude, depending on how one interprets the story.[36] I have argued above, however, that her tears express sorrow/repentance, and this posture reinforces that argument. Note that Peter falls at Jesus' knees, when he proclaims himself a sinner unworthy of Jesus' presence (5.8). Like Peter's falling, the woman's presence at Jesus' feet signifies a quest for forgiveness, rather than physical healing, and her touch has erotic implications.

---

32. In Lk. 6.19 'the crowd sought to touch him [Jesus], for power came forth and healed them all'.

33. The passage in which these themes are not repeated is near the end of the Gospel (22.51), where Jesus touched the ear of the slave of the high priest to heal him.

34. Compare this story with that of the weeping Daughters of Jerusalem in Luke 23, who are told not to weep for Jesus but for themselves and their children. In both cases the command not to weep for Jesus is a sign that he will be raised from the dead.

35. Later in the story, Jesus takes the hand of Jairus' 12-year-old daughter (8.54) and 'lays hands on' the woman with the spirit of weakness (13.13).

36. Others who are found at Jesus' feet are the man freed from demons (8.35); Jairus, who takes this posture to plead for his daughter (8.41); Mary, at the house of Martha, sits at Jesus' feet, and one of the ten lepers who was healed fell at Jesus' feet in gratitude (17.16, this scene recalls the anointing story because the leper is told that his faith made him well.)

Renita Weems calls this woman a 'sensual worshiper'.[37] In the story she wets Jesus' feet with her tears. This intimate act would necessitate her being either seated on the floor close to Jesus' feet, or if the couch on which Jesus reclined were raised, standing near his feet.[38] Her physical proximity to Jesus' feet is emphatically underscored by a sevenfold repetition of the word 'feet' (7.38, 44-46). After wetting Jesus' feet with her tears, she must move closer to wipe his feet with her hair. The word meaning 'to wipe', *ekmassō*, appears in the imperfect tense, signifying continuous action. This word is derived from the root *massō*, meaning 'to handle or touch as in a massage'. After prolonged wiping of Jesus' feet with her hair, the woman makes even more intimate contact with Jesus as she 'continually kisses' (*katephilei*, 7.38, 45) his feet.[39] Finally, she smooths ointment on Jesus' carefully caressed feet. In this scene the sinful woman is clearly depicted as a prostitute using the skills of her trade to sensually love Jesus.[40]

While this public sexual behavior may shock some modern readers and has been denied or ignored by most commentators,[41] the first-

37. Renita J. Weems, *Just a Sister Away: A Womanist Vision of Women's Relationships in the Bible* (San Diego: LuraMedia, 1988), p. 93.

38. Most commentators assume she 'stood' behind a reclining Jesus and thereby understand her to be at some distance from his feet. However, given this translation, if the couch on which Jesus reclined were raised, as Kathleen Corley suggests ('Were the Women around Jesus Really Prostitutes? Women in the Context of Greco-Roman Meals', *SBL Seminar Papers* [Atlanta: Scholars Press, 1989], pp. 491-92 nn. 21-30) the woman would be standing with her upper body in close proximity to Jesus' feet. My translation emphasizes simply her nearness to Jesus (see above, n. 12).

39. Schaberg ('Luke', p. 286) suggests that kissing feet 'was usually an act of gratitude for pardon', however, she agrees with me that her 'love' could represent 'both cause and result or sign of divine forgiveness'.

40. This interpretation stands in direct contrast to Fitzmyer's claim that 'the tears are a caution for any interpretation of the scene that the love mentioned in it was intended in an erotic sense' (*Gospel*, p. 689). I agree with Fitzmyer that her tears signify sorrow and repentance, but the actions described subsequent to the tears are certainly described in erotic language.

41. See, e.g., Creed, *Gospel*, p. 107; and Charles H. Talbert, *Reading Luke: A Literary and Theological Commentary on the Third Gospel* (New York: Crossroad, 1982), pp. 86-87, who describe her actions as 'lavished affection'. Marshall (*Gospel*, pp. 308-309) goes into elaborate detail about how the woman meant to anoint Jesus' head and then, carried away with emotion, began to weep and accidentally wet his feet with her tears. Then, in her embarrassment she wiped them dry with her hair. The kissing is explained by great reverence or gratitude, and the

century reader would have found the woman's behavior to be perfectly appropriate for the occasion. It was common in this era for prostitutes to attend formal dinners to entertain guests through dancing, singing and sexual services.[42] The sinful woman is not depicted as embarrassed about approaching or touching Jesus in this public setting.[43] Her actions are narrated in a matter of fact way, and the only emotions portrayed are weeping and sensuous loving. The Pharisee objects silently, not to the woman's presence or her actions, but to the fact that Jesus seemed not to know that it was a sinner who touched him. The issue for the Pharisee is whether or not Jesus is a prophet, for if he were, Simon supposes he would know the woman was a sinner and would not allow her to touch him.[44] The Pharisee, unlike the reader, does not understand or accept Jesus' association with sinners. This misunderstanding works ironically to mark Simon as 'one of the Pharisees and experts in the law [who] rejected God's purpose for themselves' (Lk. 7.30).

The question silently voiced by the Pharisee and the sensuous actions of the sinful woman are not the only indications she is a prostitute. In the opening of the story, the narrator emphatically refers to her

anointing of the feet remains a puzzle. Marshall says, 'From v. 46 it appears that the woman anointed Jesus' feet, an action which is unparalleled (except in Jn 12.3), since this act of honor was normally bestowed on the head'. Evidently, the Staggs (*Women*, p. 108), agree with Marshall as they call her actions, 'unplanned and unanticipated'. On the other hand, Wahlberg (*Jesus*, p. 52) focuses on the acceptability of her actions as ministry, 'Jesus saw a ministering woman whose kisses, tears and anointing he accepted with satisfaction, if not pleasure'. Luke Timothy Johnson, *The Gospel of Luke* (Sacra Pagina Series, 3; ed. Daniel J. Harrington; Collegeville, MN, The Liturgical Press, 1991), pp. 126-30, completely avoids any discussion of the erotic nature of the touching of Jesus, and focuses exclusively on purity rules from Leviticus prohibiting touching unclean things and people. Turid Karlsen Seim (*The Double Message: Patterns of Gender in Luke & Acts* [Nashville: Abingdon Press, 1994], pp. 90-94) characterizes her as a 'well-known local whore', but does not touch on the sensuous nature of her service to Jesus.

42. Corley, 'Greco-Roman Meals', pp. 487-521, esp. pp. 488-91. See also Kathleen E. Corley, *Private Women, Public Meals: Social Conflict in the Synoptic Tradition* (Peabody, MA: Hendrickson, 1993), pp. 24-70, for a more complete discussion.

43. Unlike the woman with the issue of blood who trembled after she had touched Jesus and been healed, because Jesus demanded to know who had touched him (8.47).

44. See Johnson, *Possessions*, pp. 79-126, for a discussion of Jesus as a prophet in Luke, esp. pp. 96-103 for how this passage fits into this Gospel theme.

reputation as a prostitute by calling her a 'sinner in the city'. Such a euphemism implies that she is well known in the city for immoral behavior.

> Prostitutes were therefore associated with the marketplace and other open air areas that were usually reserved for men and closed to women of good reputation. A prostitute was then, as now, characterized as a 'streetwalker'…associated with public places…[45]

Hence, the Pharisee's reference to her as a sinner reminds the reader of her notoriety as a prostitute.

In ironic contrast to the Pharisee's questioning of Jesus' prophetic skills, Jesus knows both the Pharisee's inner thoughts as well as the woman's reputation. Even so, he not only allows her sensuous actions, he gives dignity to her touch by calling it an expression of love. It is remarkable that most commentators align themselves with the Pharisee by marveling how Jesus would allow such a woman to touch him. Such amazement is based on the belief that Jesus should have been embarrassed or scandalized for being made unclean according to Jewish Law by the woman's actions.[46] However, Luke consistently shows Jesus unafraid, unembarrassed and unworried about breaking Jewish law or about touching unclean and diseased folk.[47] Therefore, it should not

45. Corley, 'Greco-Roman Meals', p. 498, and *Private Women,* pp. 124-25.

46. Lev. 15.19-22 is cited by Johnson, *Luke,* p. 127. The Staggs (*Woman,* p. 225) assert Luke depicts 'a Savior unafraid to be touched by this woman'. Wahlberg (*Jesus,* p. 51) remarks Jesus 'was not embarrassed'. Swidler (*Biblical Affirmations,* p. 187) says Jesus unconventionally spoke to her and allowed her to touch and kiss him, even though she had loosed her hair in public, which he claims was a mandatory term of divorce and therefore would have scandalized Jesus (Swidler cites Joachim Jeremias without giving the reference.) Tannehill (*Narrative Unity,* pp. 116-17) emphasizes the woman's vulnerability, as a known sinner in the Pharisee's house, who 'is a woman who does not behave properly in the presence of men' (citing Joachim Jeremias, *The Parables of Jesus* [trans. S.H. Hooke; New York: Charles Scribner's Sons, rev. edn, 1983], p. 126, who claims it was improper for a woman to let down her hair in the presence of men.) Calling her behavior 'extravagant' and 'strange', Tannehill stresses, 'Jesus came to the woman's defense'. Tannehill is right that Jesus comes to the woman's defense, but she is depicted neither by the narrator nor Jesus as behaving strangely. Corley (*Private Women,* p. 125) also, wrongly claims Luke is concerned 'that her act is immoral, given the identity of Jesus and the formal nature of the proceedings'. Corley believes Luke's concern about 'Greco-Roman propriety' prohibits him from depicting Jesus eating with 'tax collectors and sinners' (pp. 130-33). I argue the contrary.

47. Cf. 4.49; 5.12-13; 6.1-5.

surprise commentators or readers that the divine/human Jesus receives a woman's sexual expressions.

While most commentators completely avoid the sexual aspects of the story of the sinful woman, it clearly depicts erotic sexuality as a fully acceptable act—not only from a sinful woman, but also toward God's prophetic messenger. This seems radical today, because, as James Nelson puts it, 'Jesus as the Christ has been desexualized by most Christian piety throughout the ages...And about the most effective way of denying Jesus' full humanity has been to deny (outright or by embarrassed silence) his sexuality.'[48]

The depiction of Jesus' sexual touch is a healing image. Carter Heyward asserts that such activity is a basic human need in the context of a relational ethical commitment.

> Touching is a primary relational need. As a sensual, erotic pleasure, it is a life-affirming dimension of human experience. We need to touch and be touched to survive...We need to hold and be held, caressed, comforted, and enjoyed. To touch one another's bodies tenderly and respectfully is a mighty human and sacred good. It is foundational to our being fully human. From a Christian theological perspective, it is a way of anointing the body of Christ.[49]

Luke's anointing scene supports this view, and thereby offers a vision for a human sexuality affirmed by the divine. This message is especially important for women, because our bodies have been regarded as sources of temptation and evil which need to be guarded against. Ironically, at the same time women have also been seen as sexual objects to be owned, controlled and used by men. As Heyward puts it, 'Women have never had a socially established, religiously

48. James B. Nelson, *The Intimate Connection: Male Sexuality, Masculine Spirituality* (Philadelphia: Westminster Press, 1988), p. 105. There is a growing number of books dealing with developing a healthy Christian sexuality in opposition to the dualistic, misogynist views that have been historically taught by and associated with the church. See two of Nelson's earlier works, *Embodiment: An Approach to Sexuality & Christian Theology* (Minneapolis: Augsburg, 1978); and *Between Two Gardens: Reflections on Sexuality and Religious Experience* (New York: Pilgrim Press, 1983). Linda Hurcombe, *Sex and God: Some Varieties of Women's Religious Experience* (New York: Routledge & Kegan Paul, 1987); and Carter Heyward, *Touching our Strength: The Erotic as Power and the Love of God* (San Francisco: Harper & Row, 1989), both focus on women's sexuality/ spirituality.

49. Heyward, *Touching*, pp. 148-49.

affirmed, physically safe, or emotionally secure sense of our own body integrity. We have not known or loved our body selves *as our own*, for we have [had] no control over who or what passes into or out of us.'[50] However, in Luke, Jesus does not use the woman's sensuous expressions as an opportunity to exploit her sexually. He simply accepts them as acts of love and sends her away in peace.

On the other hand, while Luke portrays Jesus unembarrassed about this sexual touch, this passage also affirms sexual contact in the context of a relationship of power imbalance and outside an ethical relational commitment. The use of this passage by religious leaders to justify the unethical use of their spiritual and positional power to gain access to vulnerable congregants is a clear danger which must be warned against. When nearly 40 per cent of ministers report having sexual contact with congregants and 13 per cent report sexual intercourse with someone in their congregation, acknowledgment of the sexual aspects of this passage must be done with extreme caution.[51] It is unethical and abusive for ministers to initiate or receive sexual touching from people who come to them in a spiritual quest, as this woman came to Jesus. It is always the responsibility of the minister to maintain clear sexual boundaries in a respectful way.

Furthermore, noting the sexual dimension of this passage creates a danger it might be used to justify prostitution, because it does not acknowledge the personal and systemic abuse suffered by prostitutes in Jesus' time. During the first century many prostitutes were slaves. In an attempt to control the size of families and because of a preference for boys, baby girls were commonly exposed and left to die in garbage dumps. Some girls who had been exposed in this way were rescued and raised to work in brothels. Other prostitutes were captured in war and sold into slavery or sold by parents who could not afford to raise them.[52]

Prostitution, the 'oldest' profession, remains one of the most abusive. Even today, prostitutes report having been sexually abused by men in

50. Heyward, *Touching*, p. 25.

51. These statistics come from Richard Allen Blackmon's study for his unpublished doctoral dissertation at Fuller Theological Seminary, 1984, 'The Hazards of the Ministry'. He surveyed 300 Presbyterian, 302 Methodist, 404 Assembly of God and 190 Episcopalian clergy and found the incident of ministerial sexual abuse the same for all these denominations irrespective of gender.

52. Pomeroy, *Goddesses*; and Corley, 'Greco-Roman Meals', pp. 491-92.

their youth, often by close family members. Many young women are seduced into the profession by a pimp who initially offers the love and safety these women never received as children. These girls and women are later sold as prostitutes by the pimp for his own profit, while he controls their lives with erratic violence and terror. They face danger and life-threatening disease every day, just as they did 2000 years ago, as they are exploited by men of all social, economic and religious groups. At the same time they are condemned by society as 'the most sinful of all creatures'.[53]

Luke shows Jesus receiving the prostitute's sexual services as hope for and/or loving response to forgiveness while also marking her guilty of many sins. While Jesus is not cast in the role of an abusive pimp, the story of the sinful woman suggests her sensuous actions are related to the recognition and forgiveness given her by Jesus. Too many women feel obliged to offer sexual favors to men in exchange for love, approval, money, a few dates or the security of marriage.[54] A story suggesting that such sexual favors are accepted by Jesus in return for, or in gratitude of forgiveness is not redemptive.

The Servant

In addition to her actions being depicted as sexual expressions of love and sexual service for Jesus, these actions also depict the woman providing the hospitality Jesus expected to receive from the Pharisee. Jesus

53. Corley ('Greco-Roman Meals', p. 498) shows this attitude was also true in the Greco-Roman world. She cites an epitaph concerning a procurer or pimp from the *Greek Anthology*, v. 2, pp. 216-17: 'Pysyllus, who used to take to the pleasant banquets of the young men the venal ladies that they desired, that hunter of weak girls who earned a disgraceful wage by dealing in human flesh, lies here. But cast not stones at his tomb, wayfarer, nor bid another to do so...Spare him; not because he was content to gain his living so, but because as a keeper of common women he dissuaded young men from adultery.'

54. For discussion about the overall oppressive use of sex to exploit women in prostitution, dating and marriage, see Andrea Dworkin, *Intercourse* (New York: Free Press, 1987); Charlotte Davis Kasl, *Women, Sex and Addiction: A Search for Love and Power* (New York: Ticknor & Fields, 1989), esp. pp. 31-41, 99-110; Heyward, *Touching*, pp. 48-60; and Rita Nakashima Brock and Susan Brooks Thistlethwaite, *Casting Stones: Prostitution and Liberation in Asia and the United States* (Minneapolis: Fortress Press, 1996), esp. 183-205, pp. 235-68. For a philosophical deconstruction of prostitution including the perspective of prostitutes, see Shannon Bell, *Reading, Writing and Rewriting the Prostitute Body* (Bloomington: Indiana University Press, 1994).

contrasts Simon's lack of hospitality with that of the woman's actions. Simon gave Jesus no water for his feet, but the woman wet his feet with her tears. He gave Jesus no kiss, but the woman continued to kiss his feet. The Pharisee gave Jesus no oil, but the woman massaged his feet with perfumed ointment. The woman honored Jesus through these acts of service, omitted by Simon, the Pharisee.

This Pharisee not only fails to provide basic hospitality to Jesus, he judges Jesus for receiving it from the woman. Thus, Simon represents Luke's portrayal of contentious Jewish religious leaders who oppose Jesus. Such a depiction is dangerous, because it can be seen as a judgment of real Pharisees in the time of Jesus. Such a 'referential fallacy' has been made in the past and continues to be made by Second Testament scholars and Christian preachers, leading to anti-Jewish judgments of first-century and contemporary Judaism. However, a study of Luke's portrayal of Jews, Judaism and Jewish leaders similar to this study of the woman, would show that Luke–Acts includes both anti-Jewish and pro-Jewish sentiment.[55] In this story, the Pharisee functions as a foil, representing those who want to be with Jesus, but who oppose his keeping company with tax collectors and sinners and thereby reject the understanding of repentance and forgiveness offered through John the Baptist and Jesus.[56]

Modern religious authorities from all traditions who guard their own class, race and economic privilege should be warned by Simon's character. Those from every religious tradition and ideology who distance themselves from disenfranchised 'sinners', and who judge the worth and actions of others stand under the condemnation of this passage. On the other hand, women deemed inferior and/or especially susceptible to sin by contemporary religious authorities, may gain dignity and inner strength as they compare such authorities with the antagonist in this story. Such authorities are like those 'men of this generation who mock and criticize the messengers of Sophia, instead of justifying her'. In these ways they also fail to justify God and do not count as children of Sophia. These leaders are also like those who refuse to weep in sorrow for their own sins. They treat God's true messengers with disrespect

55. See Robert L. Brawley, *Luke–Acts and the Jews: Conflict, Apology and Conciliation* (SBLMS, 33; Atlanta, GA: Scholars Press, 1987), pp. 84-106; and Jack T. Sanders, *The Jews in Luke–Acts* (Philadelphia: Fortress Press, 1987), esp. pp. 174-78.

56. Sanders, *The Jews*, p. 177.

and judgment. Luke's story depicting Jesus exposing the Pharisee and accepting the sinful woman can sustain women in their service to God, in spite of opposition by authorities, by reminding them that they are suitable ministers.

On the other hand, this story has the potential to trap women in a system of oppression which would limit women's ministry to service and hospitality. In the contemporary church, women's service of preparing meals and cleaning the vestibules is readily accepted, but ministry involving priestly functions or verbal ministry are very often challenged. If this story is read in relation to this reality and to Luke's overall depiction of women, a critical evaluation is required.

While the sinful woman's hospitality is not called 'service' (*diakonia*), several 'model' women in Luke are described offering service to Jesus and his disciples. For instance, at the very beginning of the Gospel, Mary calls herself the slave (*doulē*, 1.38, 48) of the Lord. For her, serving also has sexual implications, because her service to God means being 'overpowered by God's Spirit', in order to bear the divine child. Anna, the prophet, serves (*latreuousa*, 2.37) in the temple night and day with fasting and prayer. After Jesus heals Peter's mother-in-law, she is said to rise up and 'serve' (*diēkonei*, 4.39) Jesus and his disciples, filling the role of hostess like the sinful woman in the Pharisee's house. In a similar fashion, the women who follow Jesus from Galilee 'serve' (*diēkonoun*, 8.3) Jesus and his apostles out of their own means. In contrast to women in the other Gospels, the women who follow Jesus in Luke 'are cast in a nonreciprocated role of service or support of the males of the movement'.[57] Later, at Martha's home, Martha complains to Jesus that she has been left alone to 'serve' (*diakonein*, 10.40), while Mary sits at Jesus' feet. While Mary's humble, passive and silent listening role is declared to be the better one, Martha's 'service' (*diakonia*) is criticized only because she is distracted by it.[58] Whether her service be seen as deaconal or preparation of a

---

57. Schaberg, 'Luke', p. 287; and Turid Karsen Seim, 'The Gospel of Luke', in Elisabeth Schüssler Fiorenza (ed.), *Searching the Scriptures: A Feminist Commentary* (New York: Crossroad, 1994), pp. 739-55.

58. See Elisabeth Schüssler Fiorenza, 'A Feminist Critical Interpretation for Liberation: Martha and Mary: Luke. 10.38-42', *Religion and Intellectual Life* 3.2 (1986), pp. 21-36, esp. p. 29, for a description of Mary's passivity and Martha's silencing by Jesus. Schüssler Fiorenza argues this is a story about the ministry of women, rather than table service. The text is ambiguous.

meal, Martha is clearly cast in the capacity of hostess to Jesus and his company in her own home.[59]

These depictions of women as hostesses and servants of God and men coincide with the 'arrogant eye' which expects women to be supporters of men. Jesus honors this kind of service through his teachings and example (cf. the Lord's supper in 22.24-27), however, women are depicted only as providers, never recipients, of such service in this Gospel. Luke clearly excludes women from the scenes where Jesus multiplies the loaves and fish and has them distributed to the crowds of 'five thousand *men*' (*andres*, 9.14). Neither Jesus nor his male disciples/apostles are ever depicted reclining with women followers at a meal or serving women.

While women are never depicted reclining at table with Jesus and his disciples, the apostles are specially invited to recline with Jesus at his last meal.[60] In the context of this meal, Jesus takes the position of servant among them, asking them to do the same. These 12 apostles are then promised places of honor at the messianic banquet as judges over the 12 tribes of Israel. No woman in Luke–Acts is offered such a privileged position, even though many are shown, like Jesus, to be faithful

---

59. Jane Via, 'Women, The Discipleship of Service, and the Early Christian Ritual Meal in the Gospel of Luke', *SLJT* 29.1 (December 1985), pp. 37-60, argues all these passages referring to women serving allude to preparing meals and waiting on tables. More accurately, the text remains ambiguous, as *none* of these references specifically describes a woman preparing and/or serving a meal. I prefer to honor the ambiguity of the text and leave open the possibility Luke might in some cases use the words 'service' (*diakonia*) and 'to serve' (*diakoneō*) to mean ministry of some other kind. For instance, Schüssler Fiorenza argues these terms point to 'eucharistic table service', as well as the 'proclamation of the word' ('Martha and Mary', p. 301). Dennis E. Smith also argues for a broader meaning in 'Table Fellowship as a Literary Motif in the Gospel of Luke', *JBL* 106.4 (1987), pp. 613-38. The term 'service' appears in Lk. 10.40; Acts 1.25; 6.1, 4; 11.29; 12.25; 20.24; and 21.19. The verbal form is found in Lk. 4.39; 8.3; 10.40; 12.37; 17.8; 22.26-27 3 times; Acts 6.2; and 19.22.

60. Quentin Quesnell, 'The Women at Luke's Supper', in Richard J. Cassidy and Phillip J. Sharper, *Political Issues in Luke–Acts* (Maryknoll, NY: Orbis Books, 1983), pp. 59-79; and Via, 'Women, Discipleship', pp. 42-44, both argue women were present at Luke's last meal. This argument is difficult to sustain in view of 22.30, where Jesus tells those at the table with him they may 'eat and drink at my table in my kingdom, and sit on the thrones judging the twelve tribes of Israel'. In fact, much of the conversation at the table focuses on members of the twelve (cf. 22.28-34).

models of servanthood. Instead, the apostles in Acts 6.2 overtly reject the kind of table service Jesus commands of them in favor of a teaching ministry.

In this context the sinful woman's repentant and loving service at a meal in the Pharisee's house, and Jesus' acceptance and commendation of her service has a different hue. Luke's depiction of women's service fits stereotypes which restricted women's options in the first century and still limit women today. 'There is a women's place, a sector, which is inhabited by women of all classes and races, and it is not defined by geographical boundaries but by function. The function is the service of men and men's interest as men define them.'[61] Instead of lending women support to escape from the 'arrogant eye', Luke glorifies and idealizes women's service to men, thereby cooperating with an oppressive world-view which constrains women's potential through both internal and external pressures.

A comparison of Jesus' attitude toward the sinful woman and his response to Peter, the sinner, confirms this world-view which places barriers between men's and women' roles. While Peter falls at Jesus' knees and confesses his sinful nature, he is never depicted serving Jesus like the sinful woman, nor is he told to go on his way in peace. Jesus calls Peter to follow him and gives Peter a special place as foremost among Jesus' apostles, but he sends the woman away.[62] In contrast to Peter and other men in the Gospel, it is also telling that no words are placed on the woman's lips, only kisses. The only words attributed to women characters in Luke–Acts are either spoken in private or disputed.[63]

---

61. Frye, *Politics*, p. 9.

62. Others sent away are those healed of physical and spiritual infirmities: the leper in 5.14, the Gerasene demoniac in 8.38-39, the woman with the issue of blood, 8.48, and the leper in 17.19.

63. Elizabeth's and Mary's words are spoken in private (1.25, 34, 38, 42-55), the words of Martha (10.40), the woman in the crowd (11.27), the maid who confronts Peter in the courtyard (23.56), are all discredited in some way. Irony involving women's speech in Lk. 24 and Acts 12 was developed in Judith K. Applegate, 'Women as Witnesses in Luke–Acts', Eastern Great Lakes Biblical Society in Pittsburgh, PA, 1990; and in Regina Plunkett Dowling, 'Bad Readers and Worse Apostles: the Vindication of Women Witnesses in Luke–Acts', the SBL meetings in Kansas City, 1991. Schaberg ('Luke', pp. 279-81) presents a sustained critique of women's speaking and lack thereof in Luke Acts. See also Mary Rose D'Angelo, 'Women in Luke–Acts: A Redactional View', *JBL* 109 (1990), pp. 441-

This final contrast demonstrates the pernicious quality of the Lukan depiction of Jesus as divine prophet who accepts the silent service of a marginal woman. Indeed, in Luke, the whole of Jesus' ministry seems dependent on the service and support of women who have received Jesus' favors of healing, exorcism and forgiveness (8.1-3). This prophet enjoys and cooperates with, rather than opposing, the reigning system of oppression and coercion which tells women they owe men service in general and especially for any favor bestowed on them.

Conclusion

This study, through a feminist literary analysis, argues that while the story of the sinful woman who anoints Jesus can be used to affirm and empower women's lives, it also contains themes and perspectives that support patriarchal systems of oppression. It offers women the promise of personal transformation, while at the same time cooperating with patriarchal messages about women's moral deficiency. It offers a glimpse of the possibility of women's sexuality being accepted and honored as sacred. However, it contains no critique of women's sexual exploitation within patriarchal structures. Finally, it provides a critique of both the rejection of women's ministry and the divine approval of women's service to men. The service portrayed by the woman in this story and the women throughout Luke–Acts is depicted as typical for women, but not for the male leaders of Jesus' new religious movement, thereby cooperating with a pervasive and oppressive stereotype of women in society.

61, for a discussion of how and why the role of prophet is denied women in this Gospel.

WHY IS SHE CRYING?
A FEMINIST INTERPRETATION OF LUKE 7.36-50*

Teresa J. Hornsby

Introduction

Virtually every study written on Lk. 7.36-50 in the past seventeen hundred years identifies the anointing woman in this pericope as a prostitute.[1] It is true that Luke calls her a sinner, but this pronouncement of sin is invariably understood to be a sexual sin. Her physical actions and displays of affection toward Jesus are marked as declarations of her shame, wickedness, and lewdness.

The label of prostitute was given to the anointing woman, I argue, because she is sensuously physical. Scholars have taken her physicality and translated it as something negative, as a cause for repentance. Such an interpretation is both misogynistic and erotophobic, nothing new in historical biblical exegesis but surprising in feminist scholarship (see, e.g., Schaberg 1992a: 35; 1992b: 186; Schüssler Fiorenza 1990: 129; Schottroff 1991: 138-57).

* This article is a revision of a paper I delivered at the 1996 SBL Annual Meeting in New Orleans, Louisiana. I owe an enormous thank you to Amy Jill Levine. Thanks also to the Vanderbilt Graduate Department of Religion Student Representatives for providing a forum in which I could discuss this project with my colleagues.

1. Particularly notable are the following: Tertullian, *Adv. Marcion* (in Roberts and Donaldson 1925: IX, 376); Origen, *Commentary on Matthew* (in Roberts and Donaldson 1925: VIII, 452); Cyril, *Commentary on the Gospel of St Luke* (1983: 171). Strack and Billerbeck 1954–56; Jeremias 1963: 126; Caird 1977: 114 (Caird does not call her a prostitute, but an 'evil woman'); Marshall 1978: 308; Fitzmyer 1981: 689; Witherington 1984; Tannehill 1986: I, 116 (he does not call her a prostitute but refers to Jeremias's statement that it was improper for women to loose their hair in public. He calls her a 'despised sinner'); Schüssler Fiorenza 1990: 129; Schottroff 1991: 138-57; Schaberg 1992a: 31-37, 51-52; Schaberg 1992b: 186; Corley 1993: 124; Seim 1994: 90; Ringe 1995: 108.

This paper first seeks to explain why feminist scholars maintain that the anointing woman in Luke is a prostitute and secondly, to suggest that there may be alternative interpretations that preserve the physicality in the text without an ascription of deviance. This pericope could, in fact, represent the anointing woman as someone who understands that physicality may be the ultimate display of love and that passion may be given as a gift to God.

The Scholarship on Luke 7.36-50

Tertullian's commentary seems to be one of the first we have on this passage.[2] Ironically, he does not consider the woman's physical attention to Jesus' body immoral; in fact, he uses the account to prove the physicality of Jesus against Marcion's claims of a docetic Christ. Tertullian does not degrade the woman at all. He cites her lavish attention to Jesus' body as evidence of an embodied rather than an ethereal divinity.

Origen, however, is the first interpreter to call the anointing woman in Lk. 7.36-50 a 'harlot'. He writes that she is 'no longer playing the harlot, but coming to the feet of Jesus, and wetting them with the tears of repentance, and anointing them with the fragrance of the ointment of holy conversation'.[3] And after Origen, most exegetes characterize the anointing woman as a prostitute or a sexually promiscuous woman, but they offer little or no basis for this assessment. I am intrigued by the persistence of the view that the anointing woman's sin in this pericope is sexual despite the lack of any evidence in the text itself to support this claim as well as ample evidence to the contrary.

There are essentially only three arguments offered by scholars to support the prostitute label. First, many authors call the anointing woman a wicked, immoral whore simply, it appears (since there are often no sources cited), because she is a woman who is called a sinner.[4] In other words, some assume that if a woman sins, the sin must be a sin

2. 'The behavior of "the woman which was a sinner," when she covered the Lord's feet with her kisses, bathed them with her tears, wiped them with the hairs of her head, anointed them with ointment, produced an evidence that what she handled was not an empty phantom, but a really solid body...' (*Adv. Marcion* 4.18 [in Donaldson and Roberts 1925: IX, 376]).

3. *Commentary on Matthew* 4, in Donaldson and Roberts 1925: VIII, 452.

4. These comments begin with Origen and continue throughout historical and form criticism.

of carnality. Though most of these arguments are in the form of moral-istic homilies that predate historical and form criticism, there are some modern examples. Luise Schottroff writes, 'the fact that a woman is portrayed as *hamartōlos* produces the association with a specifically female kind of sinfulness' (1991: 151). However, Luke uses the word *hamartōlos* five other times, all in reference to men, and none have acquired the label prostitute, nor is their sin understood to be sexual. When Peter says in Lk. 5.8, 'Go away from me, I am a sinful man', no interpreter posits that Peter has been sexually immoral. Further, the term *hamartōlos* itself in no way means prostitute (*TDNT*, I, 320-33; Balz and Schneider 1990: 65-68).

In the second argument, interpreters assume that the term 'sinner', combined with the phrase 'in the city', suggests that Luke wants the reader to understand that the anointing woman is a prostitute (Corley 1989: 498; Schottroff 1991: 150; Schüssler Fiorenza 1990: 129; Schaberg 1992b: 286). Schaberg writes, 'Luke calls her "a woman in the city, who was a sinner." It is likely that Luke means the audience to identify this woman's sin as notorious sexual activity, prostitution' (1992b: 286). Corley claims that this same phrase parallels the modern idiomatic 'streetwalker', or the Hellenistic 'public woman' (1989: 498; Licht 1953: 330-32). She writes, 'The combination of the term "sinner" with her identification as a woman known in the city makes it more than likely that Luke intends for his readers to identify her as a prosti-tute, or more colloquially, a "streetwalker" or "public woman"' (1993: 124). Corley, however, offers no primary source correlatives to the phrase 'in the city, a sinner', that would suggest a euphemism for pros-titute.[5] Elizabeth Schüssler Fiorenza clearly equates 'in the city, a sinner' with prostitute. Though she does not give a source for her claim, she writes, 'It was probably [Luke] who characterized the woman as "a woman of the city, a sinner", that is, a prostitute' (1990: 129).

The final set of arguments relies on socio-historical methods. Most

---

5.   Interpreters such as Schottroff also parallel the phrase 'she has loved much' to 'her many sins'. Therefore Schottroff equates 'love' with 'sin'. Schottroff writes: 'Although the comment 'for she has loved much' has often been interpreted as a summary of her love for Jesus, the reference to her 'many sins,' the emphasis on her many individual deeds, is intended to recall also the many love deeds the woman performed in her life as a prostitute. Thus, in my view, the central issue of the text is the interpretation of the manifold love of a prostitute as a life under God's forgiveness' (1991: 151).

cite an appendix to Jeremias's *Jerusalem in the Time of Jesus* (1963) or
Strack and Billerbeck's *Kommentar zum Neuen Testament aus Talmud
und Midrasch* (1922–61), both of which rely on third-century CE (and
later) rabbinic directives to illustrate what they consider to be the social
position of women in the first century CE. These Lukan interpreters
quote the following passage from Jeremias to assure the reader that the
anointing woman is a prostitute: 'How completely the [anointing]
woman was overcome by gratitude towards her saviour is shown by the
fact that unselfconsciously she took off her head-covering and unbound
her hair in order to wipe Jesus' feet, although it was the greatest dis-
grace for a woman to unbind her hair in the presence of men' (Jeremias
1963: 126). His reference here is *t. Soṭ.* 9.13, which dates from the third
century. However, on the use of rabbinic sources, Ross Kraemer writes,

> As more and more scholars are beginning to concede, rabbinic sources
> may at best refract the social realities of a handful of Jewish communi-
> ties, and at worst may reflect only the utopian visions of a relative hand-
> ful of Jewish men. The portrait of Jewish women that emerges from
> these writings may then be largely discounted in favor of the more
> persuasive evidence of epigraphical, archaeological, and non-rabbinic
> writings for Jewish communities both in the Diaspora and in the land of
> Israel (1992: 93).

Thus it is questionable whether third-century rabbinic writings should
be considered a valid measure for first-century Greco-Roman mores.

Still, it is the work produced by the socio-historical critics that most
concerns me. The feminist scholarship on this pericope by such
researchers as Kathleen Corley, Jane Schaberg and Turid Seim is the
most substantial interpretative work thus far. I am troubled, though,
because it is here, in feminist scholarship, where I expected to find the
'redemption' of the anointing woman. The impressive scholarship of
these women, especially Corley's work on women and meals in the
Greco-Roman world and Schaberg's rescue of Mary Magdalene, is not
aimed toward dismantling the misidentification of Luke's anointing
woman, but rather toward perpetuating the prostitute label and assuming the label to be one of deviance.

Corley places the anointing woman of Luke in the setting of a symposium. She notes that if a woman regularly eats and drinks with men,
this would be enough for her to be labeled as a prostitute in Greco-
Roman society (1989: 490). Certain women were procured for these

symposiums not only for sexual favors but also for 'their ability to participate in the conversation of men, and some were even known for their witticism, and for their rhetorical skills in philosophical repartee' (1989: 490). She goes on to say that courtesans were 'often expected to be witty, educated and involved in conversations at dinner' (1989: 490). However, this hardly sounds like the silent, weeping woman who anoints Jesus: she is neither 'procured', as a prostitute would have been, nor is she bubbling forth with witty or philosophical repartee. The anointing woman does not behave at all as Corley claims a prostitute should.

Corley's research is sound, but it should not be applied to this pericope. She has not shown that the Pharisee's dinner is indeed a Greco-Roman symposium, nor has she shown that a woman's presence at a Pharisee's house during such a meal must mean that she is a prostitute.[6] To the contrary, Corley herself notes that during the Roman era, women (usually aristocratic women) occasionally attended these meals as proper guests (1989: 492).

Like Corley, Schaberg's work is insightful in its rendering of traditionally defined roles ascribed to women. Schaberg dissects the legend of Mary Magdalene to examine why she is called a whore. Since the Gospels give little information about her life before traveling with Jesus, the whole tradition of her as a repenting prostitute seems to hinge on the story of the anointing woman in Lk. 7.36-50. The motif of 'anointing' connects Mary Magdalene (who goes to anoint Jesus in his tomb) to the anointing woman in John (who is called Mary) and the anointing woman in Luke (who is called a sinner). Schaberg's work is fascinating in its unraveling of the Magdalene's conflated image. However, she goes on to say that the unnamed woman in Luke is also linked to the woman who committed adultery (Jn 7.53–8.11), since both their sins are sexual (1992a). Even though Schaberg painstakingly separates tradition from Scripture concerning Mary Magdalene, she commits the same error she seeks to undo.

Likewise, as Seim writes to explain patterns of gender in Luke–Acts,

---

6.   Brumberg Kraus and Dennis Smith propose that the dinner at Simon the Pharisee's house in Luke is indeed a symposium. However, the arguments are constructed primarily through literary descriptions and explain the characters and their movements as literary constructs. In other words, there is no epigraphic or archaeological evidence to suggest that a Pharisaic dinner was in the form of a Greek symposium (Brumberg Kraus 1991; Smith 1987: 613-38).

she refers to the anointing woman as 'the local whore' (1994: 93). She intends to show that even though he uses 'serving' language, Luke sets up the anointing woman as a corrective to men's (in this case, Simon's) leadership. Ironically, Seim degrades the woman in order to sharpen the juxtaposition between her and the Pharisee. She writes, 'the excessive action of the despised woman is held up in 7.44-5 as a critical corrective for [Simon the Pharisee]. Through the service of a prostitute, it becomes clear what the Pharisee has failed to do' (1994: 93).[7]

The feminist interpretations of this pericope indicate a failure of feminism, as Judith Plaskow has claimed, 'to include all women within its vision' (1993: 118). Feminist writings on this passage have failed to recognize that all the previous interpretations of Lk. 7.36-50 are gender biased.[8] To my knowledge, no one has ever claimed that Peter's sins (which he admits in ch. 5) are sexual; when Jesus removes his robe to wash the male disciples' feet in Jn 13.1-17, no scholar suggests that Jesus is a gay man. Further, Peter, when he realizes what Jesus is doing, remarks, 'Lord, wash my hands and head as well'. In this instance, there are significant parallels to Luke's pericope: Peter, who has already called himself a sinner, wants Jesus to go beyond the physical attention he gives the other disciples. Peter asks for excess. Here, the subtle level of prejudice being played out in the interpretations of the anointing woman becomes apparent: If a woman, a sinner, uses her body lavishly to show love and adoration, she is a prostitute. If a man (Peter), a sinner, invites lavish physicality, he is worthy to become Bishop of Rome. Only Seim alludes to the theme of 'pleasure in excess' in this story. She writes, 'her service is not aimed at satisfying the elementary need for sustenance, or for the necessities in life. . . her service has the character of surplus... her service benefits Jesus alone' (1994: 92).

In the interpretative works, the label 'prostitute' has risen out of the theme of 'excess'. It seems unthinkable that her lavish physicality could be a proper response to Jesus. It is ironic that in the text itself,

---

7.　Seim's source for the prostitute material comes entirely from either Blank 1983, or Witherington 1984. Both these works rely primarily on rabbinic writings or, in the case of Blank, on Strack/Billerbeck, which is dependent on rabbinic writings as well.

8.　Barbara Reid (1996) offers the most positive and feminist reading of Luke 7.36-50 I have found to date. She calls into question the designation 'prostitute' and recognizes the gendered interpretations regarding the sin of Peter as compared to the sin of the anointing woman.

these excesses are received positively by Jesus. Jesus acknowledges that all her gestures are excessive: Simon does not wash Jesus' feet but the anointing woman uses her tears and hair to wash them; Simon does not kiss Jesus but the anointing woman kisses him repeatedly; Simon does not oil Jesus' head but the anointing woman puts perfumed oil on his feet. It is precisely in her physical excess that Jesus finds cause for her praise. But just as Jesus praises her for her lavish physicality, biblical scholars find cause for her degradation.

I suspect that the prostitute label remains because feminist scholars transfer the physicality in this pericope into deviant sexuality; there is still no place in critical biblical scholarship for a positive reading of women's bodies. Judith Butler and Elizabeth Grosz assert that modern feminism has neglected to dispel a misogynist philosophical assumption that lies at the foundation of Western reason. Both charge that feminism uncritically accepts that the human subject is made up of two parts: mind and body (Butler 1990: 12; Grosz 1994: 3). In the inherent polarization and hierarchy of the dichotomy, 'body comes out being the thing valued less, while mind or soul is seen as more permanent, more noble, and closer to the sphere of divinity' (Goldenberg 1985: 55-72). The body and mind/soul form a subject/object relationship; the body becomes the 'Other' that receives its definition and its legitimization through the mind or soul. This separation and ranking not only solidify the concept of 'Other', but fasten the identity of the Other securely to the body.

In Augustine, and others after him, the body and all its accompanying evil are made manifest in women. Augustine develops a theological perspective, based on Gen. 1.27, that presents the male as naturally pure in spirit and mind, and vilifies the female as the corporeal subjugate of the male. Grosz charges that most feminist theorists uncritically reappropriate Western thought and participate in 'the social devaluing of the body that goes hand in hand with the oppression of women' (1994: 10). In Lk. 7.36-50, feminist interpreters have left the dichotomy of mind/body unchallenged and have simply translated it into its Virgin/Whore correlative (Bell 1994: 2).

The Virgin, aligned philosophically with the mind, inhabits a sexless and, therefore, sinless body. Augustine proposes that the only way women can attain 'maleness', rejecting their lower corporeal female selves, is to 'become virgins', that is, to remain virgin or become celibate. Rosemary Ruether writes, 'virginity, then, is interpreted as the resurrected life of the gospel whereby woman is freed from this twofold curse of Eve of the sorrows of childbearing and male domination' (1974: 159). For fourteenth-century Tuscan women, the Virgin Mary was a 'perfect' woman at each stage of her life (Miles 1985: 3). Though she went through all the biological stages of the women who venerated her, hers was without pain, blood, suffering and death. She was physically represented but her body was not a real body. The clear message to these women was that the Virgin was free 'from biological necessity at every stage of her life...The Virgin has a characteristic female life-cycle but does not experience the biological life of human women' (Miles 1985: 3).

By contrast, the Whore is a metaphorical representation of the body. The character Mary Magdalene has accumulated these metaphorical trappings in her misidentification as a harlot. As a repenting prostitute, the traditional and conflated portrayal of the Magdalene assumes a confusing and contradictory image for women. On one hand, she is a woman who is recognized for her erotic, uninhibited and lavish use of her own body to attend to the necessity and comfort of Jesus' body (based on the image of the anointing woman in Luke as one of the traditions that was appropriated to the Magdalene). On the other hand, she must repent and denounce those gestures as deviant: her actions are interpreted as improper and dishonorable.

Because she is a female body lavishly acting upon another body, the anointing woman is called a prostitute. Since the dichotomy between body and mind has been left in place, and since a female body endowed with so much physicality cannot be designated pure, there is simply no label left to give her except Whore. When the Virgin/Whore dichotomy is left intact, the woman is defined not intrinsically but through a dualist syllogism: Woman equals Body, and Body equals Whore, therefore, Woman equals Whore.

The dualist notion of the human being also sustains the bifurcation of sex in modern feminist discourses. The feminist translations reflect a point of view that is more sharply defined within a greater conflict: a battle within feminism over who decides what is pornographic and/or obscene (Rubin 1984; Califia 1994; Strossen 1995). The sex debate (as it is now called) dissolves into two problems: Who should control women's bodies and who interprets women's physicality and sexuality. Modern feminist biblical scholars are a part of this larger debate. In the interpretations of this pericope, clearly, the message is that the graphic portrayal of women's physicality is taboo, and therefore the woman subject is maligned. Biblical feminists, perhaps unknowingly, are a part of the conservative faction of the sex debate. Their gender bias is observable not only in the label prostitute, but also in the assumption that prostitute is a degrading label.

Within the more conservative faction of feminist thought, the sexual act is either reduced to its biological function, that is, the depositing of the male seminal fluid into the female container to create another body; or, it becomes eroticized, acceptable only if physical desire transcends the body and becomes a part of the 'higher order' of soul, consciousness or spirit. Before sexuality can be controlled and deemed proper it must be either completely biologically defined, or, conversely, defined only in the language of spirituality. Sex that blurs those boundaries between body and spirit becomes deviant because it exists outside social propriety. Physicality that exists for no other reason except pleasure and that manifests strong desire for or adoration of the body is labeled pornographic, and, therefore, deviant. In Mary Douglas's model, when sex is given a proper place it is no longer perceived as dangerous. However, anything beyond the biological, that is, beyond procreative sex, is abject; it becomes unknown and threatening to the social structure (Kristeva 1982: 3). The physicality of the anointing woman occupies a place of blurred boundaries between biological propriety and 'spiritual' love. She and her gestures would be considered deviant by interpreters because they exist beyond the accepted definition of pure or proper. It is in the excess of her physical acts, kissing, weeping, caressing, that scholars have found reason to degrade her.

It is from the excessive that the Sacred emerges. Michel Foucault, following Georges Bataille, suggests that in the extremes of the profane lies the Holy (Bell 1994: 154). But to transform the danger into sanctity, Paul, for example, embraces the 'scandal' of the cross: the crucifixion, one of the most violent events in Christian history, emerges as the most sacred. The crucifixion is physicality at its most brutal, yet it is in this meridian of suffering and degradation that Christians find God's compassion. If such great love can rise out of such horrible pain, what, then, of the kisses and tears on Jesus' body at the house of Simon the Pharisee? The brutal murder of Jesus, and even the violent dismembering and sacramental eating of Jesus' body, are privileged in the tradition over the caress of the anointing woman.

In biblical discourse, there are extreme contradictions between the passion of Jesus' suffering and the passion of Jesus' pleasure. While non-violent, 'gentle' passion is privileged in expressions of sexual relationships, it is ignored (or stigmatized) in biblical scholarship. A feminist biblical discourse could dissolve the barrier by, for example, listening to those who would consider that these two passions—one fierce, one tender—are equal.

If the lavish adoration of the anointing woman is perceived as deviant, and it is, then this means that biblical scholarship has failed to recognize the potential of the Sacred in all excessive physicality.[9] The interpreters of Christianity seem to be more comfortable explaining and propagating the violent passion of Jesus rather than acknowledging any other passion concerning Jesus' body. This denunciation of passionate adoration translates into a general erotophobia in modern society. A feminist critique would not deny that there is a loving, perhaps erotic passion in Lk. 7.36-50 and other pericopes, nor would it invent theories that diminish eroticism and edify degradation. If we could acknowledge the homoerotic tension, for example, in the feet-washing scene in Jn 13.1-17, the potential for interpretation is considerable. The body, sexuality and the erotic could be an integral part of biblical studies without the intolerable label of deviance.

A feminist critique begins with the knowledge that feminist discourse should not 'assume in advance what the content of woman should be' (Butler 1990: 14). The discourses concerning women's bodies inspired by the work of Judith Butler and Gayle Rubin, for example, are integral to the development of the type of feminist hermeneutics needed in biblical scholarship. These theorists create a place for a non-subject, that is, a discussion about women and women's bodies that precludes a monolithic ideal of what 'woman' is. Therefore, if a woman is extreme in her display of physical affection, she will not be called a prostitute. If, in feminist biblical discourse, we deny certain carnality and continue

9. The word 'deviant' unnecessarily takes on a negative connotation in many discourses, especially those discourses on women, women's bodies and women's sexuality. In the scholarship of Lk. 7.36-50, the anointing woman has been labeled a prostitute. I call this label 'deviant' not because I equate prostitution with sexual deviance, but because those who label the anointing woman a prostitute intend for the ascription 'prostitute' to be a symbol of degradation. For example, Saint Cyril, Patriarch of Alexandria, calls her a wicked, hateful sinner; Caird calls her an 'evil' woman; Tannehill writes that she is a despised sinner; and another writes that she is a 'notorious harlot'. The label is meant to confine her to a place of lowest moral standards far outside the realm of propriety.

to interpret particular types of physicality as deviant, we continue to privilege the heterosexual, monogamous, procreating couple (Rubin 1984). The biblical text is a living text, written for all; it should, therefore, be interpreted in such a way that it speaks to, and gives voice to, everyone. In such an interpretation, the anointing woman's love is without debasement, her love has power, and her love is as overwhelming as his.

BIBLIOGRAPHY

Balz, Horst, and Gehard Schneider (eds.)
1990   *Exegetical Dictionary of the New Testament* (Grand Rapids: Eerdmans):
                65-68.
Bell, Shannon
1994   *Reading, Writing and Rewriting the Prostitute Body* (Bloomington:
                Indiana University Press).
Blank, J.
1983   'Frauen in den Jesusüberlieferungen', in G. Dautzenberg, H. Merklein
                and K. Müller (eds.), *Die Frau im Urchristentum, Quaestiones
                Disputatae 95* (Freiburg: Lambertus-Verlag): 9-91.
Brumberg Kraus, J.
1991   'Symposium Scenes in Luke's Gospel' (Unpublished Thesis, Vanderbilt
                University).
Butler, Judith
1990   *Gender Trouble* (New York: Routledge).
Caird, C.B.
1977   *The Gospel of St. Luke* (New York: Penguin Books).
Califia, Pat
1994   *Public Sex* (Pittsburgh: Cleis Press).
Corley, Kathleen
1989   'Were the Women around Jesus Really Prostitutes? Women in the
                Context of Greco-Roman Meals', in David Lull (ed.), *Society of Biblical
                Literature 1989 Seminar Papers* (Atlanta, GA: Scholars Press): 487-521.
1993   *Private Women, Public Meals* (Peabody, MA: Hendrickson).
Cyril (Saint)
1983   *Commentary on the Gospel of St Luke* (trans. R. Payne Smith; Astoria,
                NY: Studion Publishers).
Douglas, Mary
1966   *Purity and Danger: An Analysis of Concepts of Pollution and Taboo*
                (London: Routledge).
Fitzmyer, J.
1981   *The Gospel of Luke* (New York: Doubleday).
Goldenberg, Naomi
1985   'Archetypal Theory and Separation of Mind and Body: Reason Enough to
                Turn to Freud?', *Journal of Feminist Studies in Religion* 1: 55-72.

AN ASIAN INTERPRETATION OF PHILIPPIANS 2.6-11

Jean K. Kim

Introduction

The many forms of oppression which Asian women experience lead them to seek the cause of their sufferings. They have learned to believe that sufferings arise from human sin without considering the dynamics of exploitation and victimization. Rather than trying to find the cause of their suffering in the patriarchal social structure, they attribute their suffering to their *karma* or to their inevitable destiny as women.[1] The various religious contexts such as Buddhism and Confucianism, which have cooperated with the patriarchal system, have thus forced women to accept their suffering as inevitable rather than liberating them from it. Along similar lines, institutionalized Christianity as presented by the Western missionaries, which emphasizes the male image of God and of Jesus, has further aggravated the suffering situation of Asian women.[2]

In such a pluralistic context, where Asian Christians are still in a minority, Asian women theologians need to examine the relation between culture and the Bible. Since the Bible contains so many oppressive messages for women, critical reflection on the Bible from an Asian women's perspective is necessary for their task. One of the contradictory biblical teachings having a definite impact on Asian women is Phil. 2.6-11, which presents the contrasting images of Jesus as slave and as Lord of the world. In an Asian context, Jesus' image as Lord has been used to justify Western domination of many Asian countries in economic, political and religio-cultural spheres. Western missionaries have forced Asians to identify the Western colonizer's Lord Jesus with the Lord for Asia, claiming that their Lord is the ruler of the whole

---

1.   Rita Nakashima Brock and Susan Brooks Thistlethwaite, *Casting Stones: Prostitution and Liberation in Asia and the United States* (Minneapolis: Fortress Press, 1996), pp. 235-68.

2.   Brock and Brooks Thistlethwaite, *Casting Stones*, pp. 31-40.

universe.[3] In the final analysis, for an Asian to become a Christian meant obeying the Lord Jesus and discarding his or her Asian cultural and spiritual inheritance.

To make it worse, because of the institutionalized church, which distorted Jesus' image by emphasizing his maleness rather than his humanity, the male image of Jesus became a constitutive factor in deciding the place and role of women. Asian Christians have come to believe in twin father images: head of the world and head of families, and this conviction goes very deep into the hearts and beliefs of Asian Christians. The male images of God and of Jesus became authoritarian, and have been used to justify and to guarantee male dominance over women. On the other hand, the image of Jesus as suffering slave has been imposed upon women to persuade them to accept their suffering. According to this ideology, women ought to silently bear taunts, abuse, and even battering, and to sacrifice their self-esteem for the sake of family, nation or honor. In so doing, Asian Christian women make meaning out of their suffering through Jesus' suffering and death: they attempt to view their own suffering as redemptive. However, as Hyun Kyung Chung points out, such a making of meaning out of passive suffering is dangerous for Asian women because it can provide the oppressor with an excuse for continued oppression.[4] Furthermore, Jesus' suffering was by no means a passive suffering but rather an inevitable result of his active engagement in an anti–status quo struggle for the sake of the well-being of all living things.

As for this dangerous interpretation of Phil. 2.6-11, which associates the authoritative image of Jesus with maleness, while imposing the requirement of Jesus as suffering slave upon women, I insist that since the Bible is not an objective text but a complex product which has been shaped throughout many socio-historical contexts, every reading of the Bible should consider not only the context of the text but also the context of the flesh-and-blood reader. With this reading strategy, I would like to read Phil. 2.6-11 from an Asian perspective, which can help Asian women to resume their own subjectivities as well as their dignity

---

3. For the title, 'the ruler of the world', see Karen Jo Torjensen, '"You are the Christ": Five Portraits of Jesus from the Early Church', in M. Borg (ed.), *Jesus at 2000* (Oxford: Westerview Press, 1997), pp. 173-88 (85).

4. Hyun Kyung Chung, *Struggle to Be the Sun Again: Introducing Asian Women's Theology* (Maryknoll, NY: Orbis Books, 1990), p. 54.

by understanding that they, along with Jesus, can be divine agents in struggling for the well-being of all living things in the cosmos. For this task, firstly, by examining the tradition of christological titles about Jesus, I will argue that the problematic Christology in Phil. 2.6-11, which contains the statement of the pre-existence of Jesus, is no more than a religio-political product, which gradually became stronger during the development of early Christianity. Secondly, I will show that in his letter to the Philippians, Paul himself does not use the Philippians hymn christologically, but rhetorically in order to justify his own authority and suffering. Lastly, by introducing the *Yin* and *Yang* concept which is a basic frame of Asian thought, and *Donghak* (Eastern Learning) which is a prototype of *Minjung* theology, I would like to suggest an Asian context-oriented Christology, which can negate scriptural Christology, and move Jesus from his encasement in church tradition and doctrine to the sphere of *Minjung* where God is working.

The History of the Tradition

In his lecture on the question of how a Galilean Jew could be transformed into the decisive disclosure of God, Marcus Borg takes pains to distinguish the pre-Easter and post-Easter Jesus: 'the foundational experience that initiated the transformation from Jesus as a Galilean Jew to Jesus as the face of God and the second person of the trinity was Easter'.[5] Indeed, as Borg says, in the Gospels, Jesus is described in a programmatic way through many conceptual developments after the Easter event. The early church community confessed Jesus as the one whom God made Messiah through the resurrection (Acts 2.3-4), by which they intended to emphasize the significance and continuing validity of Jesus' authority after his death. As a Jewish title, Messiah designated the one who brought salvation, the one whose imminent return would bring with it the end of the world, the final judgment and ultimate salvation. Faith in Jesus as the one who brings final salvation presumes that Jesus is still alive, even though he died on the cross. Instead of being the shameful death of a criminal, Jesus' crucifixion thus became the most significant symbol of a salvific act, which was already ushering in the beginning of the end of time, and the group who

5. Marcus Borg, 'From the Galilean Jew to the Face of God', in Borg (ed.), *Jesus at 2000*, p. 13.

confessed Jesus as Messiah regarded themselves as the eschatological community.[6]

Among these Christian communities which were expecting the imminent end of the world, according to Martin Dibelius, sayings of Jesus were used for the purpose of exhortation (Lk. 3.7-9, 16-7; 7.18-35). Q did not intend to offer a complete summary of doctrine; it lacked the central affirmation of the death and resurrection of Jesus. The sayings in Q did not demonstrate any christological interest, but were employed as a hortatory supplement to the *kerygma*.[7] Unlike Dibelius, Bultmann insists that Q is not a simple parenesis but a preaching of the eschatological event itself, and one which had already engaged in the conceptual development about who Jesus was, for the purpose of the constitution of Christian identity.[8] Bultmann's suggestion has opened a way to understand Q as a transitional stage between the preaching of Jesus and the *kerygma* of the Hellenistic churches, as John S. Kloppenberg observes.[9] Under the influence of Bultmann, Heinz E. Todt understands Q not as parenetic supplement but as the renewed preaching of the kingdom. The resurrection of Jesus was not understood as the object of the preaching but as the authoritative basis to preach and as the validation of that preaching, and the christological perception had already occurred: the resurrection was comprehended as God's confirmation of Jesus' authority as the Son of Man.[10] Since it is more likely that when the proclaimer had become the proclaimed, the proclaimed could not have been a simple object of teaching, but rather must have become an authoritative figure, we can therefore assume that such a conceptual development as Todt proposes was already happening in the early churches.

However, nowhere in Q has the figure of the early Jesus been made divine. As Todt insists, Messiah, or Son of Man had a soteriological significance to the early church community, not the christological

6. Herbert Braun, 'The Meaning of New Testament Christology', *JTC* 5 (1968), pp. 89-127 (95-97).

7. Martin Dibelius, *From Tradition to Gospel* (trans. Betram Lee Woolf; Cambridge: James Clarke, 1971), p. 246.

8. Rudolf Bultmann, *Theology of the New Testament* (2 vols.; trans. Kendrick Grobel; New York: Charles Scribner's Sons, 1951), I, p. 3.

9. John S. Kloppenberg, *The Formation of Q* (Philadelphia: Fortress Press, 1987), pp. 22-39.

10. Heinz E. Todt, *The Son of Man in the Synoptic Tradition* (Philadelphia: Westminster Press, 1965), pp. 249-53.

significance that it later came to have with Paul and with his 'Christ'.[11]
The emphasis of the Christology of Q was not on the heavenly origin of
the Son of Man but on Jesus' authority on earth.[12] Jesus' title, Son of
God, also does not bear any marks of the heavenly being of later
Christology.[13] In Mt. 11.27, Jesus mentions 'my father', and thus
appears as the Son of God. According to Jewish tradition in Jesus'
times, as Borg explains, the 'Son of God' might mean a Jewish spiritual
person, and therefore the Son of God should be understood as a
metaphor of an intimate relationship between Jesus and God.[14] If such
is the case, the title 'Son of God' might not be intended to make a claim
for Jesus' divine sonship, but might rather be a central statement of
Jesus' own consciousness of his mission. The basic foundation of the
post-Easter concept of Jesus as the Son of God thus also does not rest
upon a pre-existent divine Sonship, but upon the praxis and preaching
of the earthly Jesus himself.

Nevertheless, as the title 'Son of God' developed in the early
Christian community, Jesus' status as the Son of God was pushed further back into his life, and even into the time before he was born, and
other more honorific titles were given to him. The intended significance
of Jesus' titles becomes clear when we observe the shift of these titles
as the gospel is propagandized in a different cultural surrounding. So
the transformation of these titles can be explained from a missiological
point of view. In the Hellenistic world, Jewish titles such as 'Messiah'
or 'Son of Man', which express the salvific significance of Jesus' life
and teaching, would be incomprehensible, or at least strange. For that
reason, the title 'Son of Man' disappeared or was modified in the
Pauline churches: 'Messiah' becomes in its Greek form *christos*, and

---

11. Todt, *The Son of Man*, p. 294.

12. Todt, *The Son of Man*, p. 296; According to Braun, the older forms of the
saying differentiate between Jesus and the Son of Man (Mk 8.38; Lk. 6.22; 9.26;
12.8-9); it is not until the later form (Mt. 5.11; 10.32-33) that the 'I' of Jesus is put
in the place of the Son of Man. This equation is also due to the christological faith,
the Easter faith, and must therefore be separated from the historical Jesus. The 'for
my sake' in the giving up of their lives by the disciples (Mk 8.55; Mt. 10.39) represents the more recent form of the saying vis-à-vis an older formulation that omits
reference to the person of Jesus, and is probably more original. Braun, 'The
Meaning', pp. 13-14.

13. Bultmann, *Theology*, p. 35.

14. Borg, 'From Galilean Jew', pp. 13-14.

the title 'the Son of God' takes on a divine meaning (Rom. 1.4).[15] In the Hellenistic sphere, Jesus is described as a redeemer in a descent and ascent mode: as a divine being who descends to earth to suffer and die for his followers, and then returns in triumph to heaven where his power resides. This transformation of Jesus' status is in itself not surprising. Just as the early church community expressed their faith in Jesus in Jewish thoughts, so now these Jewish titles are modified, and new titles are added according to Hellenistic content: the process that took place at the time of the origin of the Easter faith now occurs anew in the Hellenistic sphere. The pre-christological stage of the oldest Jesus tradition has thus given way to the stage of christological codification that happened at first in Jewish, then in Hellenistic spheres, and Phil. 2.6-11 reflects this transitional stage.

Karl-Josef Kuschel places the Philippians hymn within this development of the Jewish-Hellenistic tradition. He insists that even though the Philippians hymn contains a statement of Jesus' pre-existence, it does not contain a distinctive Christology of pre-existence: 'as a piece of great poetry, in its imagery, it can express that for which there are yet no concepts; it can boldly and metaphorically open up frontier realms of language which conceptual language is concerned to take in only a later stage'.[16] For both Aramaic-speaking and Greek-speaking Christian communities, it was not Jesus' supposed pre-existent divinity, but rather his humbling of himself which led to the cross and to his subsequent exaltation as *kyrios* and the Lord of the world, and the Philippians hymn should therefore be regarded as a deliberate literary attempt to depict the experience of the early church community regarding the Christ-event. In terms of the history of the tradition, as he explains, the Philippians hymn seems to lie on the frontier between Judaism and Hellenism. However, it would be an oversimplification to treat the Philippians hymn as purely a deliberate literary product which employs a contrasting tension of high drama to interpret the Christ-event. No writing is written in a vacuum, and each writing has its own agenda. In other words, even if the Philippians hymn was a literary

---

15. The title 'Son of God' did not come into common use until after Easter: it was given to Jesus to bestow upon him a new role which took over the duty of all earlier titles. Paul J. Achtemeier (ed.), *Harper's Bible Dictionary* (New York: HarperCollins, 1985), pp. 979-80.

16. Karl-Josef Kuschel, *Born before All Times?* (New York: Crossroad, 1992), pp. 258-63.

product, there might have been plausible reasons behind its composition and its liturgical use in the church communities.

With regard to the contradictory features of Jesus in the same document, Helmut Koester suggests that the combination of different concepts in the same document cannot be viewed primarily as a successful theological experiment but as an accomplishment of ecclesiastical politics: 'by incorporating the traditions of two very different Christian communities into one single document, both traditions were recognized as legitimate in spite of their theological disagreement'.[17] This suggestion gives a more convincing clue toward understanding the development of traditions than does Kuschel's claim. In the Philippians hymn, the crucified slave, Jesus, in the likeness of God, is proclaimed the Lord of the world. To proclaim a crucified slave as the ruler of the world, which sounds very paradoxical, might have aimed to propagate a new form of rule in the name of Christ in a new surrounding. Considering the religio-political setting of the early church community, we can assume that the transformation of Jesus' image from a Galilean Jew to the Lord of the world was contextually indispensable in coping with the tension which existed with Jewish authority, as well as with the Roman imperial cults. Against the claim that the statements about Jesus' pre-existence were merely products of intellectual effort, Helmut Merklein attempts an ideological approach from a religio-political perspective: the formation of the confession of the pre-existence of Christ does not stem from a vague and abstract Easter experience but reflects Jesus' criticism of temple and Torah and the conflict with the Jewish establishment.[18] Temple and Torah were the decisive divine authorities with which Jesus himself had already come into conflict.[19] The wisdom of God was embodied in the Torah, which had settled in the temple of Jerusalem. In contrast, eschatological salvation is embodied in Jesus' death, so the place of the revelation of God for human salvation was no longer the existing temple or Torah, but Jesus himself. The confession of the redemptive death of Jesus to critically relativize the temple and

---

17. Helmut Koester, 'Writing and the Spirit: Authority and Politics in Ancient Christianity', *HTR* 84 (1991), pp. 353-72 (367).

18. Helmut Merklein, '*Zur Entstehung der urchristlichen Aussage vom präexistent Sohn*', in *Zur Geschichte des Urchristentums* (Freiburg: Herder, 1979), pp. 53-54. Cited from Kuschel, *Born before All Times?*, pp. 265-66.

19. It was criticism of the temple and Torah which drove the Hellenists out of Jerusalem (Acts 6.11, 13-14).

Torah might thus have been a challenge to the Jews in Jerusalem, whereas the statement about the pre-existence of Jesus might have had a greater significance to the Hellenistic Christian community. On the other hand, in the first century of the Roman Empire, where the political sphere was overlapped with the religious sphere,[20] the Roman emperors claimed to be divine persons, and they set up the imperial cults, which influenced the origin and spread of Christianity.[21] According to Donald L. Jones, the Roman emperors were proclaimed as divine saviors of the world, and ascension after death became a significant symbol in emperor exaltation: Caligula, Claudius, Nero and Vepasian were all referred to as 'Savior of the World'. Also, since *kyrios*, a prominent title in the imperial cult, is also prominent in the early Christian writings like the Philippians hymn (cf. Mk 11.9-11; Mt. 21.9; Lk. 19.38; Jn 12.13), Jones claims that the early Christian proclamation of Jesus as Lord, whose purpose was to counterbalance the imperial cult, would necessarily come into conflict with Roman authority (Rom. 13.1-8; 1 Cor. 6.1; Phil. 1.13, 30; 4.3).[22] There is not much evidence in the Gospel which reveals Jesus' attitude towards Roman authority: Jesus' answer to the question regarding the payment of taxes implicitly shows the tension between the two authorities (Mk 12.13-17; Mt. 22.15-22; Lk. 20.20-26). We can see, however, in the Pauline letters that the tension contained enough potential for conflict with the Roman authority that Paul had to find a way to instruct his church communities without blaspheming God by using the same title that appertained to the emperor. In light of this religio-political background, it can be said that the early church's rejection of both the Jewish authority and the Roman imperial cult found a new expression in consistent formulations of Jesus' pre-existent divinity.[23]

Removing the christological claim of pre-existence from a theological or a doctrinal sphere to a religio-political context therefore convincingly explains its function in the early church communities. In other words, the question of Jesus' pre-existence cannot be detached from the religio-political situation of those times, and therefore the statement of

20. Richard A. Horsley (ed.), *Paul and Empire: Religion and Power in Roman Imperial Society* (Harrisburg, PA: Trinity Press International, 1997), p. 7.

21. Donald L. Jones, 'Christianity and the Roman Imperial Cults', *ANRW*, II, 23.2, pp. 1023-24.

22. Jones, 'Christianity', pp. 1027-29, 1031.

23. Horsley, *Paul and Empire*, p. 1.

the pre-existence of Jesus should be understood as a contextual product based on the early church's own self-interpretation of the Jesus-event in defense of its own community.

The Pauline Context of Philippians 2.6-11

Minjung theologian Byung-mu Ahn claims that even if the Jesus-event itself happened among the followers in private, the 'Jesus-event tradition' has been modified or used by the church authorities or apostles who were motivated by missionary or apologetic concerns.[24] Indeed, as we have examined, the transformation of Jesus' status from a Galilean Jew to the Lord of the world happened gradually according to the socio-political situation of the church communities, and we can also find this tendency in Paul's letter to the Philippians. It is generally agreed that Phil. 2.6-11 is a pre-Pauline tradition. So it can be argued that Phil. 2.6-11 has essentially nothing to do with Paul himself and must be understood as it is, without reference either to Paul or to its present Pauline context. However, all written materials we now have are composite documents. In their composition, writers of these materials employ various and even contradictory sources and traditions about Jesus when they feel that those sources are proper for their need to propagandize or instruct their communities. Paul is no exception. Paul often cites and adapts sources or traditions in his way when they fit his claims in order to elaborate or support the point he is trying to make. Therefore, even if Phil. 2.6-11 is a pre-Pauline tradition, it is not necessary to separate Phil. 2.6-11 from the overall context of Philippians. Rather, since 'Paul is the author in terms of its inclusion including all the present works', as Gordon D. Fee insists, we can analyze how Paul interprets and uses the Philippians hymn in his letter to the Philippians.[25]

In order to understand the function of the Philippians hymn in Paul's letter, L. Michael White introduces the 'friendship paradigm' theory. According to White's observation of the Hellenistic moral tradition, the ideal friendship included 'having all things in common' and 'having one mind'.[26] Friendship in the Hellenistic world was far more than a

24. Byung-mu Ahn, 'The Body of Jesus-Event Tradition', *EAJT* 3 (1985), pp. 293-307 (295).

25. Gordon D. Fee, 'Philippians 2.5-11: Hymn or Exalted Prose?', *BBR* 2 (1992), pp. 29-46 (36).

26. L. Michael White, 'Morality between Two Worlds: A Paradigm of

simple relationship; it had profound social and ethical implications which bear heavily on Paul's extensive appropriation of this language throughout the letter. The virtue of selfless, loving friendship is recognizable in the technical language of the semantic complex, especially in terms such as *koinōnia, kaiein*, and *to auto phronein*.[27] The same humility that is exemplified by Christ's 'emptying' himself to take 'the form of slave' is also the proper disposition to be maintained in all Christian relationships. White's claim that Paul adapted the ideal friendship through friendly parenesis to the Philippians to live the virtuous life in Christ is further supported by Wayne Meeks. Paul, Meeks asserts, created a moral paradigm that the world of the Philippians could understand by grounding the Greek virtue in the divine will, through the drama of Christ's humility and exaltation.[28] Gerald W. Peterman also agrees with White that 'the Christ-hymn is the hub from which the ethical injunction of the letter radiates', but he modifies White's suggestion by saying that White's friendship paradigm theory is inappropriate because every friendship contained political elements, and even the element of competition. He then affirms that this type of competitive friendship is precisely what Paul combats with his appeal to the example of Jesus.[29] In fact, in the Pauline letters, Paul mostly describes himself as 'a slave of Christ Jesus' (Rom. 1.1; Gal. 1.10; Phil. 1.1).[30] For Paul, such a total orientation of himself to the risen Lord was

Friendship in Philippians', in D. Balch (ed.), *Greeks, Romans and Christians* (Minneapolis: Fortress Press, 1990), pp. 211-12.

27. White, 'Morality between Two Worlds', pp. 214-15.

28. Wayne Meeks, 'The Man from Heaven in Paul's Letter to the Philippians', in B. Pearson (ed.), *The Future of Early Christianity* (Minneapolis: Fortress Press, 1991), pp. 335-36.

29. Gerald W. Peterman, *Paul's Gift from Philippi: Convention of Gift-Exchange and Christian Giving* (Cambridge: Cambridge University Press, 1997), pp. 116-18.

30. The vocabulary used to describe Jesus' action in the Philippians hymn has some connection with the Gospel tradition of Jesus (Mk 9.35; 10.43-45; Mt. 20.25-28; 23.11; Lk. 22.24-27). Although the terms *diakonos, diakonia* and *diakonoi*, which are prevalent in the Gospel tradition, can be distinguished from the *doulos* word group, the two word groups seem to be used here in close association. In terms of this linguistic connection, it might be the action of the earthly Jesus in submitting himself to crucifixion that provided the basis for describing Paul as *doulos*; because of these verbal similarities, L.W. Hurtardo insists that the Gospel tradition is likely to have informed Paul's uses of the key terms *doulos, tapeinos, hupēkoos*. L.W. Hurtardo, 'Jesus as Lordly Example in Philippians 2.5-11', in

also a determining factor in his relationship to the Christian communities which he founded (1 Cor. 15.8; Gal. 1.1). The obligation he felt to make them see him as 'an imitator of Christ' governs his practice of providing his readers with frequent references to his own experience. The point Paul is trying to make is that, like Jesus, he can and will sacrifice everything. In both Phil. 1.27-30 and 3.1-17, Paul relies on Phil. 2.6-11 as an exemplar or shared norm on which he bases his argument. And, as Robert T. Fortna points out,[31] the fullest expression of this is to be found in Philippians 3: 'For his sake I have suffered the loss of all things, and I regard them as rubbish in order that I may gain Christ and be found in him, not having a righteousness of my own that comes from the law, but one that comes through faith in Christ, the righteousness from God based on faith' (Phil. 3.8-9).

John Reumann suggests that the writing of such a composition might have been motivated by his suffering under Roman imperial authority during his mission.[32] Indeed, Paul deals with the affairs of the Roman state in his letter to the Philippians (Phil. 1.27; 2.10-11; 4.22). However, it is not likely that Paul addresses these matters because he cares about the Roman Empire state; rather, he is concerned about his church members in the Roman colony of Philippi. Raymond R. Brewer argues that *politeuesthe* was used to exhort the Philippians to fulfill their obligations as citizens in the way Christians should.[33] Etymologically, the word *politeuesthe* is related to the term *polis* and it was originally used of the discharge of civic duties and obligations. Because of this, Brewer could say that the Philippians are exhorted to behave as citizens of the Roman colony of Philippi. *Politeuesthe* and its related words in Philippians, however, are not necessarily about the discharge of civic duty, but convey Paul's concern for his church community, as Ernest C. Miller has already insisted.[34] Richard A. Horsley also

P. Richardson and J.C. Hurd (eds.), *From Jesus to Paul* (Waterloo, Ontario: Wilfrid Laurier University Press, 1984).

31. Robert T. Fortna, 'Philippians: Paul's Most Egocentric Letter', in R.T. Fortna and B.R. Gaventa (eds.), *The Conversation Continues: Studies in Paul and John* (Nashville: Abingdon Press, 1990), pp. 226-27.

32. John Reumann, 'Contribution of the Philippians Community to Paul and to Earliest Christianity', *NTS* 39 (1993), pp. 438-57 (456).

33. Raymond R. Brewer, 'The Meaning of *politeuesthe* in Philippians 1.27', *JBL* 73 (1954), pp. 76-83.

34. Ernest C. Miller, '*politeuesthe* in Philippians', *JSNT* 15 (1982), pp. 86-96; Davorin Peterlin also insists that the use of the noun *politeuma* shows a change of

emphasizes that Paul's communities were political as well as religious just as the term *polis* was both political and religious. Then, he affirms that Paul was trying to set up an anti-imperial alternative society by setting Christ crucified on the Roman cross in opposition to 'the rulers of this age, who are doomed to perish' and to 'every ruler and every authority and power' whom Christ will destroy (1 Cor. 2.6-8; 15.24).[35] Considering the fact that Paul refers to his conflict with the Roman authorities (Phil. 1.13) and his fears that the Philippians might experience the same struggle (Phil. 1.30), it is highly plausible that in Paul's letter to the Philippians, the Roman authority is contrasted with the divine authority: for just as Roman citizens were registered by the Roman Empire, so Christians were said to have their name written in the 'Book of Life' (Phil. 4.3).

During the time of Paul's mission, the Romans planted a colony of military veterans at Philippi, which was a cause of serious strife to the Philippians. The strife Paul presents, however, does not lie in the usual idea of war: since the ruler of the divine world is the principal example of servitude (Phil. 2.5), warfare means servitude and the victory can be won only through self-sacrifice (Phil. 3.8).[36] The contrasting images of *doulos* and *kyrios* in the Philippians hymn thus affirm that the Christ hymn was used to highlight the contrast between abasement and exaltation, which paradoxically brings hope to Paul's community. Given that the socio-historical context of Paul's mission was the Roman Empire, it is plausible to say, as Peterman suggests, that the Philippians hymn does not merely convey the ideal paradigm of virtuous friendship in a social-ethical sense, but aims to supersede the Roman imperial authority with Christ's authority through a paradoxical mode of abasement and exaltation. In addition, a close observation of the recurrence of the language and imagery of the Christ hymn throughout Paul's letter to the Philippians reveals the way in which he used Christ's experience to legitimize his own experience, thus establishing his own authority within his community and providing them with an ideal

reference and implies the universal community of believers. Davorin Peterlin, *Paul's Letter to the Philippians in the Light of Disunity in the Church* (Leiden: E.J. Brill, 1995), p. 55.

35. Horsley, *Paul and Empire*, pp. 3-8.

36. Lilian Portefax, *Sisters Rejoice: Paul's Letter to the Philippians and Luke–Acts as Seen by First-Century Philippian Women* (Stockholm: Almqvist & Wiksell, 1988), pp. 139-42.

figure: for just as Christ's abasement led to exaltation, and just as Paul takes on the role of *doulos* in following Christ, so the Christians' final experience is not an abandoned suffering, but an exaltation by God's grace. In light of this, therefore, it can be said that in the letter to the Philippians, Paul uses the Christ hymn rhetorically in order to instruct his community, which was under the Roman authority, and to give them hope, with an authority based on his self-reflection that he is the slave of Christ.

As we have examined, whatever might have been the original setting of the Philippians hymn, or its original christological affirmation, in its present form the Christ hymn does not function as a christological statement of Jesus' pre-existence but has been adapted to a new context: since Christ's own obedience to the point of death and subsequent exaltation are encapsulated in the Philippians hymn, Paul uses it as a springboard for his own protological reflection and as a model in order to shape a certain attitude of behavior in his community. Therefore, Phil. 2.6-11 should be regarded as a reworked text on the basis of the Jesus tradition for the propagation of the faith among Christians as well as being a paradigm for Paul's community in the contemporary world at Philippi, rather than as a statement per se which emphasizes Jesus' heavenly origin.

An Asian Interpretation of Philippians 2.6-11

Jung Young Lee emphasizes the necessity of the contextualization of theology because every theological statement of traditional doctrine was not formulated in a vacuum, but arose as a response to conflicting issues in contemporary times.[37] Indeed, as we have examined above, the Christian tradition that we have today is the result of contextualization throughout many centuries: when Jesus initiated his movement against Jewish religious authority in the Roman Empire situation, his following was limited mostly to a minority of Jews who, after his death, confessed him as Messiah; as early Christianity developed, it had to accommodate cultural as well as religio-political factors during its spread in the Gentile Hellenistic milieu which was under Roman control. However, after Christianity was institutionalized, it was monopolized by the West, and the dominant biblical scholarship has

---

37. Jung Young Lee, *The Trinity in Asian Perspective* (Nashville: Abingdon Press, 1996), pp. 14-15.

focused on the emergence of Christianity as universal. Owing to this strong tendency, when the missionaries brought Jesus to Asia in company with Western imperialism, they did not consider cross-cultural factors, but forced Asians to discard their cultural inheritance. In this sense, Christianity can be described as an imperial product in terms of both the historical background of the period of its origin and its ongoing propaganda. Yet, the irony of Christianity is that what started as an anti-imperial movement became the imperial religion. Against this irony, many scholars are aware that Western biblical scholarship needs to reconceptualize Christianity and biblical interpretation.[38] In fact, there was an understanding of God in Asia even before the Western missionaries brought Christianity there. In other words, since nobody claims possession of God, the transformation of Christianity into an Asian context is necessary, as Lee stresses. So in this section, I will read the Christ hymn from an Asian perspective by regarding it as a text which is part of an ongoing process of contextualization rather than as a static and finished product.

For this contextualization, the most significant task is to understand the basic frame of Asian thought, that is, the *yin/yang* principle. In Asia, all natural phenomena are conceived as the ceaseless interplay of two separated forces, *yin* and *yang*.[39] The essence of the *yin/yang* relationship is not the entity or being itself, but the dynamic act of change, because it is not the being that changes *yin/yang* into *yang/yin*, but change itself that makes it *yin* and *yang*.[40] They are existentially opposite but essentially united, so they are inseparable from each other. To put it in a more inclusive way, since *yin* and *yang* embrace each other to maintain ultimate reality by including opposites as well as transcending them, *yin* is not only *yin* but becomes *yang* through an in-between state, and vice versa. That *yin/yang* is limited by *yang/yin* thus means that the two opposites are not absolute but relative to each other, for the sake of the harmony of all living things.[41] 'Harmony' is a key word in

38. Horsley, *Paul and Empire*, p. 12; Kwok Pui-lan, *Discovering the Bible in the Non-Biblical World* (Maryknoll, NY: Orbis Books, 1995); R.S. Sugirtharajah (ed.), *Voices from the Margins: Interpreting the Bible in the Third World* (Maryknoll, NY: Orbis Books, 1991).

39. *Yin* and *Yang* represent two mutually complementary principles or forces in Asian cosmology. Fung Yu-lan, *History of Chinese Philosophy* (trans. Derk Bodde; Princeton, NJ: Princeton University Press, 1953), p. 7.

40. Lee, *Trinity in Asian Perspective*, p. 27.

41. Lee, *Trinity in Asian Perspective*, pp. 28-32.

understanding the relationship between *yin* and *yang*. Unfortunately, however, this harmony has not been emphasized horizontally, but has been used to support vertical (hierarchical) relationships between ruler and subject, husband and wife, and father and son. The main cause of this shift from a non-hierarchical relationship to a hierarchical one can be attributed to Confucianism. The all-*yang* or all-male symbol was given a great deal of attention by later Confucianism because only proper *yang* was thought to emanate from 'Heaven', even though Heaven is no more that one of the two branches which are separated from the Great One.[42] By contrast, the all-*yin* or all-female symbol was of importance only for the sake of the continuous existence of the all-*yang* or all-male being. The *yin* which was regarded as definitely inferior to *yang* by orthodox Confucianism could redeem itself only through the virtue of yielding itself to *yang*. Following this development regarding the *yin/yang* symbol, the bifurcation of gender roles and of classism thus undergirded the pretext for social and political stratification in Confucianism, and finally became fixed as a social norm.[43]

When Confucianism as the state orthodoxy became the primary ideology of the ruling civilian bureaucracy, the prejudice against *yin* in favor of *yang* became widespread throughout Chinese society. In the third century, Confucianism fell into eclipse, and yielded its dominant place to Taoism (during the third century), and then to Buddhism (during the fourth century). In the ninth century, however, intellectual interest in Confucianism revived while at the same time coming under the influence of the two other religions.[44] This revival of Confucianism is called neo-Confuciansim, which spread to East Asia as the only accepted orthodoxy. Since the main tenets of orthodoxy were based on a vast body of learning to which ordinary people and women had no access, and since neo-Confucianism represented a rigid hierarchical relationship whose goal was to emphasize responsibility in government

42. The correlations between astronomical phenomena were seen as resonant with the phenomena of the political sphere and the emperor was a direct correlate of Heaven. Fung Yu-lan, *History,* pp. 30-32; According to the *Li Chi,* one of the earliest classics of Confucianism, 'the Great One separated and became Heaven and Earth. It evolved and became dual forces'. Cited from Lee, *Trinity in Asian Perspective,* p. 24.

43. E.B. Morris, 'Deconstructionism and the "*Yin/Yang*" School', *Chinese Culture* 34 (1993), pp. 1-29.

44. Fung Yu-Lan, *History,* pp. xxii-xxiii.

and the priority of service over personal interest, it gave no voice to women and the lower classes. In the nineteenth century, when the Yi dynasty was in turmoil because of the incursion of foreign power into Korea and the internal corruption of the aristocratic class, the neo-Confucianist ideology of the Yi dynasty began to lose its authority as a state ideology.[45] In a reaction against internal corruption as well as against the overwhelming foreign power, especially the Christian missionaries who regarded Korean religious spirituality as superstition, Che-U Choe, the founder of *Donghak*,[46] inaugurated the *Donghak* peasant movement whose goal was to break sexism and classism and build an egalitarian society. He criticized the impotence of the institutionalized religions, which supported the authority of the state, and rediscovered the true meaning of the *yin/yang* principle, which was gendered by Confucianism. In addition, unlike the Chinese philosophy, which tries to explain all natural phenomena solely through the movement of *yin* and *yang, Donghak* includes Choe's development of an indigenous Korean concept of God. *Donghak*'s understanding of God agrees with the Christian concept of God in that it presents a God who intervenes in human history, but it denies the dualistic relationship between subject and object such as the 'I–Thou' relationship between God and human beings, and does not accept the conflicting relationship between nature and super-nature.[47] Throughout their 5000-year history, Koreans have been a religious people, but they have never named God nor tried to describe God in an anthropomorphic way. For them, God is an absolute being who transcends natural phenomena, but at the same time, God is an intimate being who dwells both in human beings and in the cosmos. In contrast to the Western concept, God is not understood as a transcendent Lord of the world who judges this world as evil; God exists in the cosmos not only as the creation process, but also as human beings themselves, who are given the mission to coexist with all living things according to the *yin/yang* principle. So *In-Nae-Chun* thought,[48] which is the core of *Donghak*, emphasizes the dignity of human beings:

---

45. The Yi dynasty is the last royal dynasty of Korea (1392–1905).

46. Literally, it means 'Eastern learning', which aims to counterbalance Western Learning, that is, Christianity; Ki-baik Lee, *A New History of Korea* (trans. Edward J. Shultz; Cambridge, MA: Harvard University Press, 1984), pp. 258-59.

47. No-rim Yoon, 'The World View of *Donghak*', in Hyun-hee Lee (ed.), *Donghak Thought and Donghak Movement* (Seoul: Cheong-Λ, 1984), pp. 143-70.

48. *In-Nae-Chun* means that human being is God.

since God dwells in human beings, we should respect each other as we should respect God.[49] The idea of divine presence in a human being may not be unusual in a religious sphere. However, *Donghak* is substantially different from Christianity in the idea that God is present in every human being regardless of race, class and sex, and not necessarily restricted to a certain person, and in the idea that God is working through humanity as a creation process.

Sheila Briggs, in her discussion of Phil. 2.6-11, stresses that the belief that all human beings are slaves by virtue of their humanity and that Jesus willingly took on the slavery status of a human being does not produce a social leveling effect. She then continues to argue that, since the emphasis on Christ's original equality with God indicates that Christ's existence did not start with a slavery status, this kyriocentric statement therefore does not challenge the interests of the slave-master, but rather simply provides an ideal example of the slave's role.[50] Indeed, as Briggs insists, since slaves are those who have no choice or power in themselves to resist, but must obey their master, the statement that Jesus took on a slave's form does not suggest any initiative to change social injustice but simply justifies the virtue of obedience. From *Donghak*'s point of view, however, human beings are not slaves by nature, but divine persons who convey a divine power,[51] which can transform the disharmonious relationships which cause pain and suffering into harmonious relationships. And, this transformation happens through 'voidness'. At the heart of the *yin/yang* system, the 'void' constitutes the third term, and with it, a binary system becomes ternary, which tends ceaselessly toward the unitary, that is, the oneness of the *yin*-and-*yang* circle. This concept of 'void' can be equated with the Christian concept of *kenosis*. However, the concept of 'void' does not mean merely 'sacrifice' or 'obedience', but rather it means an active engagement for an acquiring of genuine life by being a true part of the organic chain of the cosmos.[52] In this cultural context, which is based on a cosmo-anthropology, the conflicting image of Jesus as a slave as well as the Lord of the world is unacceptable. The salvific power is not

49. Yoon, '*Donghak*', pp. 164-70.

50. Sheila Briggs, 'Can an Enslaved God Liberate?: Hermeneutical Reflection on Philippians 2.6-11', *Semeia* 47 (1989), pp. 143-49.

51. Also, one of the most important doctrines of Buddhism is that all living things have the nature of Buddha.

52. Ji-ha Kim, *Rice* (Waekwan: Bundo, 1990), p. 153.

simply that of Jesus, but is embedded in every human, and we all have the potential to be divine agents of the creator of the cosmos. In other words, Jesus was neither a slave nor the only Savior of the World, but a divine human being who engaged actively in social transformation toward an egalitarian world where all living things can live harmoniously. In so doing, Jesus showed a way through which people can engage in ongoing transformation: Jesus was a divine agent whose goal was to invite people into social transformation through his *kenosis* (voidness). This contextualized Christology can not only provide Asian women with a source of the liberating power with which they can resist the oppressive patriarchal society, which is the cause of disharmony, but can also lead them to engage in an ongoing transformation as subjective agents, rather than remaining as passive recipients who have to accept a hopeless, suffering reality as their inevitable destiny.

Conclusion

Early Christianity began as an anti-imperial movement, and was enriched through many steps of transformation, and finally became an imperial religion. In order to negate the imperialistic as well as patriarchal characteristics of Christianity, I have shown that the Philippians hymn was not a statement of Jesus' pre-existence but a contextualized statement which was formed in the Christian religio-political milieu, and that in the letter to the Philippians, Paul does not use the Christ hymn christologically, but rhetorically in order to affirm his position as suffering *doulos* and to give hope to his church members. Then, from an Asian perspective based on the *yin/yang* principle and *Donghak*, I suggested that Jesus was neither a slave nor the only Savior of the World, but a divine agent who was actively engaged in an ongoing creation process by allowing himself to be an entry into areas of social transformation.

Unfortunately, the so-called Truth of Christianity has become the instrument of mastery, so that its ignorance of others has been embedded both in the story told and in the telling of the story. However, since truth is produced and extended according to the regime in power, what is put forth as truth is often nothing more than a meaning to a certain people in a certain context. So, when we are suspicious of the truth, we come to enter the terrain in which speaking subjects appear and disappear. Just as the moon waxes and wanes according to the *yin/yang* principle, the old form of subject continues to mutate between loss and gain, and the new form of subject appears from voidness in order to invite a different entry into areas of social transformation.[53] The abdication of the subjective position (Western/men), however, is not a distortion of truth, but an enrichment of it through plurality, which can deliver the text from its enslavement to mastery. If the core of Christianity is Jesus, then Christianity cannot remain as an imperial religion, but should also be renewed, like Jesus who invited people into social transformation, through self-critical assessment and the process of mutual transformation. On the other hand, displacement involves the invention of new forms of subjectivities and of relationships which accompany the continuous renewal of critical work, as Trinh T. Minh-ha emphasizes: 'the displacer [non-Western/women] proceeds by unceasingly introducing differences into repetition by questioning over and over again what is taken for granted as self-evident, by reminding self and other of the unchangeability of change, by dissipating what has become familiar and finally by participating in the transformation of received values, and of other selves through one's own self'.[54] In the process of mutual transformation, just as *yin/yang* changes into *yang/yin* through 'voidness' there is no real subject (Western/men) or object (non-Western/women) as a being in itself. Only through this mutual transformation can we hope to see an age of harmony and mutual coexistence where all of us, regardless of our race, sex, and class, can live together not as 'object' or 'the other' but as divine agents for the goodness of all.

---

53. I am indebted for this idea to Trinh T. Minh-ha, *When the Moon Waxes Red: Representation, Gender and Cultural Politics* (New York: Routlege, 1991).
54. Trinh, *When the Moon Waxes Red*, pp. 19-21.

II

INTERROGATIONS: METHODOLOGICAL ESSAYS

What Makes a Feminist Reading Feminist?
A Qualified Answer

Phyllis A. Bird

Neither my published work, nor the other forms of biblical interpretation in which I engage readily fit the description 'feminist reading(s)'. I therefore feel obliged to question the constraints imposed by defining the subject of discussion as 'a reading'. I could formulate my opinion differently by employing a broader understanding of 'reading', but I would still want to make the same points.

My answer to the question addressed to this panel requires definition of the terms 'feminist' and 'reading'. I understand feminism as a critical and constructive stance that claims for women the full humanity accorded to men, insisting that women be represented equally in all attempts to describe and comprehend human nature and that they be full participants in the assignment and regulation of social roles, rights and responsibilities.[1] Feminism articulates its gender-inclusive view of human nature and responsibility over against historical and contemporary systems of thought and social organization that make males the norm and give men, as a class, power and priority over women. It does this by focusing on women, moving women from the margins to the center of inquiry and action. Feminism begins with critique of existing patriarchal and androcentric forms of thought and organization, and commitment to the realization of alternative forms. It is thus a political movement for change,[2] grounded in social analysis and drawing on

---

1. Formulated negatively, feminism may be described as a commitment to assert the full humanity of women wherever that is denied, diminished or subordinated to male models.

2. For me, feminism is also theologically grounded and is central to my theological understanding. To insist that the movement is fundamentally political does not entail denial or qualification of its theological meaning. Nor does its theological grounding exclude common analysis and action with feminists of other or no religious persuasion. My theological understanding does affect my hermeneutics

women's experience as the primary source for its critical and constructive work.[3]

There is no single feminist program or analysis. Feminist analysis and aims differ in relation to individual and class experience, intersecting loyalties and identities (such as ethnic, national and religious identities), understanding of the root problem, and view of scriptural authority or normativity. As a consequence, specific goals and strategies of feminist action will differ. There is also an essential openness and tentativeness in feminist constructions. When feminism moves from critique of oppressive systems and practices to vision and construction of new alternatives, it moves into the realm of the unknown, and its formulations must be constantly reassessed in the light of new experience.

How does such a movement find expression in biblical interpretation? I am dubious about the possibility or usefulness of identifying a feminist perspective or commitment with any readily discernible feature(s) of the content of a reading viewed in isolation from the circumstances of its production and reception. My initial response to the question addressed to this panel was to say that what makes a feminist reading feminist is a feminist reader—implying first the producer of the reading, and secondly, the recipient. I recognize that this is not wholly satisfactory; I can enumerate some signs that fit my own feminist understanding. But I want first to register my discomfort, as a feminist biblical interpreter, with the focus of the question on 'a reading'.

I assume that a 'reading' describes some form of literary (or possibly oral?) production in which a biblical text is interpreted for some audience—that is, it is not simply an immediate and private response to a text, but a communicative act that means to influence a wider audience. For me, the anticipated audience is critical to the production of the reading. A focus on the reading alone narrows attention to a single moment or element in a complex process of communication and does

however, especially when I interpret biblical texts within and for the community of Christian believers. As I shall argue below, the context of interpretation is decisive for hermeneutics.

3. It is also a modern phenomenon of the last two centuries, dependent on economic and technological advances in the West and a natural-rights philosophy grounded in biblical tradition, but now transformed into a global movement drawing upon a variety of cultural and philosophical traditions. The fact that the philosophical roots of the movement may be traced to biblical origins does not, in my view, justify retrojecting feminist perspectives into biblical texts.

not take account of the occasion, purpose or audience of the work. It makes a discrete literary product carry the full weight of the feminist interpretative agenda in dealing with the Bible or biblical texts.[4]

My complaint arises from the fact that my own approach to the Bible, as a feminist and as a Christian believer, is fundamentally dialogical, requiring as its first step an attempt to formulate the sense of the text in its ancient social and literary context—viewing the text as itself a response to a conversation in the author's own time, an effort to persuade an ancient audience of a new or alternative view. My response to the text comes only after I have clarified its terms—just as my response to a modern dialogue partner demands that I first attempt with all the means at my disposal to hear as accurately and as sympathetically as possible what he or she means to say. I do not imagine that I escape the hermeneutical circle by this sequencing or that my hearing is devoid of bias or interest; I only insist that my first obligation is to the text as a distinct voice, an other whose integrity must be respected in the same manner as a face-to-face conversation partner or a contemporary composition.[5] Thus I want to separate analytically and operationally the

4.   This narrower understanding of 'reading' identifies it with literary approaches to interpretation and observes a close identification of 'feminist' interpretation with such approaches, as exemplified in the text-immanent 'readings' of Phyllis Trible, Cheryl Exum, Danna Fewell and Mieke Bal. I am inclined now to extend my definition of 'reading' to encompass all forms of interpretation, following John Barton, *Reading the Old Testament: Method in Biblical Study* (Louisville, KY: Westminster/John Knox Press, rev. edn, 1996). Cf. also Anthony C. Thiselton, *New Horizons in Hermeneutics: The Theory and Practice of Transforming Biblical Reading* (Grand Rapids: Zondervan, 1992). My concern remains nevertheless with those forms of interpretation that do not fit the narrower class of literary approaches.

5.   I do not insist that this is the only way, or even *the* 'right' way, to approach the text. I do believe, however, that I have an ethical obligation to the ancient authors to try to hear them as they wished to be heard—despite a history of interpretation that has erased the author or constructed the author in its own image (the concept of canon does not, in my view, cancel the notion of individual authors, whose imprint is indelibly inscribed in the text). As a modern, historically conscious reader, with means of reconstructing the past (however limited), I believe I have an obligation to undertake such reconstruction as these means allow, even when the resulting message is at odds with the church's interpretation and/or my own sensibilities. That obligation is not substantially qualified by the fact that I can never know whether my reconstruction is 'correct' or even close to the 'original' intention (which can only be tested by alternative reconstructions). Nor is it

horizons of production and reception, even as I acknowledge their inevitable interpenetration. The model of dialogue better suits this aim than the model of 'reading' that collapses the two moments of interpretation.

A reading that attempts only the first descriptive and analytical task may not contain any clearly recognizible feminist message—although I do think that signs of feminist analysis may be observable in the categories and concerns of reconstructing the 'original' message. It may nevertheless play an essential role in feminist response to the text in preaching, Bible study, classroom discussion, and scholarly debate. Feminist aims may be served by readings that do not inscribe feminist messages or values in the text. A reading that contains no explicit feminist critique may serve feminist interests either by providing a springboard for feminist reflection or a fresh interpretation of a text aimed at eliciting broad discussion in which feminist voices may play a role. I see advantages in construing the arena of discussion as broadly as possible and the terms of debate as openly as possible, so as to move feminist interpretation out of the ghetto of exclusive feminist rhetoric. Feminist hermeneutics pertains to the whole work of biblical interpretation and not simply to productions that are recognizible as 'feminist readings'.

This is obviously not the place for a defense of historical-critical method, but in light of the widely accepted view that historical criticism is fundamentally antithetical to feminist epistemology and hermeneutics,[6] I must at least insist that it is indispensable to my own

diminished by recognition of multiple authors in the production of the present text (which makes the analysis of speaker and context more complex, but does not invalidate the model). See further below.

6.   The notion of a tension between historical-critical scholarship and feminist biblical interpretation in the service of a movement toward social reform is the underlying theme of the volume of essays edited by Adela Yarbro Collins, entitled *Feminist Perspectives on Biblical Scholarship* (SBL Biblical Scholarship in North America, 10; Chico, CA: Scholars Press, 1985). See esp. Collins, 'Introduction', pp. 3-4. The discussion in this volume is dominated by Rankean notions of 'scientific objectivity' that do not seem to me to be essential to distinguishing past and present meanings or to efforts to identify and control reader bias. I find Gordon Leff's views of historical 'objectivity' congenial, as cited from *History and Social Theory* (Garden City, NY: Doubleday, 1971) by Elisabeth Schüssler Fiorenza in 'Remembering the Past in Creating the Future: Historical-Critical Scholarship and Feminist Biblical Interpretation' (in Collins, *Feminist Perspectives*, pp. 43-63,

feminist understanding of Scripture. I find no tension between historical criticism and feminist commitment, between an attempt to view the past on its own terms and a commitment to change the terms of participation and discourse generated by that past. I see no reason why an attempt to enter sympathetically into the minds or consciousnesses of historical persons and empathize with their feelings, motives and actions should exclude critique and ultimate rejection of those views. Why should an ancient author be denied the critically sensitive hearing demanded by a modern speaker just because he or she cannot speak back? The fact that all historical interpretation, as all cross-cultural interpretation, will fail to represent the other fully or adequately is no reason to abandon the attempt. Dismissal of historical criticism simply means that unexamined assumptions are read into the text. Historical criticism makes no claims concerning the normativity, or representativeness, of the ancient texts; in fact, it alerts readers to the dangers of such assumptions by considering the perspective, location and interests of the ancient author (including class, gender, religious party, etc.).[7]

An underlying problem in much of the debate concerning methods of interpreting biblical texts is differing, and often unstated, assumptions about the normativity of the text, more particularly assumptions about the *way* in which Scripture exercises authority for contemporary belief and practice. Strategies of interpretation are related to notions of the nature and consequences of biblical authority. Without attention to this question discussions of hermeneutical options, feminist or other, remain relatively meaningless, in my view, and fraught with misunderstandings.

With this too-brief excursion into method let me now attempt to identify some signs of feminist orientation in readings of biblical texts,

p. 49), and I generally concur with Schüssler Fiorenza's reformulation of the criterion of objectivity when she describes historical judgments as 'intersubjectively understandable and intersubjectively verifiable' ('Remembering the Past', p. 53). I also agree with her in regarding the Bible as a thoroughly androcentric document, but I do not find this sufficient reason to deny it authority as a source for Christian faith—or feminist theology. No historical writing, or experience, has escaped this cultural conditioning. See Bird, 'The Authority of the Bible', in *The New Interpreter's Bible*, I (Nashville: Abingdon Press, 1994), I, pp. 33-64.

7.   Feminist critique joins historical-critical analysis in insisting that the texts that carry the sacred message are human, historically and culturally conditioned vehicles. Feminist analysis of patriarchy is essentially a historical-critical understanding. It needs to be sharpened as a hermeneutical tool, not blunted or discarded.

confining my attention to the Old Testament, or Hebrew Bible.[8] For me, the essential signs or ingredients of feminist interpretation are *systemic analysis* of gender relations and a *critique* of relationships, norms and expectations that limit or subordinate women's thought, action and expression. Highlighting of women alone, either as heroines or victims, does not constitute feminist interpretation, in my view, if it lacks systemic analysis. On the other hand, gender analysis alone, without critique of the asymmetrical distribution of power and prestige within the society is not feminist interpretation, although it may be essential to a feminist reading.

If the combined criteria of systemic gender analysis and critique of androcentric and patriarchal privilege establish a reading as feminist, or at least as indispensable to such an identification, the adequacy of the reading must still be tested. Feminist readings can distort ancient meanings to suit modern sensibilities and needs. Are such readings acceptable if they serve feminist goals? What standards of judgment are to be used in assessing readings? Must all readings be accorded equal value? Whom does the reading serve? Who is a competent judge of a reading? Who is a competent reader? For me, these are the critical questions. I have not tried to answer them, because they lie outside the bounds of this assignment.[9] I venture, however, to suggest two further criteria for judging a feminist reading:

(1) It must make sense of women's experience, or 'ring true' for women readers. Here one must immediately ask, Which women?, and recognize the danger of simply conforming to the perceptions of contemporary Western women, European-American women, or other interested parties. Since this danger exists in all readings, however, it can only be controlled by engaging the broadest audience possible and by encouraging dialogue between women of different class and cultural

8.   I must note briefly that where readings of biblical texts are carried out within or for religious communities, there is no common or neutral language to describe the earliest canon of Scriptures (again the issue of audience is critical to interpretation).

9.   I recognize as feminist, readings and analyses with which I disagree, as, e.g., treatments of women in patriarchal societies that view them as powerless victims, failing to see how they profit from the system and exercise power within it (cf. Schüssler Fiorenza, 'Remembering the Past', pp. 58-59), or treatments of women's status that equate economic contribution with social recognition and power.

experiences. In the final analysis the rule holds: women have preferred place as judges of a feminist reading.

(2) Ultimately it should make sense to men as well. Feminism, and feminist interpretation, is not idiosyncratic, concerned only with female history and female nature, but aims to provide a more adequate account of our gendered human nature and history. Feminist reading should strive, I believe, for universal acceptance (recognizing that no interpretation gains such assent)—even if it seeks only the emancipation and empowerment of women. Its power lies in exposing the limits and distortions of past and prevailing readings and conceptions. I do not underestimate the difficulty of creating a shared world-view—especially where biological and socio-cultural factors are so inextricably intertwined—but feminist goals cannot be achieved by women alone. Feminism is concerned with wholeness, which can only be achieved through dialogue/interchange in which women have positions of power. Feminism seeks to enable that dialogue by empowering women.[10]

A final note on tactics and content of feminist reading. Feminist aims in biblical interpretation may find expression in a wide variety of ways depending on the audience, occasion and desired effect of the reading. Shocking exaggeration or assuming a view opposite to that expressed in the text may achieve recognition of previously unseen or misinterpreted gender perspectives in the text. Lifting up women alone to create a history of biblical women may serve to provide an essential sense of a female past for women (and men) accustomed to viewing the Bible as essentially male history.[11] Feminist midrash can provide a bridge from patriarchal past to feminist future by recasting biblical accounts. Imaginative reconstruction to fill the silences of the text with unseen or unheard women can bring recognition of the limits and biases of the sources so they are not read unconsciously as inclusive. And inclusive readings can claim the whole history and literature for women whether that was the original intention or not. This is hardly an exhaustive

10. One of the consequences of the patriarchal monopoly of power for social planning is that women are often unable to envision larger goals and may be trapped by a 'victim' mentality or an encapsulated sense of self and world. But they may also be freer to dream the 'impossible'.

11. While I rejected such constructions above, I recognize the usefulness of partial and counter treatments in contexts where full analysis is impossible. For laywomen deprived of biblical images of women by a canon and lectionary that contain few images of women, such selective readings may convey an essential feminist message of identification and empowerment.

catalogue of approaches, but it brings me back to my original point that feminist reading is determined by criteria that lie outside the reading itself. These various ways of reading in the service of feminist aims represent different ways of understanding the role of the Bible for the reader. That remains a critical question for determining the adequacy, usefulness or credibility of a reading.

WHAT MAKES A FEMINIST READING FEMINIST?
ANOTHER PERSPECTIVE

Pamela Thimmes

For several months I asked colleagues, friends and students the question this topic asks me, 'What makes a feminist reading feminist?' Apart from a few serious attempts at fumbled articulation, modest lectures about asking questions that require neat generalizations and playing to type, and even a few silent stares, my hopes for probing questions and ideas and/or musings that might spark the imagination remained unfulfilled. Perhaps this is a customary response to questions of methodology. Why is this question so difficult to answer? Why do attempts to answer it raise many more difficult questions?

Since this is a question about interpretation, my responses come from a particular socio-political framework: first, my own response recognizes *difference* (there is no such thing as one feminism or a single voice for women); secondly, it comes from a particular social location. The adage 'What you see depends on where you stand', can refer to questions of methodology as much as to the act of writing, or to reading strategies and interpretation. So my own reading and interpretation comes from a particular social location—some of my personal locators mirror majority positions in the academy and society, and some locators clearly position me as a minority in both the academy and society. These locators serve as the lenses through which reading and interpretation proceed.

The question at hand, 'What makes a feminist reading feminist,' is a methodological question. In a search for a starting point I moved beyond the friends/colleagues interview mode to a review of the literature in both biblical studies and literature. It became evident that, while methodological questions marked the early years of feminist literary theory and feminist biblical hermeneutics, until recently there was less attention given to describing and clarifying method, and more emphasis on praxis, literally *doing* feminist hermeneutics.[1] In retrospect, both the diversity of approaches and the continual movement from theory to praxis exemplifies the nature of the discipline. In important ways the development of literary feminism is similar to the development of feminist biblical hermeneutics, and as a practitioner who has had a foot in both disciplines I find myself moving easily back and forth between literary theories and biblical methods in my own reading and interpretation. As a result, I see that similar questions are of concern in both areas. For example, Nina Bayim notes, 'Perhaps the central issue in academic literary feminism right now is theory itself'.[2] Similar sentiments are voiced in feminist biblical hermeneutics, but they are framed in terms of cautions. Alice Bach warns, 'Feminist criticism must remain fluid, not fixed, so that each of us can contend with the ripples and waves of the dominant culture, diving into language to recover everything that is duplicitous and resistant and confounding'.[3]

In response to the question 'What makes a feminist reading feminist?' my own thinking moves in a circular pattern, encompassing a

---

1. For example, in literary theory, see Diana Fuss, 'Reading like a Feminist', *differences* 1 (1989), pp. 77-92; Joyce Quiring Erickson, 'What Difference? The Theory and Practice of Feminist Criticism', *Christianity and Literature* 33.1 (1983), pp. 65-74; Elizabeth Gross, 'What is Feminist Theory?', in her *Feminist Challenges: Social and Political Theory* (Boston: Northeastern University Press, 1986); Nina Bayim, 'The Madwoman and her Languages: Why I Don't Do Feminist Literary Theory', in her *Feminist and American Literary History* (New Brunswick, NJ: Rutgers University Press, 1992), pp. 199-213; Josephine Donovan (ed.), *Feminist Literary Criticism: Explorations in Theory* (Lexington: University of Kentucky Press, 1975); Mary Eagleton (ed.), *Feminist Literary Theory: A Reader* (New York: Blackwell, 1986); Elaine Showalter (ed.), *Feminist Criticism: Essays on Women, Literature and Theory* (New York: Pantheon Books, 1985); Gayle Greene and Coppelia Kahn (eds.), *Making a Difference: Feminist Literary Criticism* (New York: Routledge, 1986).

In biblical studies see Elisabeth Schüssler Fiorenza, *But She Said: Feminist Practices of Biblical Interpretation* (Boston: Beacon Press, 1992); as well as *Bread Not Stone* (Boston: Beacon Press, 1984); Janice Capel Anderson, 'Mapping Feminist Biblical Criticism: The American Scene, 1983–1990', *CR* (1991), pp. 21-44; Mary Ann Tolbert, 'Defining the Problem: The Bible and Feminist Hermeneutics', *Semeia* 28 (1983), pp. 113-26; and 'Protestant Feminists and the Bible: On the Horns of a Dilemma', in Alice Bach (ed.), *The Pleasure of her Text: Feminist Readings of Biblical and Historical Texts* (Philadelphia: Trinity Press, 1990), pp. 5-23.

2. Bayim, 'The Madwoman and her Languages', p. 199.

3. Bach (ed.), *The Pleasure of her Text*, pp. ix-x.

number of ideas and presuppositions that find clarity only in partnership with the other elements contained in the circle. This paradigm is
marked by particular elements that serve as arcs constituting various
portions of the circle and is, at root, an ecological paradigm. That is, no
element in the circle works independent of the other elements; rather,
this interdependent relationship is what constitutes the circle, and the
circle is the methodological enterprise. I see four elements necessary in
feminist hermeneutics:

> (1) *Feminism*—is a political category understood and practiced as a lib-
> eration movement, critiquing the oppressive structures of society;[4] (2)
> *Experience*—is not simply a *construct*; it also *constructs*;[5] (3) *Culture*
> (social location)—mediates our experience, and thus our worldviews or
> paradigms; (4) *Reading/Interpretation (Language)*—language is more
> than simply a non-material tool, it is an expression of a particular
> understanding of reality.[6] It is in language that social locators (gender,
> race, class, etc.) are first noticed and first submerged.[7]

These elements function together seamlessly in the methodological
enterprise, as I understand it. However, I will try to make some specific
comments that will clarify the question at hand and the interrelationship
of the elements.

I understand *feminism* as both a political term and as a political category because it is, essentially, a liberation movement that not only critiques the oppressive structures of society but, by its various voices and

---

    4.   Tolbert, 'Defining the Problem', p. 115.
    5.   Robert Scholes, 'Reading Like a Man', in Alice Jardine and Paul Smith
(eds.), *Men in Feminism* (New York: Methuen, 1987), p. 215.
    6.   Roland Barthes, *The Pleasure of the Text* (trans. R. Howard; New York:
Hill & Wang, 1975); Basil Bernstein, *Class, Codes, and Control*. I. *Theoretical
Studies towards a Sociology of Language* (4 vols.; London: Routledge & Kegan
Paul, 2nd rev. edn, 1974); Roland Champagne, 'A Grammar of the Languages of
Culture: Literary Theory and Yury M. Lotman's Semiotics', *Literary History* 9
(1977–78), pp. 205-10; Jonathan Culler, *Structuralist Poetics: Structuralism,
Linguistics and the Study of Literature* (Ithaca, NY: Cornell University Press,
1975); Jacques Derrida, *Of Grammatology* (trans. G.C. Spivak; Baltimore: The
Johns Hopkins University Press, 1976); *idem*, 'Structure, Sign and Play in the
Discourse of the Human Sciences', in R. Macksey and E. Donato (eds.), *The
Structuralist Controversy* (Baltimore: The Johns Hopkins University Press, 1970);
Joshua A. Fishman, *Readings in the Sociology of Language* (The Hague: Mouton,
1970).
    7.   Bach (ed.), *The Pleasure of her Text*, p. xii.

approaches, works for transformation.[8] As a political category feminism grew and grows out of *women's* experience and makes explicit the interconnections among all systems of oppression. Liberation movements work for justice, and ultimately for transformation. So, just as feminism affirms and promotes the full humanity of women it rejects and denies anything that diminishes the full humanity and equality of women,[9] as well as sexism, racism, classism, ageism, or any other dominance pattern that seeks to separate, alienate and oppress. From the beginning feminism has offered a broad-based critique built from the experience of women, but not exclusive to women. Elisabeth Schüssler Fiorenza suggests,

> A 'feminist' reading…must time and again rearticulate the categories and focus its lenses of interpretation in particular historical situations and social contexts. It may not subscribe to a single method of analysis nor adopt a single hermeneutical perspective or mode of approach. It also may not restrict itself to one single reading community or audience…At stake here is a theoretical shift from the paradigm of domination to one of radical equality. Emancipatory movements have to create discursive communities based on shared assumptions and values that define boundaries and validate claims to authority.[10]

The ideology that motivates critique (against paradigms of domination) and advocacy (toward a paradigm of radical equality) is an ideology that deconstructs *and* constructs. It is this ideology that is foundational to feminist hermeneutics. However, feminism as both critique and ideology raises a number of questions for feminist interpretation: Because a scholar is a self-defined feminist, does that mean any interpretation offered by that scholar is feminist? Does the gender of the interpreter automatically presume a feminist or non-feminist reading? Is a

8. Schweickart reminds us, 'Feminist criticism…is a mode of *praxis*. The point is not merely to interpret literature in various ways; the point is to *change the world*. We cannot afford to ignore the activity of reading, for it is here that literature is realized as *praxis*. Literature acts on the world by acting on its readers'. See Patrocino P. Schweickart, 'Toward a Feminist Theory of Reading', in Elizabeth A. Flynn and Patrocinio P. Schweickart (eds.), *Gender and Reading: Essays on Readers, Texts and Contexts* (Baltimore: The Johns Hopkins University Press, 1986), p. 39.

9. Letty Russell (ed.), *Feminist Interpretation of the Bible* (Philadelphia: Westminster Press, 1985), p. 16.

10. Elisabeth Schüssler Fiorenza, 'Transforming the Legacy of *The Women's Bible*', in *Searching the Scriptures: A Feminist Introduction*, I, p. 18.

particular reading strategy or interpretation feminist because feminists agree that it is? Does placing women's experience, ideas, values, visions at the center of an interpretation make that interpretation feminist?[11] These, and other questions seem to be part of the methodological minefield, part of the contested territory that the academies continue to crawl through in defining, appropriating and utilizing feminist hermeneutical perspectives.

Within the last decade there has been an ongoing conversation about the centrality and importance of *gendered* reading in feminist hermeneutics, bringing this question to the fore. Privileging women's experiences, voices, values, concerns, differences and critiques is the heart of feminist hermeneutics, and will remain so. Gender is a fundamental organizing category of experience and reading is a social activity that involves a complex interweaving of 'structures of power, gender and identity'.[12] We now know that gender is central to any reading experience, and there is provocative research that argues that because the framework of literature (in terms of what is considered classic, good or canonical literature) has been driven by male paradigms, that is, a patriarchal conceptual framework (a situation analagous to the biblical 'canon'), women have been *immasculated* by the very reading process in which they participate.[13] There are also indications that men, reading literature written by women and expressive of women's experience, have a difficult time engaging in and

11. For a discussion that asks many of these questions and provides various views on each question, see Eagleton, *Feminist Literary Theory*, pp. 149-54.

12. Nancy K. Miller, 'Arachnologies: The Woman, the Text and the Critic', in Nancy K. Miller (ed.), *The Poetics of Gender* (New York: Columbia University Press, 1986), p. 272. Also see Bonnie Zimmerman, 'What Has Never Been: An Overview of Lesbian Feminist Literary Criticism', in Greene and Kahn (eds.), *Making a Difference: Feminist Literary Criticism*, pp. 177-210. Reading, says Annette Kolodny, is a 'learned activity...inevitably sex-coded and gender-inflected', quoted in Elaine Showalter, 'Critical Cross-Dressing: Male Feminists and the Woman of the Year', in Jardine and Smith (eds.), *Men in Feminism*, p. 119.

13. The term was originally coined by Judith Fetterley in *The Resisting Reader: A Feminist Approach to American Fiction* (Bloomington: Indiana University Press, 1987). See Schweickart, 'Toward a Feminist Theory of Reading', pp. 49-50: 'a crucial feature of the process of immasculation is the woman reader's bifurcated response. She reads the text both as a man and as a woman. But in either case, the result is the same; she confirms her position as other'.

appropriating the framework necessary to the reading and interpretation of those texts.[14]

On the one hand, some would argue that revisionist reading or reading *against* patriarchal texts offers little protection.[15] But what happens to the reader in the reading experience? Harold Bloom cautions, 'You *are* or *become* what you read [my emphases]'.[16] In many cases, the female reader must construct herself as *Other*, when she is required to identify with the male as universal and dominant in a text.[17] In reading, 'what we engage are not texts but paradigms'.[18] Thus the feminist reader, reading biblical texts, is required to be a resisting reader. Kolodny explains, 'we read well, and with pleasure, what we already know how to read; and what we know how to read is to a large extent dependent upon what we have already read (works from which we developed our expectations and learned our interpretative strategies)'.[19]

On the other hand, revisionist readings, reading against the text 'can remind us of the powerful effects readers have on texts, and conversely of the powerful effect texts have on readers...'[20] Schweickart notes, 'Feminist criticism...is a mode of *praxis*. The point is not merely to interpret literature in various ways; the point is to *change the world*. We cannot afford to ignore the activity of reading, for it is here that literature is realized as *praxis*. Literature acts on the world by acting on its readers.'[21] Joyce Erickson agrees and adds, 'for both feminist and

---

14. See the section Annette Kolodny devotes to structures of signification and reading in 'Dancing through the Minefield: Some Observations on the Theory, Practice and Politics of Feminist Literary Criticism', in *The New Feminist Criticism: Essays on Women, Literature and Theory*, pp. 148-219. Elaine Showalter joins the conversation herself when she reports, 'Heath concludes that a man reading as a feminist always involves a strategy of female impersonation. But is there not also a mode of impersonation involved when a woman reads as a feminist, or indeed, when a woman reads as a woman?', 'Critical Cross-Dressing', pp. 128-29.

15. See Hélène Cixous, 'Language conceals an invisible adversary because it's the language of men and their grammar', in 'The Laugh of the Medusa', *Signs* 1 (trans. Keith Cohen and Paula Cohen; Summer 1976), pp. 875-93.

16. Harold Bloom, *Kabbalah and Criticism* (New York: Seabury Press, 1975), p. 96.

17. Elizabeth Struthers Malbon and Janice Capel Anderson, 'Literary-Critical Methods', in *Searching the Scriptures*, p. 251.

18. Kolodny, 'Dancing through the Minefield', p. 153.

19. Kolodny, 'Dancing through the Minefield', p. 154.

20. Erickson, 'What Difference?', p. 71.

21. Schweikert, 'Toward a Feminist Theory of Reading', p. 39.

Christian [biblical] critics the high value accorded literature and art is
linked to the conviction that they have the power to affect human life, a
power that extends into the future'.[22]

These two positions offer plausible arguments. Reading is not done
in a vacuum and the activity of reading imperils the status quo. For me
the question of what 'reading' we do as biblical critics concerns, not
only what reading *is*, but what it *does* to the reader and to the community in which it is read. The old, often asked question, 'does the text
construct the reading subject or does the reading subject construct the
text?'[23] has a place in a discussion about gender and reading. Diana
Fuss suggests,

> In reading…we bring (old) subject-positions to the text at the same time
> the actual process of reading constructs (new) subject-positions for us.
> Consequently, we are always engaged in a 'double reading'…in the
> sense that we are continually caught within and between *at least two*
> constantly shifting subject-positions (old and new, constructed and con-
> structing) and these positions may often stand in complete contradiction
> to each other.[24]

Is feminist hermeneutics, then, a reading strategy, a methodology, that
because of its origins, history, and context, can only be done by
women? Is gender the only determiner of feminist reading? Fuss notes
that 'feminism seems to take for granted among its members a shared
identity'.[25] If feminism is understood as a political construct, then
fidelity to the ideology must be borne out in the praxis, that is, in the
methodologies utilized. For me, then, what makes a feminist reading
feminist has less to do *today* with the gender of the person offering the
reading and more to do with the coherence the reading has with a feminist ideology. However, I make this statement well aware that there are
serious problems inherent in both the appropriation of feminism by
men, and with the assumption that men can read like women. Showalter
notes that this functional view of reading might be both superficial and
politically suspect—can feminist reading be reduced 'to a cognitive
skill easily transferable to male texts or critical theories?'[26]

22. Erickson, 'What Difference?', p. 71.
23. Fuss, 'Reading Like a Feminist', p. 86.
24. Fuss, 'Reading Like a Feminist', pp. 86-87.
25. Fuss, 'Reading Like a Feminist', p. 77.
26. Showalter, 'Critical Cross-Dressing', p. 119.

Experience, *culture* and *reading/interpretation* are difficult to separate in the feminist methodological circle because all are mediated
through *social location*. For me, *social location* means that the
paradigms or world-views we hold are a result of complex patterns
including a number of factors that provide a lens focusing and shaping
experience, from which is abstracted a particular view of reality. These
factors include gender, age, race, religion, education, class, sexual orientation, physical abilities, geography, environment, politics, culture
and family. The result is a socially constructed world-view that indicates *place*, or *where I stand*. Mary Ann Tolbert reminds us, 'most of
us (though not all) have multiple *perspectives* from which we may
interpret texts…We do not exist in one social context but many'.[27]

If the four arcs I propose are facets of a feminist reading, the relational nature of these elements serves as a model for the process of
reading/interpretation that characterizes a feminist reading. As feminists we bring a shared ideology to the discussion, as well as a variety
of interpretative strategies for reading. We need to be reminded that we
never *just* read, that we always read *from somewhere*,[28] and that
'reading is, after all, a learned skill, taught according to conventional
rules devised by the cultural elite of any literate society. It is thus a kind
of socialization into the values and stereotypical roles expected by that
society'.[29] There are among us many voices and many *somewheres*, a
diversity of experiences, a diversity of readings, and in an ecological
framework, diversity is the life-force of the system. We might better
ask the methodological question in light of this diversity, 'What makes
feminists' readings feminist?'[30]

Earlier I noted that feminist hermeneutics has been primarily concerned with the practice of reading. Is there a difference between the
theory and practice of feminist hermeneutics? I think not. If we argue
there is a difference, we concede that theory is an esoteric luxury
and an elitist pastime that has alienated itself from its roots.[31] As a

---

27. Mary Ann Tolbert, 'Reading for Liberation', in Fernando F. Segovia and
Mary Ann Tolbert (eds.), *Reading from this Place: Social Location and Biblical
Interpretation in the United States* (Minneapolis: Fortress Press, 1995), I, p. 274.

28. Fuss, 'Reading Like a Feminist', p. 89.

29. Tolbert, 'Reading for Liberation', p. 274.

30. 'Only by emphasizing the differences and multiplicities of knowers and
known can hierarchy and dominance be overcome', Anderson, 'Mapping Feminist
Biblical Criticism', p. 26.

31. See Bayim, 'The Madwoman and her Languages', p. 199: 'Feminist

liberation movement founded out of the oppression of women, feminist hermeneutics, in practice and theory, and in partnership with other feminist perspectives,[32] not only works for justice but is actively engaged in transformation—it not only *deconstructs*, it *reconstructs*, and it *constructs*.

At the beginning of this essay I spoke about the parallel routes traveled by literary feminism and feminist biblical hermeneutics. Literary feminists frequently speak about 'second-wave' feminism as the 'discovery that women writers had a literature of their own…'[33] and now feminists speak about the 'third wave'. If we, as biblical scholars, can talk about a 'second wave' in feminist hermeneutics, it is very different from that of literary feminists. We cannot claim a 'literature'(in the canonical sense) of our own. Increasingly, though, and particularly with the publication of expressly feminist commentaries and introductions, feminist biblical hermeneutics has moved into a new arena. I would suggest that 'third-wave' feminist hermeneutics is at hand, if not here, the time when feminist monographs, commentaries, dictionaries, etc. that deal with the entire canon (and non-canonical literature) will sit side-by-side on library shelves with the androcentric voices that have dominated the cultural landscape. However, I suspect (and hope) that by the time that horizon is realized we will see that biblical studies has been revolutionized by a multiculturalism that exemplifies both the value of diversity and the importance of social location in any hermeneutic, the foundation of which was laid by feminist hermeneutics.

hermeneutics oscillates between two perspectives: pluralism and legalism. The pluralist perspective recognizes that the very act of reading implies interpretation, and with any number of readings and individuals engaged in readings, there will be a variety of interpretations—one expects the unexpected and diversity is encouraged. The legalist perspective attempts to "locate the correct positions and marshal women within the ranks".' Of the two perspectives, the pluralist position has dominated biblical studies. Bayim continues, 'As for recent literary theory, it is deeply legalistic and judgmental. Infractions—the wrong theory, theoretical errors, or insouciant disregard for theoretical implications—are crimes. Pluralists "dance"; theorists "storm" or "march" ', pp. 199.

32. Bayim, 'The Madwoman and her Languages', p. 204.

33. Elaine Showalter, 'Introduction: The Feminist Critical Revolution', in *The New Feminist Criticism*, p. 6. Also see Nina Bayim's assessment of the 'second wave': 'Matters for Interpretation: Feminism and the Teaching of Literature', in *Feminism and Literary History*, pp. 214-15.

READING THE BIBLE WITH AUTHORITY:
FEMINIST INTERROGATION OF THE CANON*

Mary Ann Tolbert

No issue arouses more acrimonious debate among Christians, especially Protestant Christians,[1] than the problem of the authority of the
Bible. From the fundamentalists' cry of inerrancy to the liberals' designation of 'classic text', each group, each denomination, indeed, one
often thinks, each individual Christian upholds a competing view of the
Bible's function, use, and particularly its present authority over the
lives of believers. For Christian feminists, the question of the Bible's
authority is notoriously troublesome because it has been appealed to so
often as providing a divine mandate for their second-class status within
many church structures. Texts as diverse in historical origin, language,
and viewpoint as Genesis 2–3, 1 Tim. 2.11-15; 1 Cor. 11.2-16; 14.33-
36; and 1 Peter 3.1-6 have been used as proof that women's submission
to men in home, church and society at large is the revealed plan of God.
Yet, the difficulty women have with the issue is just a recent example

* Portions of the argument have appeared—sometimes in a more developed
form—in other articles I have published over the last decade. See esp., 'A Response
from a Literary Perspective', in R.A. Culpepper and F.F. Segovia (eds.), 'Literary
Perspectives on the Gospel of John', *Semeia* 53 (1991), pp. 203-12; 'Afterwords:
Christianity, Imperialism and the Decentering of Privilege', in F.F. Segovia and
M.A. Tolbert (eds.), *Reading from This Place*. I. *Social Location and Biblical
Interpretation in Global Perspective* (Minneapolis: Fortress Press, 1995), pp. 347-
61; and '"A New Teaching with Authority": A Re-Evaluation of the Authority of
the Bible', in F.F. Segovia and M.A. Tolbert (eds.), *Teaching the Bible: The
Discourses and Politics of Biblical Pedagogy* (Maryknoll, NY: Orbis Books, 1998).

1. In the discussion which follows, I will be addressing the issue of biblical
authority primarily as it occurs in Christian circles and indeed in Protestant
Christian circles. There are clear differences between the ways biblical authority
functions in Protestant Christianity and the use, authority and understanding of
Tanakh in the various forms of contemporary Judaism.

of a longer, deadlier dynamic, for only a little over a century ago, this same claim of biblical authority was employed by many Euro-American Protestant southerners, citing passages like Col. 3.22-24; 1 Tim. 6.1-2; and 1 Pet. 3.18-25; to justify as divinely ordained the despicable evil of racial slavery. Moreover, throughout Christian history the negative polemic against the Jerusalem Jews found in the canonical Gospels has been appealed to as the warrant for every form of anti-Judaism from exile to pogroms to genocide.

Indeed, from just a superficial overview of Christian history since the Reformation when the doctrine of *sola scriptura* came to the forefront of theological debates, the invocation of the tenet of biblical authority has been remarkably negative; that is, it has been used most often to *exclude* certain groups or people,[2] to *pass judgment* on various disapproved activities,[3] and to *justify* morally or historically debatable positions.[4] I am *not* saying that the Bible has been primarily negative in its influence over the centuries, for that assertion would be easily challenged by the lives of many good-hearted Christians working for peace,

2. E.g. although their aim was to correct church abuses and give individual Christians greater freedom in determining their own practice of religion, by making the authority of the Bible supreme over all other traditions, the Protestant Reformers exercised one of the greatest exclusions in Christian history which resulted in the division of Western Christianity. Moreover, the tendency to use biblical interpretations to create boundaries between 'us' and 'them' continues in the proliferation of Protestant denominations. Within present ecclesiastical organizations, biblical warrants may be claimed to exclude women from ordination or positions of power in the church structures, to exclude homosexuals from ordination, to forbid divorce or remarriage, etc.

3. E.g. the prohibition movement earlier in this century, especially in the form of the Woman's Christian Temperance Union, posited a biblical mandate for prohibiting the use of alcohol; many current state laws prohibiting some homosexual practices are often argued on biblical grounds; anti-abortionists cite the commandment against killing as legitimating their fight for the unborn; etc. This use of biblical authority to authorize national political agendas makes the issue of the appeal to the authority of the Bible one of concern to all citizens and not just Christians or Protestant Christians.

4. E.g. slavery would certainly be a morally questionable position supported by appeals to biblical authority, and historically problematic claims for creationism and the repudiation of evolutionary theory in favor of the literal existence of the Garden of Eden or the great Flood of Noah, all stem from attribution of authority to the Bible. Again, especially at the state level, these claims are often politically mounted to affect the curricula of public school systems or the selection of textbooks.

liberation, justice and human salvation, who have drawn much of their inspiration from the Bible. Nor am I arguing that attempts to formulate the place of the Bible theologically in relation to the Christian life have always arisen from necessarily exclusivistic aims,[5] although that might well sometimes have been the case. It is not the Bible itself but the overt, often institutionally based appeal to an already-formulated *doctrine of biblical authority* that displays this generally negative, exclusivistic pattern. It is this use of biblical authority by various ecclesiastical bodies, especially in contemporary situations, that requires serious investigation. In the following essay I will attempt to explore from an explicitly feminist standpoint some of the motivations and dynamics behind these claims for the authority of the Bible.

At the outset it is important that I indicate my own ideological stance, since it quite clearly affects the arguments I will make. One of the crucial issues facing feminists—and, I would suggest, those involved in other liberation movements as well—is whether the goal of liberation is equal access to the present power structures of a racist, patriarchal society, assuring, in other words, that we get our share of the pie, or whether it is the disruption of that order entirely and the gradual evolution of something new under the sun, providing perhaps bread for the world rather than pie for the privileged few. Partially because I have come to believe very strongly that 'equal access' for women and other 'outsiders' is contrary to the fundamental organization of patriarchal society, but mostly because I am increasingly convinced that equality is not something I want, if being equal means acting as those presently in power act, I wish to stand and speak in

---

5.   Theological formulations concerning the authority of the Bible have generally been attempts to understand the place of the Bible in the context of revelation, faith and the workings of the Holy Spirit, and they can be found in the Christian tradition as far back as Origen and Augustine. E.g. the Westminster Confession of Faith, drawn up in the seventeenth century and still the basis of many evangelical Christians' doctrine of biblical authority, argued that only through the work of the Holy Spirit in the heart of each person could that person come to understand the Bible as the Word of God, and it was a Word that contained all things necessary to human salvation and faith. For a brief discussion of various understandings of the place of the Bible in Christian tradition, see J.B. Rogers, 'The Church Doctrine of Biblical Authority', in D.K. McKim (ed.), *The Authoritative Word: Essays on the Nature of Scripture* (Grand Rapids: Eerdmans, 1983), pp. 197-224. See also D. Kelsey, *The Uses of Scripture in Recent Theology* (Philadelphia: Fortress Press, 1975).

ways as disruptive to the present system as possible and to join with all others who are attempting to imagine and evolve new ways of living together on this lovingly created planet, which is our common home. It is this ideological perspective which informs much of the following discussion. The discussion will proceed in three parts: (1) a selective analysis of some of the problematics surrounding the formulations and functions of the doctrine of biblical authority; (2) a proposal concerning the essentialistic, exclusivistic dynamics underlying appeals to that authority; and (3) a plea for envisioning the process of reading the Bible with authority in a world of difference.

The Problematics of Biblical Authority

The authority the Bible exercises over believers can be seen as deriving from at least three different sources, which, while they may overlap, should be carefully discriminated from each other. First, we may speak of the authority any text conventionally exerts on its readers by means of its aesthetic or existential insight into the paradoxes of human life in the world, regardless of cultural milieu or historical particularity. Texts as different as Homer's *Iliad*, Shakespeare's *Hamlet*, or the *Tao Te Ching* carry a kind of narrative authority even for contemporary readers by the quality of the thoughts they provoke in their audiences. 'Classic' texts from whatever period or culture are generally said to bear this kind of authority; they are classics because of the durability of their depiction of human existence.

Secondly, texts may gain authority, not necessarily because of the profundity of their insight, but because by reason of historical setting they have in some sense come to be part of the formation of individuals and communities. The United States Constitution or the Declaration of Independence would be good examples of documents bearing such authority. For people formed by the public school system of the United States under the influence of these documents, it is almost incredible to think that there was a time not very long ago when few people believed that all 'men' had certain basic, 'inalienable rights to life, liberty, and the pursuit of happiness'. Although the framing 'fathers' of the Constitution did not themselves see fit to extend these rights to women or slaves, so thorough has been our contemporary formation by these founding texts that our arguments now concern whether or not two-celled embryos also have such rights. If one extends the notion of text to cover other cultural artifacts, as recommended by deconstruction, one might recognize this same type of authority functioning in long-running television series, like *M*A*S*H* or *Star Trek* with their faithful community of followers (e.g. the 'Trekkies').

Thirdly, texts may be designated as authoritative by some institutional body with the power to require obedience from its constituents and deliver punishment for disobedience, however that punishment may be understood (e.g. as physical restraint, expulsion, ostracism, etc.). This doctrinal or legal view of authority depends primarily on the power of the institutional base for its effectiveness, and if the institution wanes, so does the authority of the texts. Legal codes from Hammurabi's to Napoleon's are good examples of such texts. The canonization process itself reflects this institutional pattern, and the adoption of various doctrines of biblical authority by ecclesiastical bodies continues the tradition.

Clearly, some texts may bear only one of these forms of authority, while others bear two or all three.[6] It is important to distinguish among them, however, because the *source* of authority, or what makes the texts seem important and powerful, is different in each case. The Christian Bible derives its standing, I would like to suggest, from all three forms of authority, but the one that is most problematic and most often discussed is the last, its doctrinal or institutionally sanctioned authority over the actions of believers. I will focus the remainder of my critique on this form of authority, withholding a discussion of the Bible's possible narrative authority and formational power for a future essay.

A number of scholars in recent years, most notably James Barr in several publications,[7] have pointed to difficulties in the formulations

6. These three forms of textual authority I am suggesting bear a very rough correspondence to the three forms of social authority posited by Max Weber: Charismatic (narrative), Traditional (formational) and Rational (doctrinal). For a discussion of Weber's views on authority, see S. Lukes, 'Power and Authority', in T. Bottomore and R. Nisbet (eds.), *A History of Sociological Analysis* (New York: Basic Books, 1978), pp. 663-65.

7. See, e.g., his *The Scope and Authority of the Bible* (Philadelphia: Westminster Press, 1980); and *Holy Scripture: Canon, Authority, Criticism* (Oxford: Clarendon Press, 1983); see also, L.W. Countryman, *Biblical Authority or Biblical Tyranny? Scripture and the Christian Pilgrimage* (Philadelphia: Fortress Press, 1981); D.K. McKim (ed.), *The Authoritative Word: Essays on the Nature of Scripture* (Grand Rapids: Eerdmans, 1983); and J.D.G. Dunn, *The Living Word*

and uses of the Protestant doctrine of biblical authority. The foremost problem, stated in its baldest form, is that the orthodox Protestant doctrine of taking the Bible as the ultimate authority in all doctrinal matters cannot *itself be verified from the Bible*. The 'biblical world', that historical period in which God's revelation occurred as witnessed by the biblical writings *antedates* those writings themselves. The Word of God did not come to Isaiah as a document to be interpreted, and although Jesus and Paul, the major characters in the 'New Testament period' had, unlike Moses and Isaiah, a scriptural tradition to use, the freedom with which they altered it, repudiated it or interpreted it is striking.[8] Indeed, James Dunn, in arguing for an evangelical perspective on the authority of the Bible based on 'the New Testament attitude to, and use of, scripture' must deny 'that Christians today can necessarily treat the scriptures...with the same sovereign freedom exercised by Jesus and Paul',[9] thus leaving evangelicals in the contradictory position of both appealing to the New Testament as norm and at the same time denying the current applicability of what is found there. The problem, seen in relation to the specific issue of canon, can also be found in Chapter 1 of the seventeenth-century Westminster Confession, the document upon which the Reformed tradition continues to base its doctrine of scriptural authority: The Confession states that only the 66 books of the (Protestant) canon compose Scripture as inspired by God and therefore provide the sole basis of all doctrinal formulation; yet, *no* passage in any of those 66 books provides a list of which texts are inspired or which are not, nor a numerical limit to that group.[10] Evidence for the canon of Scripture and its precise limits can only be found *outside* the canon!

In addition to this major doctrinal difficulty of being unable to ground the authority of Scripture in Scripture itself, most formulations of the doctrine of biblical authority evince obvious inconsistencies by

(Philadelphia: Fortress Press, 1987).

8. Barr, *Holy Scripture*, pp. 12-19. As Barr notes, 'The authority attached to the Old Testament within the New did not mean that New Testament Christianity took pre-existing scripture as its dominant and controlling ideological base...The undoubted authority of the Old Testament as Word of God does not alter the fact that for the New Testament it is no longer the unique starting point: its positions may be criticized, may be modified, and it is no longer an absolute. Its authority is relative to the supreme authority of Jesus Christ' (pp. 18-19).

9. Dunn, *The Living Word*, p. 127.

10. See the discussion of the canon in Barr, *Holy Scripture*, pp. 23-28.

tending to see some elements of Scripture as more authoritative than others. The 'canon within a canon' pattern is quite ancient and could, in fact, claim as scriptural warrant the story of Jesus' declaration of the two great commandments, love of God and love of neighbor, as the essence of all the law and the prophets (Mt. 22.36-40). Luther's view of Christian salvation as 'by grace through faith' had the effect of elevating the writings of Paul and dooming the Epistle of James, among others, to ridicule or oblivion. One might then suppose that the point of developing a doctrine of biblical authority was to underline major themes within biblical material as essential to Christian faith today. However, James Barr has argued quite convincingly that the main reason was precisely the contrary: traditional Protestant orthodoxy needed the authority of an inspired canon, not to emphasize dominant biblical patterns, but rather to elevate as essential theological beliefs 'elements which had comparatively slight and even marginal representation within the biblical material: the virgin birth, predestination, the inspiration of scripture'.[11] Consequently, the *doctrine of biblical authority* supplies ecclesiastical bodies with power to proclaim as normative Christian belief, not love of God and love of neighbor, but those peripheral and 'thinly evidenced' (by one, two or three separate proof texts) issues like the subordination of women, the legality of slavery or the sinfulness of homosexuality. Moreover, because these elements are often so rarely addressed within the canon as a whole, both changing social values within the broader, contemporary society and dissenting interpretations by other Christian groups can sometimes erase or deny formerly 'essential' biblical teachings (like, e.g., 'slaves obey your masters' or the definition of predestination). Thus, the *doctrine of biblical authority* has generally functioned to assure, not the continuing importance of widely attested or programmatic themes in Scripture, but rather the divine inspiration of the tenuous and the marginal.

Although several further difficulties with the formation and use of doctrines of biblical authority could be listed, for our purposes only one other major problem needs to be raised: the singularity of *the Word* of God. In §4 of Chapter 1 of the Westminster Confession, the authority of Scripture is said to rest on the fact that God is its sole Author.[12] As a result, the Bible as a whole 'was one body of material all of which alike uniquely came from God, and which had the same attributes

11. Barr, *Holy Scripture*, p. 39.
12. Rogers, 'The Church Doctrine of Biblical Authority', p. 213.

throughout...'[13] Protestants refer to the Bible as the Word of God, and that use of 'the singular ('Word', not 'words') is hardly an accident'.[14] From the early medieval period almost to the Enlightenment, the necessary unity of the biblical point of view, derived from the unity of its Author's divine will, was not in dispute. Indeed, it was undergirded by two dominant conventions of biblical reading: harmonization and allegory. Since the Bible was the definitive revelation of the eternal and unchanging God, whatever was found in one place could be used to complement different material found in another place. As Barr illustrates, 'Though it was possible to write a Gospel which did not mention the Virgin Birth, the mention of it, where it *was* mentioned, was allowed to complement the non-mention of it elsewhere'.[15] Varying reports of the same event were understood to supplement each other rather than contradict or undercut each other. Hence, biblical material could be added all together to form a harmonized reading of the whole. Moreover, the elaborate, encyclopedic programs of allegorical interpretation discovered the complete history of salvation and its culmination in the life of Christ throughout the entire canon, including the books of the so-called Old Testament. Regardless of the putative reference of the literal level of the text, the several allegorical levels could reveal the divine 'treasures' of Christian theology behind that 'veil'. And although Luther and some of the other early Protestant Reformers criticized the excesses of allegorical interpretation, they were willing enough to continue the practice to show that salvation 'by grace through faith' everywhere filled the Bible.[16]

With the advent of modern biblical scholarship during the eighteenth and nineteenth centuries, encouraged by the Enlightenment's new historical consciousness and elevation of individual freedom, these two conventional supports for the unity of the Word of God increasingly came under attack. The view that past times and cultures had an integrity of their own, which needed to be acknowledged and reconstructed, doomed allegorical readings of Scripture to the realm of

---

13. Barr, *Holy Scripture*, p. 3.

14. Countryman, *Biblical Authority or Biblical Tyranny?*, p. 99.

15. Barr, *Holy Scripture*, p. 3.

16. For a discussion of allegorical interpretation, especially as it affected the parables of Jesus in the New Testament, see M.A. Tolbert, *Perspectives on the Parables: An Approach to Multiple Interpretations* (Philadelphia: Fortress Press, 1979), pp. 26-28.

fantasy or wishful thinking, and careful, critical analyses of biblical texts began to show time and again that they often contained very different, indeed even contradictory, points of view and were perhaps created and used by very different, maybe even opposed, groups of people. Under the sharp eye of the trained biblical scholar the singular Word of God began to splinter into a cacophony of separate voices.

Not surprisingly, many within orthodox Protestantism saw the rise of 'higher criticism' as dangerous to the faith, a view that still exists in some circles, but as the evidence uncovered by biblical criticism began to mount, many Protestants embraced the new perspectives by empha- sizing that Scripture was intended to lead people to salvation, not to provide correct scientific, historical or geographical data. For conserva- tive Protestants, however, such accommodation was decried as sacrificing the unity and truthfulness of God's revelation to the critical stance of the modern world, and they instead countered the claims of 'higher criticism' by a doctrine of biblical authority now heightened into an assertion of inerrancy.[17] Among present-day Protestant evangel- icals inerrancy is by no means universally approved, for if it is difficult to establish biblical authority on the basis of the Bible itself, it is impossible to establish inerrancy. As James Dunn puts it, arguing for biblical inerrancy is 'to out-scripture scripture'.[18] A doctrine of biblical authority that begins with inerrancy not only rejects the critical stan- dards of contemporary society (catering to the perennially popular acceptance of anti-intellectualism), but it also makes of the Bible a magical book with infinite applicability and vision, *when properly interpreted*. Magic is perhaps the oldest form of religious belief, and its revival in the 'bibliolatry'[19] of the most fundamentalist segments of modern Protestantism has been accompanied by a corresponding increase in the personal power of the pastor, who now sometimes func- tions as the only fully initiated medium of true interpretation.[20] I would

17. For the various responses of Protestants in the nineteenth century to the rise of biblical criticism, see the brief history in Rogers, 'The Church Doctrine of Biblical Authority', pp. 215-24.

18. Dunn, *The Living Word*, p. 126.

19. Dunn, *The Living Word*, p. 126.

20. The recent history of the Southern Baptist Convention is an excellent example of this process. Despite their historic belief in the 'priesthood of every believer', Southern Baptist delegates to the annual convention meetings have in recent years not only passed resolutions on the inerrancy of Scripture and the need for inerrantists to be appointed to their seminary faculties but also resolved that

like to suggest that this correspondence between inerrancy and rising pastoral authority is not simply coincidental. As I will argue more thoroughly in the next section, doctrines of biblical authority serve primarily as masks for human drives to power, and moreover, they generally cover a power that is totalitarian in intent.

If the most conservative wing of Protestantism attempts to preserve the unitary truth of Scripture by claims of inerrancy, can we assume that in acknowledging the historical and narrative diversity of the Bible revealed by modern criticism, other Protestants (and Catholics) have basically abandoned the wish for a singular, authoritative Word? I think not. In moderate or liberal Protestantism and especially in the scholarship produced by and for this broad group, the quest for unity has survived in at least two main ways: the continuing significance of scholarly appeals to 'authorial intention' and most important of all, the growth in the last two centuries of the 'quest of the historical Jesus'. While recognizing the multitude of voices and perspectives in Scripture, modern biblical scholars often tend to use a claim of 'authorial intention' to argue for the superiority of their interpretations over those of their fellows in the academy. And this claim is effective because 'authorial intention' is currently accepted by the guild as a conventional criterion of 'truthful' research. So, although there may be a variety of texts in the Bible, each text reflects only its own author's intention, thereby giving the illusion, if not in fact the reality, of limitation to the process. The singular Word of God is not restored, but the cacophony is sharply reduced.

Restoring the singular Word, however, is, I would like to suggest, the primary driving force behind that most ubiquitous and persistent obsession of modern New Testament scholarship, the quest for the historical Jesus. Although I have not actually tallied the numbers, I feel safe in betting that 80 per cent to 90 per cent of all New Testament scholarship in the last two centuries has had as some part of its impetus this quest for Jesus. Whether it is trying to reconstruct the social, political, religious or linguistic ethos of first-century Palestine or trying to reconstruct the sources of the Synoptic Gospels or trying more directly to argue for specific statements, canonical or non-canonical, that might have some probability of going back to him (regardless of how this is done, by writing articles or voting with colored marbles), lying behind

pastors should be given greater authority in church matters and greater respect by church bodies.

all of this research and providing its *raison d'être* is the urge to reach the words, thoughts and life-world of the historical Jesus. Why? Through most of the centuries of the Common Era, the Christian church has not displayed an obsession with Jesus. Only in the last two hundred years or so has this dynamic surfaced. Granted that the awakening of historical consciousness in the Enlightenment fractured naive assumptions that the Gospel depictions of Jesus were simple reality and in so doing created problems where few had existed before; still, the response to these problems might have been simply to recognize the ideological dimensions of the Christian writings and go on from there to discuss the formation of early Christianity and its contemporary relevance, as some scholars like Rudolph Bultmann, for example, in fact did. Indeed, Bultmann around the middle of this century reiterated what Albert Schweitzer at the beginning of the century had so thoroughly and eloquently argued: the quest for the historical Jesus is fruitless because the sources do not provide the information needed, and what one gets in the various 'lives of Jesus', scholarly or popular, is, as Schweitzer documented, mainly the writer's own face reflected in the wishing well of the historical Jesus.[21]

Yet, the quest for the historical Jesus appears to have more lives than the proverbial cat, for no matter how many times its death has been announced, despite all the logical and clear-cut evidences of its failure, it keeps popping up again in new forms. Why? I submit that the chronological correspondence between the development of modern biblical criticism, which broke up the unitary Word of the Divine Author, and the emergence of the various quests for the historical Jesus is, again, *not* merely coincidental. If the authors of biblical books speak with many voices and diverse points of view, surely Jesus himself spoke with only *one*. And if the best that can be claimed about the New Testament texts is that they form the earliest existing witness to the divine revelation of the incarnation, life and death of Jesus the Christ, surely what the historical Jesus may have said, done and thought is of a much higher order of authority, for he himself *is* that revelation. The singular, authoritative Word of God is restored to modern Protestantism by seeking the singular, authoritative voice of the historical Jesus. It is this prevailing desire for a unitary authoritative word, I wish to argue,

21. See Schweitzer's discussion of this tendency in *The Quest of the Historical Jesus: A Critical Study of its Progress from Reimarus to Wrede* (intro. J. Robinson; trans. W. Montgomery; New York: Macmillan, 1968), pp. 4-8.

that continues to resurrect quests for the historical Jesus regardless of recurrent proofs of their demise.

The persistent allegiance of most Christian bodies to doctrines of biblical authority despite the many theoretical and practical problems with their formation and use, just like the dogged pursuit of the historical Jesus despite its apparent scholarly futility, ought to raise the issue of what motivates these problematic positions. After all, they are issues that dominate the ethical, doctrinal and theological discussions of numerous Protestant denominations and the pages of innumerable articles and books. What lies behind the dominance of these concerns? Or in the terms I think women and other 'outsiders' should always raise the question, *cui bono*? to whose good is it that these problematic positions shape our discourse? To an exploration of this question, we now turn.

The Power behind the Authority

The Bible is a written text, or collection of written texts. How do written texts mean and how do people know what they mean? Can they mean only one thing or many things? In the long history of Western literary criticism from Plato to the present, three major alternatives have surfaced to explain textual meaning, each focusing on one of the three elements of the communication process: the sender, the message or the receiver. Of the three, the least supported and supportable is the focus on the message itself. The recent American school of New Criticism almost alone of all the literary theories propounded through the centuries asserted that meaning was to be found in the configurations of the autonomous literary work cut off from its author, its audience and its language world. The New Critics believed 'in the irreducible givenness of the literary text and in the coercive power of its features to control reading'.[22] Readers in this view become primarily textual consumers who have no choice but to passively ingest the text, either well or poorly. Although some principles of the New Critics provided a needed antidote to earlier critical practices, their insistence on the autonomy of the text could not be sustained, for texts clearly have important connections to their authors, their readers, and the cultural matrix out of which they come, even if those connections are hard to specify exactly.

22. J.A. Radway, *Reading the Romance: Women, Patriarchy and Popular Literature* (Chapel Hill: University of North Carolina Press, 1984), p. 7.

Focusing on the sender has been a more popular choice, although it is now historically dated. If a text is understood solely as the creation of an author, then the author is the one who gives a meaning to his or her text. Hence, establishing the author's (singular) intention becomes the ultimate goal of all reading.[23] Obviously, privileging the claim of authorial intention in evaluating competing biblical interpretations advocates this option. Moreover, the formation of most Protestant doctrines of biblical authority assumed such a connection by deriving the **author**ity of the text from its revelation of the divine **Author**'s will. Interestingly, the predominant form of English literary criticism in the seventeenth and eighteenth centuries, the period from which the Westminster Confession and other early Protestant arguments about biblical authority come, was the biography; as Samuel Johnson's *Lives of the Poets* amply demonstrates, for that period the meaning of a literary work was to be sought in the life of its author. Not surprisingly, then, doctrines of biblical authority bear the indelible intellectual stamp of the historical age in which they were developed. In an era that understands the relation among authors, texts and readers quite differently, as does our own, these doctrines face the additional problem of sounding very anachronistic.

For a variety of reasons few literary critics today subscribe to the alternative of the author's meaning, or indeed have subscribed to it in the last century. Authors often say more than they intend or less than they intend or other than they intend; they may well not know exactly what they intended to say at all. As the New Critics pointed out in developing the 'intentional fallacy', authors who can actually be questioned about their works prove notoriously unhelpful in discussing them, and most authors of classic works of literature returned to dust centuries before anyone ever thought of questioning them. It was against the position of literary criticism as biography that the New Critic's emphasis on the text itself provided a much-needed corrective.

The contemporary understanding of the meaning of the text—one that has also often surfaced over the centuries—focuses on the receiver or reader, and its present intellectual heritage is not only New Criticism but also semiotics and post-structuralism; however, it begins with practical, cross-cultural observation: looking at the history of any text—and the Bible is an *excellent* example—shows that many different meanings

23. For one of the best attempts in recent years to argue for this position, see E.D. Hirsch, *Validity In Interpretation* (New Haven: Yale University Press, 1967).

have been posited for the same text by different groups of people in the same period or by people in different periods. How is this multivalency to be explained? If a text can have only one meaning (the author's, for example), then the explanation is that one reading only is correct and all the others are wrong. But which one is correct? And by what criteria is that correctness to be determined? Observation, again, demonstrates that the 'correctness' of a reading is generally determined by the dominant group in any cultural period according to its own current intellectual criteria and all other readings are rejected as wrong,[24] but those rules of 'correctness' themselves change over time (e.g. in the twelfth century allegorical readings were deemed correct, intended by God, but in the twentieth century under the dominance of the historical paradigm, allegorical readings are wrong). It is difficult to avoid the conclusion that texts have different meanings for different groups of readers, and thus, that textual meaning in some very significant ways is, and always has been, reader dependent. The reader, then, attributes meaning to the text, but the reader does that on the basis of conventional cultural strategies of reading that she or he has been taught. In the language of semiotics, reading 'is a process of making meaning, a process of sign production where the reader actively attributes significance to signifiers on the basis of previously learned cultural codes'.[25] Readers at the very least are co-creators of the meaning of any text, and some reader-response critics and deconstructionists would go considerably further by arguing that no text exists until a reader construes its meaning.[26]

Understanding meaning as the production of readers according to learned conventions explains both the presence of multiple meanings for any text and the shifts in those meanings over time and across

24. See Hayden White's discussion of the importance of noting who has the authority in any situation to determine, not only the meaning of a text, but even what questions are proper to put to a text, in 'Conventional Conflicts', *The New Literary History* 13 (1981), pp. 145-60.

25. Radway, *Reading the Romance*, p. 7.

26. For a discussion of the variety of reader-response criticisms, see S. Suleiman and I. Crosman (eds.), *The Reader in the Text: Essays on Audience and Interpretation* (Princeton, NJ: Princeton University Press, 1980); J. Tompkins (ed.), *Reader-Response Criticism: From Formalism to Post-Structuralism* (Baltimore: The Johns Hopkins University Press, 1980); and J. Culler, *On Deconstruction: Theory and Criticism after Structuralism* (Ithaca, NY: Cornell University Press, 1982).

cultures; it also exposes any attempt to assert a singular, universally correct meaning as an act of power and control rather than a 'simple' reading of 'just what is there'. Appealing to authorial intention in our present intellectual climate as proponents of biblical authority or questers for the historical Jesus are still inclined to do, not only springs from an obsolete theory of texts and reading but reveals a considerably more important, if mostly hidden, political agenda. As Michel Foucault has asserted about authorial intention:

> ...the author is not an indefinite source of significations which fill a work, the author does not precede the works; he is a certain functional principle by which, in our culture, one limits, excludes, and chooses; in short by which one impedes the free circulation, the free manipulation, the free composition, decomposition, and recomposition...The author is therefore the ideological figure by which one marks the manner in which we fear the proliferation of meaning.[27]

If Foucault is correct about the ideological dimension of contemporary claims for authorial intention, as I firmly believe he is, calling upon the image of the divine Author or the historical Jesus is an act of power calculated to limit and exclude the meanings of others. Moreover, if readers or interpreters of Scripture are the ones who are actually construing its meanings, the practice of naming that meaning as God's or Jesus' disguises its real source. Indeed, such naming acts to give a divine face to a very human process and to give divine sanction to human drives to power over the opinions of others. Robert Morgan in his recent discussion of biblical interpretation admits as much without seeming to realize the political implications of the admission. In discussing the variety of conflicting interpretations of the Gospel of Mark, he says

> This great variety of conflicting possibilities makes it impossible to believe that many of the subtleties perceived by interpreters were intended by the evangelist. That is not necessarily a problem for literary critics. They can disregard the author's intention and enjoy the variety. But Christian interpreters have good reasons for maintaining their hope that what they say about Mark is what Mark intended, however mistaken the great majority of them must be.

So, Morgan says there are 'good reasons', but what are these good

---

27. Foucault, 'What is an Author?', in P. Rabinow (ed.), *The Foucault Reader* (New York: Pantheon, 1984), p. 119.

reasons? A better theory of textual meaning? Not at all, for Morgan
goes on to say,

> Without this claim that their interpretations represent the author's inten-
> tion, theologians cannot usually persuade others in the religious commu-
> nity to listen. What the latest professors say about God on their own
> authority has less claim upon the community's attention than what they
> say (with whatever authority their scholarship bestows) that Mark or
> Jesus were saying about God.[28]

According to Morgan, then, the claim of authorial intention is important to scholars and church leaders in order to give *their own views*
greater authority in the religious community. Thus appeals to the
authority of the Bible or the historical Jesus function as masks for
human interpretations, and they are extremely valuable masks—too
valuable to be dropped just because the theoretical or intellectual bases
on which they were constructed have crumbled (or never existed in the
first place)—both because they confer a transcendent, divine authority
to human words and because the power they supply is a singular,
exclusive power to limit or deny the meanings of others, a power, in
other words, which is basically totalitarian. This disguising of human
intention under a divine cloak is especially evident in various attempts
to conjure up the historical Jesus, since claims for his revelatory
authority can be so much greater and the actual data available is so
slight that the special concerns of the interpreter have considerably
freer reign, as Schweitzer pointed out almost a century ago.

It might be objected here that not *any* interpretation of any theologian, biblical scholar or church leader is given an attentive hearing, as I
seem to be suggesting. To be able to appeal convincingly to biblical
authority or the historical Jesus the reading proposed must be
'plausible'[29] to the dominant scholarly community or ecclesiastical
body. Raising the criterion of plausibility or persuasiveness underscores
the fact that readers comprehend textual strategies on the basis of
learned cultural conventions. We are, in other words, taught to read as
we do. To say that a reading is plausible is to say that it accords with
the current cultural rules of discourse. In fact, readings that harmonize
closely with whatever the going rules are, tend to appear 'natural' or
'neutral'. To claim that an interpretation is unbiased is really only to

---

28. R. Morgan with John Barton, *Biblical Interpretation* (Oxford Bible Series;
Oxford: Oxford University Press, 1988), pp. 235-36.
    29. Morgan and Barton, *Biblical Interpretation*, p. 236.

indicate that its particular bias agrees with that of the dominant discourse. But those rules of discourse can and do change; indeed, they may even vary radically among different groups within the same culture or across different cultures within the same historical period.[30] The questions to ask are *where do the rules come from, who determines them and who enforces them*? And the answer to those questions is fairly self-evident: those people who lead and control the dominant cultural institutions in any historical period. Moreover, the rules of discourse they support generally work to maintain the status quo and protect their own vested interests, and before any new members can be added to that leadership they must be so shaped and molded that their vested interests, their job security, financial stability and reputation, also depend on continuing the tradition of the dominant discourse.

Really none of what I have just said is especially new. Any modest foray into the works of Foucault, Derrida or most feminist scholarship in literature, history or psychology would encounter many of the same arguments, perhaps even more forcefully put. It worries me that there is less of this kind of analysis in feminist scholarship in religion than one might expect, and less of it in various liberation theologies than one might hope. Actually, what one finds more often in feminist, especially Protestant feminist, biblical research and in many forms of liberation theology are arguments designed to show that the authority of the Bible and the revelatory authority of the historical Jesus are on the side of liberation and equality. In addition, much of this work depends upon the very same androcentric and patriarchal modes of discourse and methods of research that have been in the past and continue in the present to be used to exclude women, racial and ethnic minorities, disabled persons, homosexuals and others from equal respect and equal access. Feminist biblical hermeneutics has in general attempted to counter one claim to the singular, authoritative Word by challenging it with another claim to the singular, authoritative Word. As a political strategy, usurping the opposition's authoritative foundation has obvious and important advantages. At the very least, it demonstrates that the exclusion of these groups is not so universally and unambiguously supported by biblical texts, even when current modes of critical discourse are being employed, as the dominant group would like everyone to believe,

30. For a discussion of the radical variability of reading conventions, see S. Fish, *Is There a Text in This Class? The Authority of Interpretive Communities* (Cambridge, MA: Harvard University Press, 1982).

and that is a great gain, for it discloses the fact that bias and not neutrality has been shaping interpretations of the Bible; man and not God has been oppressing and demeaning other human beings.

Nevertheless, the difficulty with a strategy of calling upon biblical authority to counter biblical authority is that while it may change the players, it does not change the game. As long as one claims to speak with the singular, authoritative Word of the divine Author, the meanings of others must be excluded. There must continue to be an 'us' and a 'them', insiders and outsiders, the chosen and the rejected, the right and the wrong. For women, especially, the danger of continuing the patriarchal game has been illustrated time and again throughout at least the past five thousand years of human history, because whenever an outsider group has finally been able to wrest power from those in control, whenever a revolution has occurred, whenever some new order has finally won the day, women are still the losers, still a commodity of exchange between vying groups of men. As long as this game of domination and subordination holds out its 'pie in the sky' for the winners to divide among themselves, some may be fed, but most will starve. Should we not try to conceive of another game entirely?

Reading with Authority in a World of Difference

As long as there are winners, there must be losers; as long as there are insiders, there must be outsiders; one group cannot exist without the other. Such dualisms, always hierarchically ordered with one element in the superior position and one in the inferior, are the basic building blocks of patriarchal culture. For a new game to be imagined, they must be broken apart. They must be shown to be cultural constructions, constructions that can in fact be changed, and not the primal organization of the human mind or the natural order of the cosmos. We must come to see what dualistic language tries to prevent us from seeing: instead of living in a world of binary oppositions, we actually live in a world of difference. There are not just two voices speaking but many voices, both within each of us and across the world around us. To explain what I mean by 'a world of difference',[31] I need to analyze

31. The term 'world of difference' is derived from the work of the brilliant geneticist, Barbara McClintock; see the discussion of her 'different' perspective on science in E.F. Keller, *Reflections on Gender and Science* (New Haven: Yale University Press, 1985), pp. 158-76. Much of the argument throughout this section

more closely the dynamics of hierarchical dualisms to show that what appears to be two is in fact only one.

The groundwork for that analysis has already been brilliantly developed in relation to the dualisms governing sexuality, male versus female, by Luce Irigaray, perhaps the most prominent of the 'French Feminists'.[32] In examining Freud's theories about female sexuality, Irigaray argues that Freud never actually describes *two different sexes* but rather only *one* and its opposite: 'The "feminine" is always described in terms of deficiency or atrophy, as the other side of the sex that alone holds a monopoly on value: the male sex.'[33] In the language of sexuality, the female is granted no importance integral to herself, no description specific to her own body. The dynamics of her psychosocial development, according to Freud and his large company of psychiatric followers, are defined completely by what she *lacks*. Even her 'mature' sexual pleasure, the much-debated and never proven 'vaginal orgasm', is determined, not by her own physiology, but by the sexual anatomy of the male. Irigaray demonstrates that in Freud's discourse on sexuality, 'Woman herself is never at issue...the feminine is defined as the necessary complement to the operation of male sexuality, and, more often, as a negative image that provides male sexuality with an unfailingly phallic self-representation'.[34] While Irigaray goes on to begin the task of exploring female sexuality on its own terms by positing touch and multiplicity, rather than the male passion for sight and singularity, as the basic sensibility underlying a specifically female sexuality, for my purposes her most remarkable revelation is that hidden beneath the apparent dualism of male versus female is actually a *monism*. There are not two distinct and opposed elements, but only one and its negative projection of itself onto the other. The other is defined as lack, atrophy

on fractured identities and the nature of the Other draws on the insights of S. Harding, *The Science Question in Feminism* (Ithaca, NY: Cornell University Press, 1986), pp. 163-96.

32. For discussions of the work of the French Feminists and their debt to Lacan, see A. Nye, *Feminist Theory and the Philosophies of Man* (London: Croom Helm, 1988), pp. 115-71; T. Moi, *Sexual/Textual Politics* (London: Methuen, 1985); E. Marks and I. de Courtivron, *New French Feminisms* (Brighton: Harvester, 1981); and C. Weedon, *Feminist Practice and Poststructuralist Theory* (Oxford: Basil Blackwell, 1987), pp. 63-73.

33. L. Irigaray, *This Sex Which Is Not One* (trans. C. Porter; Ithaca, NY: Cornell University Press, 1985), p. 69.

34. Irigaray, *This Sex Which Is Not One*, p. 70.

or diminution of the dominant element, not as an entity with its own integrity, specificity and value.

What Irigaray has shown to be the case for the apparent dualisms of sexuality, I want to argue is also the case for all the other hierarchical dualisms of patriarchal culture. Whatever group or class or gender or sexual orientation is considered inferior or rejected by the cultural hegemony is described *in terms of that hegemony*—as its lack, its atrophy, its diminution or the projection of what it fears in itself. Hence, not only is women's sexuality defined solely in relation to men but also their personality traits: they are weak, easily frightened, passive, nurturing children, and they must be that way for men to be able to define themselves as strong, courageous, brave, aggressive, independent adults. Women provide the negative mirror image to assure men of their masculinity. Yet, the same mechanism, and many of the same traits, can be found in the descriptions of other groups of 'outsiders' to the cultural hegemony: adult African Americans are called 'boy' or 'girl' (a diminution) or in need of restraint because of their uncontrollable aggressive tendencies (a projection); the poor are castigated as lazy or irresponsible (atrophy); homosexuals are fantasized as possessing rampant sexual urges (a projection); Native Americans are patronized as weak-minded children, who must be protected on reservations (atrophy and diminution); physically disabled persons are treated as mentally retarded as well (atrophy); and so on. The purpose of these descriptions is to provide an apparent contrast, assuring the dominant group that they are mature men and women, in full control of their anger and sexuality, mentally and physically whole and, thus, deserving of the freedom and rewards the system accords them. It is not just that those persons whose identities place them outside the cultural hegemony are viewed as Other, but that the very description of their Otherness is controlled by the dominant discourse in terms of itself and then attributed to the Other; who these Others may be in their own specificity, integrity and diversity is *never* allowed to surface as a possible question. In terms biblical scholars especially should understand, the ones who have the power to name, name all the world in relation to themselves, in their own image. At the heart of hierarchical dualisms stands a dominant narcissistic egoism that defines everyone and everything in terms of its own values and its own fears.

For those Others whose natures are defined for them and projected on them by the dominant discourse, the results are devastating. They are allowed neither their own integrity and specificity as human beings nor do they have a language with which to explore their own identity and diversity. What they are encouraged to believe about themselves, they may know at some deep level is not true, but they have little power to object. What is occurring in many liberation movements, I would like to suggest, are attempts to remedy these distortions, to fill in the silences, to claim the power to speak for themselves. Reconstructing history, rediscovering the lives, words and sufferings of foremothers and forefathers, understanding one's roots, are all extremely important paths to developing a sense of integrity that has been denied by the dominant culture. For oppressed racial and ethnic minorities, particularly, the revitalization of their own languages, traditions and history provide a vast resource for exploring who they are and have been and may be *on their own terms*.

Furthermore, what the monism of patriarchal culture hides most thoroughly are the very real differences among people. All 'minorities' are not the same, even though the use of a single term (minority) to cover all of these different groups of people suggests that they are. As hard as it is for some to accept, all women are *not* alike; we do not all look the same, although the cosmetic and fashion industries, not to mention the media, strive mightily to make it seem so; we do not all act the same or think the same or love the same. Yet, according to the dominant discourse we are ideally identical—nurturing, loving, dependent, passive, non-ambitious, weak in math and science, very much in need of a man, and so on. One of the hardest realizations for women but one of the most important is the recognition that the way we have been described (and socialized) by patriarchal culture has never taken into account who we might be in our own integrity. Consequently, the exploration of individuality is one of the first and most essential tasks of liberation for women. It has also caused major problems for the women's movement. I think that the much-vaunted factionalism and elitism of the women's movement springs from the failure of women to throw off the ideological trappings of patriarchal culture and appreciate the profound differences among us, while at the same time acknowledging the congruence of many of our goals. Having for so long had others speak for us and about us, as we gain our own voices we resent anyone—even another woman—saying what 'all' of us want or need or think. However, this individuality is not the 'rugged individualism' of American myth but the understanding of who we are in relationship with and in differentiation from others; it is a radically interconnected individuality. Moreover, because a working-class woman, an African American woman, a Jewish woman, an Asian-American woman, a lesbian or a disabled woman experiences oppression not only because of her gender but also because of her economic, ethnic, class, racial, religious or sexual identity, we are forced to recognize that real differences exist *within* us as well as between us.[35] Women often find within themselves conflicting allegiances, which can be extremely painful to negotiate. Yet, all of these differences are denied reality by the monistic narcissism of the cultural hegemony. Such monism simplifies the world around us and within us, to be sure, but it also profoundly distorts it.

What would it be like to live in a world of difference? To live in a world in which that which is integral to each of us is acknowledged and valued, not ignored or disdained by the language of hierarchical dualism? How would one read the Bible in that world? I do not know, for I do not live in such a world. But at the very least, I would imagine that the meanings of others would not be excluded or rejected by appeal to a singular, authoritative divine Word. Moreover, since in all of our differences the Bible is one text that we share, by reading it together and really hearing the varieties of meanings other people out of their own experiences create in that text, I might actually come to understand who those others are in their differences and who I am in mine considerably better than I do now. And because I believe that intimate attention to the particularity of another or of others is the only basis for love and also that whatever truth there is in this world is not to be found within me or within you but somewhere *between* us, I would not only enjoy the variety of these interpretations but also perhaps find in the process a hint of that long-awaited messianic banquet. Of course, inviting all the world to sit at table and share the great feast is extremely risky; after all, they just might come.

35. My thinking along these lines was stimulated by hearing a paper presented by Professor Sheila Briggs, 'The Politics of Identity and the Politics of Interpretation', given at the conference on 'Gender, Race and Class: Implications for Interpreting Religious Texts' at Princeton Theological Seminary, 16–18 May 1988.

TRANSLATION HAPPENS:
A FEMINIST PERSPECTIVE ON TRANSLATION THEORIES

Tina Pippin

> To refuse translation is to refuse life.
> (Derrida 1985b: 137)
>
> Paradise marks the end of translation.
> (Rafael 1988: 175)

Translating Theory/Theorizing Translation

All readers of the Bible are translators. A translator is anyone who reads between the lines, or on top of the lines, or over the lines, or on the other side of the lines, or in reverse and upside down, by using mirrors, by burning the pages, setting the words on fire. Modern and postmodern assumptions about meaning and difference bring the translator to look at the ideological grounding of how and why translation occurs. What is the social location of the translator? What is the ethical responsibility of the translator? Is an anti-oppression/colonizing translation of the Bible possible? What are the possible responses to the silence of popular and legitimized academic translations on issues of gender, race and class? Where has the heritage of Bible translations left us? What are the liberatory options in the translation process?

In the beginning was the word, language and speech that began the process of translation. For many early Bible translators, the original language was Hebrew; God spoke Hebrew and gave it to Adam in Eden. Postcolonial theorists show how the search for the 'original' language helped Christian missionaries claim superiority for their religion over indigenous religions, even though languages such as Sanskrit were older than Hebrew (Said 1979: 136). The languages of the *textus receptus* of the Tanakh and the New Testament—Hebrew, Aramaic and Greek—show the diverse relationship of these languages to their religious cultures. Hebrew and Aramaic both derive from the Canaanite language (and the Phoenician alphabet) or the Ethiopian language (Lambdin 1971: xiii). Greek is the language of the colonizers, a unifying trade language that linked the nations to Greece and later to Rome. The Septuagint and the New Testament and later the Vulgate in Latin reflect the language of empires. Even within these biblical languages are different dialects. There is no pure or 'original' biblical language, only traces of autographs, echoes of stories told.

One 'universal' in translation theories is that there is no ideal translator and no ideal translation. Translations lead to indeterminacy of meanings, in a scattering of dialects and social contexts that occurred at Babel. The translation of the biblical stories occurs as soon as they are spoken. The King James Version and the New Revised Standard Version are versions of versions of versions (and on into infinity) of stories. Translation theorist Gregory Rabassa asks if Bible translators are translating or creating new versions; he says the KJV is 'almost another book in itself. It is a version indeed, much like the variants of folktales and legends' (1984: 24). A 'version' is an adaptation when it relates to secular literature, but it stands for Bible 'translation'. Instead of the New Revised Standard Translation, there is Version, but Translation is intended. The NRSV is in a sense as Version both a translation and an adaptation of ancient literary works. In some sense the multiple Versions of the Bible are also a/versions, where feminists or the colonized or subjugated races or classes turn away from the authority of Scripture and rewrite their own stories into the text.

The history of Bible translation is much like that of the many editions of the Brothers' Grimm fairytales. The many versions of Little Red Riding Hood, for example, have different ideologies and endings based on the social desires and needs of specific times and cultures (see Zipes 1993). Is every translation of the Bible, then, a rewriting of the text? The Bible has a history of different authoritative claims, sacred text from sacred language. Every translation is a push away from the Hebrew and Greek, yet Bible translations have claimed special inspired status. If the biblical texts are inspired (directly by God, mediated by an author and editor or whatever), then translation must also connect with this divine inspiration. This notion makes translation a metaphysical activity, relegated to an ethereal realm. The missionary context of many biblical translations claims, often implicitly, to be engaged in a special, sacred activity that is different from the translation of 'secular' texts.

There is the sense in the history of Bible translation that the translator must remain faithful to the biblical text. Walter Benjamin introduced the concepts of fidelity and freedom in translation in his influential article, 'The Task of the Translator'. On the issue of faithfulness to the original Benjamin stresses, 'Fidelity in the translation of individual words can almost never fully reproduce the meaning they have in the original' (1968: 78). Benjamin is not interested in a translation's audience, since the translator has constructed the audience (1968: 69). Benjamin privileges the text but in a different way than the dynamic equivalency theory in Bible translation. The original has an 'afterlife' only in translation so that 'no translation would be possible if in its ultimate essence it strove for likeness to the original' (1968: 73). Benjamin calls for a transparent translation (1968: 79), and the only way for the original to be present is through an *interlinear* version. He elaborates this point:

> Just as, in the original, language and revelation are one without any tension, so the translation must be one with the original in the form of the interlinear version, in which literalness and freedom are united. For to some degree all great texts contain their potential translation between the lines; this is true to the highest degree of sacred writings. The interlinear version of the Scriptures is the prototype or ideal of all translation (1968: 82).

Thus in translation the original languages of the Bible are scattered as at Babel; the original is in fragments of originals and translations. By setting these side by side the translation can harmonize with the original (Benjamin 1968: 79). There is no one fixed text but multiple texts, and the sacred, poetic possibilities have room to play.

Paul de Man evaluates Benjamin's discussion of fidelity and freedom in the act of translating and notes that a translation is more canonical than the original: 'That the original was not purely canonical is clear from the fact that it demands translation; it cannot be definitive since it can be translated' (1986: 82). This deconstructive statement echoes Derrida's concern that Benjamin posits an untouchable, sacred kernel in an original text, and this idea is untenable for Derrida, since such a kernel is a myth (1985b: 114-16). Perhaps Benjamin desires a virginal kernel of the sacred in translation (Derrida 1985b: 115-16), in other words, the desire for the space of pure language in the gaps between the columns in the interlinear Bible. In any event, the authority of the text, original or translation, is up for grabs.

Carol Jacobs deconstructs Benjamin's article and states that his translation theory is ambiguous and leads to a 'monstrosity' of a translation (1975: 761). In this fidelity-freedom discussion where do the translators's loyalties lie?—with the text, the context, the Word, community? Do translators have to chip away at the authority question as they translate? At what point does the reality of the struggles of people affected by the translation come to bear? Is the problem with the word/s of the text (either original or translated or both) or with the ideologies of the translators? Does Benjamin's privileging of the text place too much emphasis on the high ideals of the translation project that the Romanticists (like Schleiermacher) held as the appropriate bourgeois activity? Is a transparent translation an appropriate or ethical goal in the context of the history of violence of claims of objectivity? Is rehearing, retelling, rediscerning the Bible in highly (and proudly) subjective ways more important than remaining 'faithful' to it?

Fidelity to the text often means bringing in all the oppressive material. Rabassa relates, 'There are tremendous temptations to improve, enhance, or personalize, often a chance to make the translation a better book' (1984: 36). When translating for race and class, how much should the translator be faithful to the text, and when does faithfulness lead to an abusive translation? Sometimes the translation itself supports (consciously or not) racist or classist agendas, and the translator has the role of reconstructing a more authentic translation. But if the text is sexist, racist and/or classist, should the translator let these negative pieces be, or change them to make the text more inclusive, to make a better book?

The New Revised Standard Version is basically regarded as a 'faithful' translation, even though there is little attention to race, class (or gender) in this translation. This version is used worldwide and is the guide for translations into many languages. Dynamic equivalency theory reigns, if there is such a thing as 'equivalency' in translation. Translator Lawrence Venuti states that 'Fidelity cannot be construed as mere semantic equivalence' and 'canons of accuracy are culturally specific and historically variable' (1995: 37). Venuti exposes the myth of the invisible translator, what he calls 'the illusion of transparency' (1995: 1). Certain Bible translations are so familiar that their translation is the 'natural' one. The long romance with the KJV or the Authorized Version produces the difficulty in introducing new versions into communities loyal to these older traditions. Venuti's problem with dynamic equivalency theory is that it reinscribes the target language with the cultural and ethnocentric values of the source language; in other words, the translator hauls his or her own ideologies into the translation. Venuti critiques Eugene Nida's ideal of a natural translation and states strongly:

> Communication here is initiated and controlled by the target-language culture, it is in fact an interested interpretation, and therefore it seems less an exchange of information than an appropriation of a foreign text for domestic purposes. Nida's theory of translation as communication does not adequately take into account *the ethnocentric violence that is inherent in every translation process—but especially in one governed by dynamic equivalence* (1995: 22; emphasis mine).

Translator, missionary and Christ are one in Nida's dynamic equivalency translation. There is an urgency to translate the Bible into as many languages as possible.

Liberating Translation

Focus on gender, race and class takes the translation act out of the scientific and technical realm: translation affects real human lives. Spivak offers that translation is always about a cultural politics of difference that affects women's lives. The translator has an ethical responsibility to what she is making accessible (1993: 191). Spivak notes, 'The task of the feminist translator is to consider language as a clue to the workings of gendered agency' (1993: 179), while keeping in mind the knowledge of 'the heritage of imperialism' (1993: 193) that has had a great effect on women's lives in the Third World. For Spivak, 'Translation is the most intimate act of reading', an erotic act of surrender on the part of the translator (1993: 180-83). To read is to translate. Spivak moves translation theory out of the realm of science (Nida and Taber 1982; see Gentzler 1993: ch. 3, on 'The "Science" of Translation') into the realm of the emotive.

'Translation' has been traditionally defined from the Latin *translatio* in the sense of 'transporting', or the German *Übersetzung*, 'crossing or jumping over'. The Indonesian words for 'translation', *terjemahan*, *pertalan* and *penjalinan*, come from the root 'to bear a child or to change one's clothes' (Raffel 1993: 1303). Translation is physical and mental and sensual, the mind–body link. One of the noises of translation is the life of the translator, the translator's body on the body of literature, the loyalty to self and body in the face of a text of power.

The act of translation changes the meanings of words and texts. Then are parts of the Bible untranslatable? Does every translation represent loss—some loss of the original? Is it possible to become lost in translation? Is it impossible for the translator to disappear into the language, or is it always an attempt to step 'inside' the text while simultaneously remaining clearly outside? These boundary lines between 'inside' and 'outside' the text are blurred. Vicente Rafael questions the boundaries of 'translation' even further and points out: 'The Spanish words *conquista* (conquest), *conversión* (conversion), and *traducción* (translation) are semantically related' (1988: ix). Translation is about changing something into something else. The interests of the translator are part of the process of translation. Thus, the multiple definitions of the word 'translation' reveal issues of power and ideology.

In his discussion of Benjamin, Homi Bhabha emphasizes the space of untranslatability and the part of any original text that resists translation. Bhabha engages Benjamin on this point:

> The migrant culture of the 'in-between', the minority position, dramatizes the activity of culture's untranslatability; and in so doing, it moves the question of culture's appropriation beyond the assimilationist's dream, or the racist's nightmare, of a 'full transmissal of subject-matter', and towards an encounter with the ambivalent process of splitting and hybridity that marks the identification with culture's difference (1994: 224).

Bhabha also takes issue with Benjamin's desire for a transparent translation, since all translations are culturally bound: 'Cultural translation desacralizes the transparent assumptions of cultural supremacy, and in that very act, demands a contextual specificity, a historical differentiation within minority positions' (1994: 228). Bhabha's interest is in the 'foreign element' in translation 'that has to be engaged in creating the conditions through which "newness comes into the world"' (1994: 227). Bhabha's emphasis on the foreignness of translation is very different from Schleiermacher's romanticized version in the nineteenth century. For Bhabha racist myths are central in colonial texts.

An example of how the 'foreign element' is identified and subverted comes from Aboriginal translators. Hendrik Spykerboer raises important issues from Aboriginal biblical scholars and their 'movement to translate the biblical message into aboriginal cultural forms' (1993: 776). He states that this movement questions 'whether Western biblical interpretations are not more influenced by prejudices related to Western civilization and culture than has often been thought' (1993: 776). Western hegemonic biblical interpretation is challenged.

Bible translation has traditionally been a strategy of containment— the containment of the Other in Western hegemonic terms. Bhabha notes that a liberatory movement is 'caught in the discontinuous time of translation and negotiation' (1994: 38). Anti-oppression translating brings the translator (and reader) to a different space, a historical space where past, present and future intersect. Liberatory translation is caught in this 'Third Space' (Bhabha 1994: 39), where translation is a political act reclaimed on different terms by the Other.

The 'authority' of the canon reflects the 'authority' of Western culture, and translating in the Third Space undermines both these grounds of authority. The Bible is different from other sacred texts in its authoritative reach. In Islam the sacred text of the Quran is only authoritative and authentic in Arabic—never in translation. The Bible is authoritative in translation, and even in paraphrase, as the popularity of The Living Bible proves. Still, the concerns of race and class are absent from most translations, like in some biblical epic film of the 1950s in which all the performers are Anglos, even the Egyptians. Even the NRSV catches only the most obvious past translation mistakes by making the change to 'I am black and beautiful' in Song 1.5. There is no systemic, theoretical commitment to issues of race and class in Bible translation in the West, and no concern for the role of the powerful in the Third Space where 'authority' is questioned and sometimes protested, sometimes refused.

Many feminist and postcolonial translators are calling for and doing 'activist translation', transformational translation or translation for social change. Derrida posits translation as transformation (Derrida 1985b: 95-6; 1978: 20). His claim that translation is both 'necessary and impossible' (1985a) relates to the reality of translating in the Third Space. Translation theorist Edwin Gentzler describes deconstructive translation: 'Deconstructionists go so far as to suggest that perhaps the *translated text writes us* and not we the translated text' (1993: 145). Translation is a survival technique in which the variables of race and class continue to operate. The notion of the objectivity of these variables is so ingrained that they are taken to be normative and are second nature; they are seen as not needing to be questioned because readers accept the normativity of them. There is a devaluing of any culture in making race, class and gender invisible. Many translators are not even aware of the ideological underpinnings and the ways social conditions effect language. There are a multitude of ways to translate for race and class, and they are all culturally specific and haunted by the very present ghosts of hegemonic English translations.

Feminist Translation Theory as a Journey in the Third Space

> The site of translation is always an arena of struggle.
> (McLaren 1994: xxv)

My earliest memory of translating the Bible occurred when I was about five years old in a Sunday school room in the back of a tiny Episcopal church: An adult said to me, 'The story of Adam and Eve is like Aesop's Fables; the Bible is like a fairy tale'. I immediately translated the whirl of fantastic tales of talking snakes and supernatural events and magic into the realm of the unreal. Fantasy theorist Rosemary Jackson states, 'all literary works are fantasies' (1981: 13), and I easily fit the Bible into this mode. She offers a definition: 'The fantastic traces the unsaid and the unseen of culture: that which has been silenced, made invisible, covered over and made "absent"' (1981: 4). Translation attempts to enter the fantasy in various ways—both a possible and impossible task of looking for the cultural traces of other languages, times and voices. To translate is to be lost in texts, in their fantasy worlds which are part historical novel, part fairy tale. Feminist translation theory reminds us of the dangers that lurk in these patriarchal textual/narrative worlds—and the necessity and responsibility of facing these dangers. A central question for me is: Does feminist translation theory of the Bible necessarily lead to the production of a liberatory (anti-oppression) text? Should it?

For 2000 years the biblical texts are in various stages of decay. In the midst of this decay the fragments of translation are found. The postmodern political move is to focus on the fragments and push against the traditional myth of a 'pure' translation and translator faithful to the text to the exclusion of other loyalties. Suzanne Levine (1984; 1991) speaks of 'the (sub)version of translation' as a postmodern move that raises the issues of gender, sexuality, class and race as legitimate, crucial and critical, but formally protected by the privilege/s of the translator. Gayatri Spivak uses the phrases 'the politics of translation' and 'the cultural politics of difference' to expose the motivations and loyalties of the translator. As Elizabeth Castelli points out in investigating *les belles infidèles*, 'Translations, the argument runs, are like women: the faithful ones are homely, while the unfaithful ones are beautiful. Theorists of translation almost always situate fidelity in some relation to women, whether by explicit analogy or underlying structure of their arguments' (1993: 196). If the Bible is held as a 'sacred text', then this issue of fidelity is especially important, since there is often an obsession with the Word of God, a desire to hear God's voice.

God's 'voice' is one of many noises in the translation process. When translators are aware of their multiple positions and privileges, they make 'translation noises' of cultures and tongues and echoes (Derrida's 'the irreducible multiplicity of tongues'). Where do the translator's loyalties lie? In the text, context, word, community? Do we have to chip away at the authority question as we translate? The reality of our own struggles (and privileges) are at stake in the gendered translation.

What if the translation brings us bad news of a sexist, patriarchal order? This question points to the basic choices for feminist readers of the Bible: (1) there is a basic humanistic, egalitarian, non-patriarchal root to the biblical text which only needs uncovering and corrective translation; (2) there are sexist and non-sexist parts in the Bible and only the later are revelatory; (3) the Bible is entirely patriarchal and sexist and is not a liberatory document for women (see Carol Christ's categories, 1987: 144). Is a task of the feminist translator to make the biblical text better than (read: more ethical, less sexist, less imperialist, less oppressive) the 'original?' Or to expose the sexism, denounce it and move on to other texts?

Even if moving on is the choice made, the biblical culture of the United States is everywhere—translated in literature, politics, popular culture and media. The lure is always to translate and translate the translations. Spivak relates translating to the realm of the erotic, for translation is seductive: 'It is a simple miming of the responsibility to the trace of the other in the self' (1993: 179) and 'To surrender in translation is more erotic than ethical' (1993: 183). We are not like the biblical people in the texts we translate. There is, again, a cultural politics of difference that causes ruptures, impossibilities and pleasures in the translation process. Babel may be untranslatable (Derrida), but since Babel we translate. We desire Babel nonetheless, and it sure is a fantastic story.

Translation has become such a serious enterprise/exercise. Translators have often forgotten to play. This notion of play is linked with the notion of the need for multiple translations instead of the ideal-istic/utopian search for one, monolithic, true/pure translation. The Bible has become a 'fixed' text in the minds of so many of my students. About half of my students operate under a 'dogmatic' translation theory and use defensive speech to provide quick answers. One recent semester a student in my Hebrew Bible class asked who the 'us' was in Gen. 3.22 ('the man has become like one of us'), and a fundamentalist Christian student provided the answer: 'Oh, that's the Father, Son and the Holy Ghost!' If and when they become 'translators' on their own terms, they begin to play. One example is in the scene of Ruth and Boaz on the threshing floor and the debate about the euphemistic mean-ing of 'feet' and the imagining of what is happening in this story. The multiple voices, scattered possibilities (and impossibilities) ring out. Gaps upon gaps, ruptures upon ruptures, translations upon translation. What is 'true' becomes less stable—and more playful.

Stepping 'inside' the text while simultaneously remaining clearly outside; these boundary lines are blurred. One can never completely disappear into the language, without a trace or echo. Translation is and is not a magic trick. My students are working with a translation of the Hebrew into English, but even Hebrew scholars read the Tanakh in translation. Reading is writing notes in the margins, being a marginal reader, choosing to read as/over/against the marginalized. As Derrida notes, translating is how we understand ourselves and life. 'To refuse translation is to refuse life' (1985b: 137). In the words of a mock bumper sticker I imagine, Translation Happens.

One dimension of feminist translation of the Bible, it seems to me, is along the lines of Nelle Morton's idea of 'hearing each other to speech' (1985: 127-29). Perhaps we should 'hear each other to translation' or 'hear the text to speech'. If we did this, what would we hear? Hetero-glossia? Nothing at all? These are the questions of deconstruction. Perhaps Adrienne Rich provides a clue: '*You must write, and read, as if your life depended on it*' (1993: 32). Adding Derrida, you must translate as if your life depended on it. To return to Rich (and play with her text):

> To [translate] as if your life depended on it would mean to let into your reading your beliefs, the swirl of your dreamlife, the physical sensations of your ordinary carnal life; and, simultaneously, to allow what you're reading to pierce the routines, safe and impermeable, in which ordinary carnal life is tracked, charted, channeled...To [translate] as if your life depended on it—but what [translation] can be believed? Isn't all

[translation] just manipulation? Maybe the [translator] has a hidden program—to recruit you to a cause, send you into the streets, to destabilize,
through the sensual powers of language, your tested and tried priorities?
(1993: 33).

To translate as if your life depended on it means listening to the echo of
the 'original' in the multiple cultural expressions of the biblical text
over time (Benjamin 1968: 76). As Benjamin relates, 'For to some
degree all great texts contain their potential translation between the
lines; this is true to the highest degree of sacred writings. The interlinear version of the Scriptures is the prototype or ideal of all translation'
(1968: 82). The postmodern bible is one of multiple translations, inter
and intralinear—and spiral—reading between the lines and breaking
through the flat, silent page to hear and participate in an infinite
conversation.

BIBLIOGRAPHY

Bannerji, Himani
1995   *Thinking Through: Essays on Feminism, Marxism and Anti-Racism*
            (Toronto: Women's Press).
Benjamin, Walter
1968   'The Task of the Translator', in Hannah Arendt (ed.), *Illuminations* (New
            York: Schocken Books): 69-82.
Bhabha, Homi K.
1994   *The Location of Culture* (New York: Routledge).
Buber, Martin, and Franz Rosenzweig
1994   *Scripture and Translation* (trans. Lawrence Rosenwald with Everett Fox;
            Bloomington: Indiana University Press).
Budick, Sanford, and Wolfgang Iser (eds.)
1996   *The Translatability of Cultures: Figurations of the Space Between*
            (Stanford: Stanford University Press).
Castelli, Elizabeth
1993   '*Les belles infidèles*/Fidelity or Feminism? The Meanings of Feminist
            Biblical Translation', in Elisabeth Schüssler Fiorenza (ed.), *Searching the
            Scriptures: A Feminist Introduction* (New York: Crossroad): 189-204.
Christ, Carol P.
1987   *The Laughter of Aphrodite: Reflections on a Journey to the Goddess* (San
            Francisco: Harper & Row).
Derrida, Jacques
1978   *Positions* (trans. Alan Bass; Chicago: University of Chicago Press).
1985a   'Des Tours de Babel', in Joseph F. Graham (ed. and trans.), *Difference in
            Translation* (Ithaca, NY: Cornell University Press): 167-85.

1985b   *The Ear of the Other: Otobiography, Transference, Translation* (ed. Christie V. McDonald; trans. Peggy Kamuf; New York: Schocken Books).

Dimock, Wai Chee, and Michael T. Gilmore
1994   'Introduction', in *Rethinking Class: Literary Studies and Social Formations* (New York: Columbia University Press): 1-11.

Eco, Umberto
1995   *The Search for the Perfect Language* (trans. James Fentress; Cambridge: Blackwell).

Gentzler, Edwin
1993   *Contemporary Translation Theories* (New York: Routledge).

Gold, Victor Roland, Thomas L. Hoyt, Jr, Sharon H. Ringe, Susan Brooks Thistlethwaite, Burton H. Throckmorton, Jr and Barbara A. Withers (eds.)
1995   *The New Testament and Psalms: An Inclusive Version* (New York: Oxford University Press).

Greenstein, Edward L.
1989   *Essays on Biblical Method and Translation* (Atlanta: Scholars Press).

Herzog, William R., II
1994   *Parables as Subversive Speech: Jesus as Pedagogue of the Oppressed* (Louisville, KY: Westminster/John Knox Press).

Jackson, Rosemary
1981   *Fantasy: The Literature of Subversion* (New York: Methuen).

Jacobs, Carol
1975   'The Monstrosity of Translation', *Modern Language Notes* 90: 755-66.

Jasper, David (ed.)
1993   *Translating Religious Texts: Translation, Transgression and Interpretation* (New York: St Martin's Press).

Joyce, Patrick (ed.)
1995   *Class* (New York: Oxford University Press).

Lambdin, Thomas O.
1996   *Introduction to Biblical Hebrew* (New York: Prentice–Hall).

Levine, Suzanne Jill
1984   'Translation as (sub)version: On Translating Dante's Inferno', *Sub-stance* 42: 85-94.
1991   *The Subversive Scribe: Translating Latin American Fiction* (New York: Graywolf Press).

Man, Paul de
1986   'Conclusions: Walter Benjamin's "The Task of the Translator"', in *The Resistance to Theory* (Minneapolis: University of Minnesota Press): 73-105.

McLaren, Peter L.
1994   'Foreward', in Miguel Escobar, Alfredo L. Fernández and Gilberto Guevara-Niebla with Paulo Freire, *Paulo Freire on Higher Education: A Dialogue at the National University of Mexico* (Albany: State University of New York Press): ix-xxxiii.

Metzger, Bruce M., Robert C. Dentan and Walter Harrelson
1991   *The Making of the New Revised Standard Version of the Bible* (Grand Rapids: Eerdmans).

Mohanty, Chandra Talpade
1991   'Introduction: Cartographies of Struggle: Third World Women and the
              Politics of Feminism', in Chandra Talpade Mohanty, Ann Russo and
              Lourdes Torres (eds.), *Third World Women and the Politics of Feminism*
              (Bloomington: Indiana University Press): 1-47.
Morton, Nelle
1985   *The Journey Is Home* (Boston: Beacon).
Nagele, Rainer
1997   *Echoes of Translation: Reading between Texts* (Baltimore: The Johns
              Hopkins University Press).
Nida, Eugene A., and Charles R. Taber
1982   *The Theory and Practice of Translation* (Leiden: E.J. Brill).
Niranjana, Tejaswini
1992   *Siting Translation: History, Post-Structuralism, and the Colonial Context*
              (Berkeley: University of California Press).
Philip, Marlene Nourbese
1992   'Preface: An Extract from "Discourse on the Logic of Language"', in
              Susheila Nasta (ed.), *Motherlands: Black Women's Writing from Africa,
              the Caribbean and South Africa* (New Brunswick: Rutgers University
              Press): xi-xii.
Rabassa, Gregory
1984   'The Silk Purse Business: A Translator's Conflicting Responsibilities', in
              William Frawley (ed.), *Translation: Literary, Linguistic and
              Philosophical Perspectives* (Newark: University of Delaware Press): 35-
              40.
Rafael, Vicente L.
1988   *Contracting Colonialism: Translation and Christian Conversion in
              Tagalog Society under Early Spanish Rule* (Ithaca, NY: Cornell
              University Press).
Raffel, Burton
1993   'Translation', in Alex Preminger and T.V.F. Brogan (eds.), *The New
              Princeton Encyclopedia of Poetry and Poetics* (Princeton, NJ: Princeton
              University Press): 1303-1305.
Rich, Adrienne
1993   'As if your life depended on it', in *What Is Found There: Notebooks on
              Poetry and Politics* (New York: Quality Paperback Book Club): 32-33.
Robinson, Douglas
1996   *Translation and Taboo* (Urbana: Northern Illinois University Press).
Said, Edward
1979   *Orientalism* (New York: Vintage Books).
Smalley, William A.
1997   *Translation as Mission: Bible Translation in the Modern Missionary
              Movement* (Macon: Mercer University Press).
Spivak, Gayatri Chakravorty
1993   'The Politics of Translation', in *Outside in the Teaching Machine* (New
              York: Routledge): 179-200.

Spykerboer, Hendrik C.
1993   'Australian Aboriginal Languages', in Bruce M. Metzger and Michael D.
            Coogan (eds.), *The Oxford Companion to the Bible* (New York: Oxford
            University Press): 775-76.
Steiner, George
1992   *After Babel: Aspects of Language and Translation* (New York: Oxford
            University Press).
Venuti, Lawrence
1995   *The Translator's Invisibility: A History of Translation* (New York:
            Routledge).
Weems, Renita
1991   'Reading her Way through the Struggle: African American Women and
            the Bible', in Cain Felder (ed.), *Stony the Road We Trod: African
            American Biblical Interpretation* (Minneapolis: Fortress Press): 57-77.
Zipes, Jack (ed.)
1993   *The Trials and Tribulations of Little Red Riding Hood* (New York:
            Routledge).

WHY *THE NEW TESTAMENT AND PSALMS*:
AN INCLUSIVE VERSION?

Burton H. Throckmorton, Jr

Recently someone sent me a cartoon that had been adapted from *The New Yorker*. Two women are talking. One says, 'I don't like the idea of this passage calling the deity a "him".' And the other responds: 'Nonsense, that's a transcript by a scribe who had neglected his grammar. There are many such errors in all ancient scriptures. Thank heaven that today we have such good clerks.'

Which, in a circuitous way, leads me to raise the question of why the committee on which I served for many years was engaged in preparing the recent Oxford University Press publication, *The New Testament and Psalms: An Inclusive Version*, which has caused such a hullabaloo, not only in this country, but also throughout the English-speaking world.[1] I have spoken on talk shows all over this country, as well as in Canada, the United Kingdom and even South Africa. I am interested now, however, in the 'why' rather than the 'what' of the new version—the 'what' is very well explained in the 'General Introduction'.

But first a few preliminary words. We are in an age, now, of postmodern theology (like postmodern science and postmodern philosophy), and one aspect of this is a shift from a patriarchal stance to what I would like to call a *human* stance. But our world does not yet know how to understand itself in terms of what it *is*, but only in terms of what it has *just-now-ceased-to-be*. We are flailing around a bit, trying to find ways of talking and writing and translating that represent the way we are relating to each other. We are undergoing a transvaluation of values which, as Nietzsche observed, 'can only be accomplished when there is a tension of new needs, and a new set of needy people who feel all old

---

1.   Victor Roland Gold *et al.* (eds.), *The New Testament and Psalms: An Inclusive Version* (New York: Oxford University Press, 1995).

values are painful—although they are not conscious of what is wrong'.[2]
And further complicating the whole matter is the fact that, so far as
translating goes, we all bring a world to a text, and each of us hears the
same text in terms of our own private worlds.

Translations—all translations—are notoriously difficult. How liter-
ally must one translate in order not to falsify? And further, how literally
is it *possible* to translate? The questions cannot be answered in princi-
ple, I think, but can only be dealt with, case by case, as one translates.
Let me cite an instance of translation from the world of the writer
Samuel Beckett. It is generally known that Beckett, who was born in
Ireland, spent much of his life in Paris, and wrote in both French and
English. Sometimes he did his own translation into the other language.
In one of the plays he wrote in French we have the following dialogue:

> NAGG: (geignard ['whining']): Qu'est-ce que c'est?
>
> CLOV: C'est le biscuit classique. ('biscuit' or 'pastry'—something
> vaguely to do with food in France.)
>
> Beckett has translated this exchange as follows:
>
> NAGG: (plaintively): What is it?
>
> CLOV: Spratt's medium. (Also extremely vague.)

Now one might say that Beckett has not translated his French at all; and
the critic Hugh Kenner has written that Beckett's English is 'a desperate equivalent for the aloof precision of "le biscuit classique".'[3] But
Beckett believed that his English version was less misleading than a
literal translation would have been. In fact, if literalness were a necessary and inherent characteristic of translation, then Beckett would not
have translated his own words at all. But he thought he had!

Of course, in one sense an accurate translation from one language to
another is really impossible—to which anyone who has read
Shakespeare in French or German will attest ('Être ou ne pas être' is
fascinating French!). But on another level translation is of course possible, and we must do it, and we look for the closest equivalent we can
find in the receptor language.

And often something quite different from what was written is

2.   Quoted by Mary Daly, *Beyond God the Father* (Boston: Beacon Press,
1973), p. 98.

3.   Hugh Kenner, *Samuel Beckett: A Critical Study* (Berkeley: University of
California Press, 1968), p. 95.

required in translation. For example, how would one translate into French the complimentary closing often used in business correspondence, 'Very truly yours'? Surely not literally, 'Très vraiment à vous!' So we ask what would be said in French. Perhaps 'Sentiments distingués', of which the English equivalent is certainly not 'With my distinguished sentiments'. We must look for the nearest equivalent of the *meaning* of words in the current idiom, for what is sometimes called the 'dynamic equivalent'. In the 'inclusive version' of the New Testament and the Psalms we have been far more literal, of course, than Beckett was, but we have tried to allow the church's Scriptures to address all believers equally, and directly, in current English usage.

It should be added that when you translate from one language to another you do not simply translate *words*, disregarding their meaning in the cultural context in which they were written. You must translate the meaning the words had in their original context into an equivalent meaning in a different cultural context. This is what Beckett knew. And this is what the revisers of the New Revised Standard Version disclose when, for instance, they translate the Greek *adelphoi* as 'brothers and sisters', knowing full well that in its original context it meant only 'brothers'.

But I would like to go now specifically to what we have done with biblical language referring to God, where we have often found strong opposition—even, sometimes, bordering on the hysterical. What I have heard from people who have called in on radio talk shows reveals how angry some of them have become because their traditional English version of Scripture has been 'tampered with'. For many religious people, often unbeknownst to them, androcentric God-language serves to legitimize and intensify women's subordination, alienation and powerlessness. With the patriarchal hierarchy of man over woman, of husband over wife, of male clergy (still predominantly) in the church, and of male clergy still at the top of the hierarchy of clergy; with almost entirely male images and metaphors used in the church's Scriptures, prayers, liturgy and hymns; with a male Jesus Christ, and with a male God at the head of it all, patriarchy is sewed up and airtight. How is that patriarchal nut to be cracked? Did the *New Revised Standard Version* manage to do it? I think quite clearly, no. It did very well indeed, as I have twice acknowledged in long reviews, with language referring to human beings, but with language referring to God it did nothing. Which leaves us, still, with very little total progress, because it is the God language in the church that both discloses and reinforces patriarchy.

We are told by those who think that while the church can tolerate reading and hearing its Scripture in the contemporary inclusive idiom referring to human beings, the church cannot cross the line—I would say the absolutely decisive line—that allows Scripture to be heard as Word from other than a male God. Of course it is repeatedly said that such images and metaphors as 'Father' and 'King', as well as the masculine pronouns 'he,' 'his' and 'him' have no sexual connotation at all, and are, therefore completely compatible with the belief that God transcends sex, as the church has always held; but we are also told that such images and metaphors as 'Mother' and 'Queen', and the pronouns 'she' and 'her' are, on the contrary, sexual terms which, when used in the same contexts as their non-sexual counterparts, give them sexual connotations. I am completely unable to comprehend that logic. But I do know that there is in the church an enormous vested interest in assuring that no one seriously tamper with the perception that God, the ultimate Reality, the One Who Is, is the great Protector and Preserver of Patriarchy.

The bottom line is that we can be as inclusive of *each other* as our language will allow, but it remains the case that if we are permitted to perceive *God* only through male metaphors and on male analogies, nothing will have changed.

The assumptions we make about ourselves and the assumptions we make about God all fit into and are determined by the patriarchal construct we have all inherited. This means that if we are to be inclusive in our language about ourselves, and renounce androcentric language with reference to human beings, we must oppose the construct of patriarchalism, and all androcentric language that derives from it, not only in reference to human beings, but also in reference to God, for it is our theology that ultimately legitimates our practice, and thus it is our God-language that validates our language about each other. Our practice and our intentions are grounded in our assumptions about God. God and I never disagree fundamentally about anything!

The reason for the changes that are made in translations of the Bible in every generation is that the biblical books are canon in the church. The new inclusive version has been prepared for the *church*. Between 1900 and 1982, 159 different translations of the whole Bible or large parts of it were published in English. Why so many? Because in the church the Bible is read so that a Word from God may be heard and appropriated. But the church has not believed that it is a *male* God who addresses men and women, but a God who transcends sex, and may be perceived and heard as readily and as naturally by women as by men, by people of color as well as white people, and in fact by all kinds of human beings, equally.

I have been asked on call-in radio shows why I have not tried to bring Shakespeare up to gender snuff. The answer is simple: Shakespeare is not canon. But believing communities, Jewish and Christian, require that their Bibles be made available in their current idiom. The inclusive New Testament and Psalms grew out of, among other things, a pastoral concern.

In the Introduction to the New English Bible, prepared by a committee chaired by the great New Testament scholar, C.H. Dodd, and first published in 1961, we read the following statement: 'We have conceived our task to be that of understanding the original as precisely as we could... and then saying again *in our own native* idiom what we believed the author to be saying in his' (p. ix, italics mine; 'his' an acceptable pronoun in this context in 1961). Our committee has done, once again, that very same thing. Our work is but one small segment, in a long trajectory of versions, that seeks to allow the Bible to address believers in their current language. We believe that in our own day, we have said in inclusive idiom, in a new and different context and culture, what the biblical authors were saying in theirs. In any case, this is what we attempted to do.

WAS IT REALLY RAPE IN GENESIS 34?
BIBLICAL SCHOLARSHIP AS A REFLECTION
OF CULTURAL ASSUMPTIONS

Susanne Scholz

In recent years biblical scholars have begun to examine critically the impact of the Bible on Western culture. For example, J. Cheryl Exum states that 'perhaps no other document has been so instrumental as the Bible in shaping Western culture and influencing ideas about the place of women and about the relationship of the sexes'.[1] Vincent L. Wimbush maintains that the Bible has 'profoundly affected the imagination of Western culture'.[2] A group of scholars calling themselves 'The Bible and Culture Collective' argue that 'the Bible has exerted more cultural influence on the West than any other single document'.[3] These and other scholars claim that the Bible has shaped culture and vice versa.

This growing demand to investigate the Bible as 'cultural heritage'[4] has already led to numerous publications with varied subject matters and methodological approaches. Some studies examine biblical interpretations of different historical and social perspectives to demonstrate the interpretative diversity available.[5] Others juxtapose biblical themes

1. J. Cheryl Exum, 'Feminist Criticism: Whose Interests Are Being Served?', in Gale A. Yee (ed.), *Judges and Method: New Approaches in Biblical Studies* (Minneapolis: Fortress Press, 1995), pp. 65-90 (66).

2. Vincent L. Wimbush, 'Biblical-Historical Study as Liberation: Toward an Afro-Christian Hermeneutic', *Journal of Religious Thought* 42.2 (Fall–Winter 1985–86), pp. 9-21 (15).

3. The Bible and Culture Collective, *The Postmodern Bible* (New Haven: Yale University Press, 1995), p. 1.

4. Wim Beuken and Sean Freyne (eds.), *The Bible as Cultural Heritage* (Concilium, 1; Maryknoll, NY: Orbis Books, 1995).

5. Theophus H. Smith, *Conjuring Culture: Biblical Formations of Black America* (New York: Oxford University Press, 1994); Brian K. Blount, *Cultural*

and characters with cultural sources, such as film, art, literature and music.[6] Several works analyze how different communities located within and without the United States interpret the Bible.[7] *The New Interpreter's Bible* acknowledges the emergence of biblical cultural studies. The first volume includes several introductory essays that describe reading strategies of Bible readers from marginalized social locations. The essays discuss particularly the approaches of women, African Americans, Hispanics and Native Americans.[8]

The analysis of readers has thus become crucial in biblical cultural studies. Fernando F. Segovia stresses this methodological turn when he writes, 'This new development posits...a very different construct, the flesh-and-blood reader: always positioned and interested; socially and historically conditioned and unable to transcend such conditions...It is a development that I would describe in terms of "cultural studies"—a joint critical study of texts and readers, perspectives and ideologies...'[9] Rejecting objective, value-free and universally valid reconstructions of the biblical past, cultural critics assume that no one reads from the vantage point of neutrality or impartiality. Thus George Aichele and Gary A. Phillips maintain that 'meaning can no longer be thought of as an objective relation between text and extratextual reality, but instead it arises from the subjective, or ideological, juxtaposing of text with text *on behalf of* specific readers in specific historical/material situations'.[10]

Interpretation: Reorienting New Testament Criticism (Minneapolis: Fortress Press, 1995); Stephen Breck Reid, *Listening In: A Multicultural Reading of the Psalms* (Nashville: Abingdon Press, 1997).

    6.   Bernard Brandon Scott, *Hollywood Dreams and Biblical Stories* (Minneapolis: Fortress Press, 1994); J. Cheryl Exum, *Plotted, Shot, and Painted: Cultural Representations of Biblical Women* (JSOTSup, 215; Sheffield: Sheffield Academic Press, 1996); Alice Bach, *Women, Seduction, and Betrayal in Biblical Narrative* (Cambridge: Cambridge University Press, 1997).

    7.   Fernando F. Segovia and Mary Ann Tolbert (eds.), *Reading from This Place*. I. *Social Location and Biblical Interpretation in the United States*. II. *Social Location and Biblical Interpretation in Global Perspective* (Minneapolis: Fortress Press, 1995); Bible and Culture Collective, *Postmodern Bible*.

    8.   *The New Interpreter's Bible: A Commentary in Twelve Volume*, I (Nashville: Abingdon Press, 1994), pp. 150-87.

    9.   Fernando F. Segovia, '"And They Began to Speak in Other Tongues": Competing Modes of Discourse in Contemporary Biblical Criticism', in Segovia and Tolbert (eds.), *Reading from This Place*, I, pp. 28-29.

    10.   George Aichele and Gary A. Phillips, 'Introduction: Exegesis, Eisegesis, Intergesis', *Semeia* 69.70 (1995), pp. 7-18 (15).

And so 'readers become as important as texts'[11] in the investigation of the relationship between the Bible and culture.

The methodological implications of this development are significant. Whereas earlier interpretative paradigms, such as historical criticism, assumed a neutral and disinterested reader who put aside her or his presuppositions during the process of the interpretation, biblical cultural criticism posits that interpretation is always perspectival. A cultural critic acknowledges assumptions and, in fact, constructs the interpretation accordingly. This understanding of the interpretive process has consequences for the meaning of exegesis. Segovia claims that 'all exegesis is ultimately *eisegesis*'.[12] A statement of Edward L. Greenstein stresses a similar point, 'To engage in Biblical Criticism means we must exercise our beliefs'.[13] Also Exum explains, 'To think that interpretations can be neutral or objective would be to assume that meaning resides in the text. My position…is that meaning resides in the interaction between reader and text'.[14] Hence, biblical cultural critics uncover and examine the various interests and positions of the readers and discuss the findings in relation to the broader culture.

Biblical cultural studies offers the opportunity to understand the contribution of biblical scholarship to culture and, indeed, to the world. Focusing on the readers and their interpretations, cultural critics describe how interpreters use biblical texts to support cultural, political, economic and societal developments. Different critics emphasize different aspects in this critical work. For Segovia, biblical cultural criticism begins a process of liberation and decolonization. For Brian K. Blount, culturally diverse readings of selected biblical texts show that the final, definitive interpretation of a text will always be unattainable. For Exum, the various 'cultural afterlives' of women pose the question whether contemporary readers can avoid the gender bias present in biblical texts and in the history of interpretations. For Alice Bach, biblical cultural studies give women analytical guidance to extricate themselves

---

11. Segovia, 'Other Tongues', p. 32.

12. Fernando F. Segovia, 'Cultural Studies and Contemporary Biblical Criticism: Ideological Criticism as Mode of Discourse', in Segovia and Tolbert (eds.), *Reading from this Place*, II, p. 16.

13. Edward L. Greenstein, 'Theory and Argument in Biblical Criticism', in *idem, Essays on Biblical Method and Translation* (BJS, 92; Atlanta: Scholars Press, 1989), p. 68.

14. Exum, *Plotted*, p. 90.

from 'the androcentric logic of the roots of Western culture'.[15]

Biblical cultural studies are not restricted to the historical examination of biblical texts or to the literary study of the text itself. Rather, they seek an interdisciplinary conversation with other academic and non-academic discourses. They encourage a critical analysis of biblical scholarship in light of contemporary concerns. And they challenge contemporary 'flesh-and-blood' readers to consider the ethical consequences of their interpretations.[16]

Rape and the Case of Genesis 34

Since biblical cultural criticism regards all interpretative approaches as constructs of 'real readers', the examination of these constructs identifies the views and agendas of the readers. Such an examination works particularly well in the case of Genesis 34, the story about the rape of Dinah. Containing a complex account, the chapter provokes scholars to state clearly their views on rape. Therefore, the interpretations of Genesis 34 show whether biblical scholars accept or criticize those views. They exemplify the connection between biblical scholarship and contemporary assumptions about rape.

Only a relatively limited number of interpretations exist because Genesis 34 is not a popular story among critical interpreters.[17] One reason might relate to the literary position of the chapter. Placed within the Jacob cycle (Gen. 25.19–35.22), Genesis 34 is often classified as an independent later source difficult to date within Israelite history. Although the existing interpretations are often short, they contain excellent information about assumptions concerning rape in biblical scholarship.

15. Segovia, 'Cultural Studies', p. 16; Blount, *Cultural Interpretation*, p. 184; Exum, *Plotted*, p. 9; Bach, *Women*, p. 1.

16. Pamela J. Milne, 'Toward Feminist Companionship: The Future of Feminist Biblical Studies and Feminism', in Athalya Brenner and Carole Fontaine (eds.), *Reading the Bible: Approaches, Methods and Strategies* (Sheffield: Sheffield Academic Press, 1997), pp. 39-60 (55-56).

17. Note that major feminist biblical publications do not interpret the chapter in detail, e.g. Phyllis Trible, *Texts of Terror* (Philadelphia: Fortress Press, 1984); Letty M. Russell (ed.), *Feminist Interpretation of the Bible* (Philadelphia: Westminster Press, 1985); Katheryn Pfisterer Darr, *Far More Precious than Jewels: Perspectives on Biblical Women* (Louisville, KY: Westminster/John Knox Press, 1991); J. Cheryl Exum, *Fragmented Women: Feminist (Sub)Versions of Biblical Narratives* (Valley Forge, PA: Trinity Press, 1993).

The story in Genesis 34 is as follows: Dinah, the daughter of Leah and Jacob, is raped by Shechem, the prince of the land, when she goes to visit women in her neighborhood. Lusting after her, Shechem abducts Dinah and asks his father, Hamor, to assist him with his plan to marry her. In the meantime Dinah's father, Jacob, and her brothers hear about the rape. The brothers react strongly. When Shechem and Hamor negotiate the marriage, the brothers request that all the Canaanite males in the town be circumcised. While the male Shechemites lie in pain after the circumcision, Dinah's brothers attack the city and kill all the males, including Shechem and Hamor; they then abduct the women and children of the city. When Jacob hears about these actions, he condemns his sons. They ask in return if their sister should be treated like a prostitute. With that question the story ends.

The summary demonstrates that this narrative includes complicating factors, such as the revenge of Dinah's brothers. The following examination does not highlight these factors, but concentrates instead on the rape. Often this focus evokes fear and fury. Rape victim-survivors and their supporters are reminded of the enormous injustice and powerlessness they have experienced. Others want to resolve the emotions by emphasizing the complications of the story. The focus on rape, however, confronts the extent of rape-supportive scholarship and culture. Such a confrontation is certainly not easy.

The present article assumes a feminist value system 'to demonstrate more transparently the importance of our [feminist biblical scholars'] contributions to the goals of the feminist movement'.[18] Since the 1970s feminist scholars have researched the problem of rape.[19] They explored it from the perspective of the victim-survivor, traced the history of the contemporary rape prevalence, and argues that numerous strata of society contribute to the high statistics. Grounded in feminist assumptions, this article demonstrates that prevailing interpretations of Genesis 34 support what some feminists have called the contemporary 'rape culture'.[20]

18. Milne, 'Feminist Companionship', p. 60.

19. For an analysis of the feminist work on rape, see Susanne Scholz, 'Rape Plots: A Feminist Cultural Study on Genesis 34' (PhD Dissertation, Union Theological Seminary, New York, 1997), pp. 75-104. For an abbreviated version of this analysis, cf. Suzanne Scholz, 'Through Whose Eyes? A "Right" Reading of Genesis 34', in A. Brenner (ed.), *Genesis* (The Feminist Companion to the Bible, 2nd series, 1; Sheffield: Sheffield Academic Press, 1998), pp. 150-71.

20. For an elaboration of this concept see Emilie Buchwald, Pamela R. Fletcher

Obfuscating Rape: Contemporary Interpretations of Genesis 34

Scholars employ various arguments to interpret the rape in Genesis 34. Four are particularly significant. One refers to a textual argument, another to historical considerations, the next to source critical observations and the last to an anthropological comparison. They are all based on standard scholarly methodologies.

Was it Love? A Textual Argument

Already the beginning verses of Genesis 34 present a challenge for many readers.[21] Did Shechem fall in love with Dinah (v. 3) after he raped her (v. 2)? Was 'it' not rape because he loved her? Contemporary Bible versions translate only hesitantly that Shechem raped Dinah. For example, the NRSV reads v. 2b, 'He seized her and lay with her by force'. The REB presents the same verse slightly modified, 'He took her, lay with her, and violated her'. The new JPS *Tanakh* translation states that he 'took her and lay with her by force'. Showing some hesitancy in v. 2, many translations accept v. 3 as a straightforward reference to love. The NRSV states, 'And his soul was drawn to Dinah daughter of Jacob: he loved the girl, and spoke tenderly to her'. The REB insists: 'But Shechem was deeply attached to Jacob's daughter Dinah; he loved the girl and sought to win her affection'. The new JPS *Tanakh* translation concedes: 'Being strongly drawn to Dinah daughter of Jacob, and in love with the maiden, he spoke to maiden tenderly.' These translations exemplify that contemporary Bible committees emphasize the description of love in v. 3 after an initial moment of force, violence, or even rape in v. 2.

Contemporary scholars support this decision. Terence E. Fretheim reasons that 'many-faceted love' overrules the rape, so that 'this turn of events shifts the reader's response to Shechem in more positive directions'.[22] Indeed, 'Shechem proceeds to act in a way *atypical* of rapists: He clings to Dinah...loves her...and speaks to her heart...The latter phrase *may* cause Dinah's positive response' [stress added].

and Martha Roth (eds.), *Transforming a Rape Culture* (Minneapolis: Milkweed, 1993).

21. For a complete discussion of interpretations from 1970 to 1996, cf. Scholz, 'Rape Plots', pp. 105-47.

22. Terence E. Fretheim, *The Book of Genesis: Introduction, Commentary, and Reflections* (Nashville: Abingdon Press, 1994), pp. 574-81.

Furthermore, Shechem 'seek(s) to make things right'. He offers gener-
ously to marry Dinah although 'such generosity was certainly not necessary'. The marriage proposal suggests to Fretheim that 'Shechem's
offer was in Dinah's best interests' within the legal tradition of ancient
Israel.

While Fretheim stresses Shechem's love and generosity, he describes
Dinah's brothers as suspicious characters and finally unacceptable:
'They use religion as a vehicle for their deception'. A reference to Gen.
49.5-7 supports this negative view about Dinah's brothers. Fretheim
claims that the 'sharp and unambiguous judgment (indeed, a curse!) by
Jacob on the violence of Simeon and Levi must stand as the primary
clue about how we should interpret this chapter (Gen. 49.5-7)'. For this
scholar the violence of the brothers and not the rape constitutes the
interpretative key. He recommends to follow Jacob's model and to
reject the brothers because they use 'their sister's predicament as an
excuse to perpetrate violence'. They kill the 'rapist and lover of Dinah'.
Rejecting the brothers, Fretheim underlines Shechem's good intention,
the love and generous marriage offer. Shechem turns into an 'atypical
rapist'.

Sharon Pace Jeansonne also highlights v. 3. Interested in the
'relevance of the women within the ancestral history of Israel', she asks
where the reader's 'sentiments' should lie when Genesis 34 ends. She
finds in the narrative 'unresolved ambiguities'. For example, she asks
whether Shechem was 'sincere in his professed love'[23] and concludes
that 'Shechem truly loved Dinah after the assault'. For Jeansonne, love
demonstrates the 'many aspects of this crime and its repercussions' in a
story characterized by ambiguities.

George W. Coats offers a concise interpretation that also stresses the
significance of v. 3.[24] He announces that the problem arises when
'Shechem rapes Dinah but also loves her' and wants 'to convert the
strained relationship into a permanent one' [stress added]. The brothers, however, oppose Shechem's 'folly'. The story is, therefore, a story
about the men: the brothers, 'principally Simeon and Levi', and
Shechem along with his father Hamor. Acting violently, the brothers

23. Sharon Pace Jeansonne, *The Women of Genesis: From Sarah to Potiphar's
Wife* (Minneapolis: Fortress Press, 1990), pp. 87-97.
24. George W. Coats, *Genesis with an Introduction to Narrative Literature*
(The Forms of the Old Testament Literature, 1; ed. Rolf Knierim and Gene Tucker;
Grand Rapids: Eerdmans, 1983), p. 234.

plunder the city which 'leads to complications in the relationship between Israel and Shechem'. And so the 'simple plot [is] focused not on the rape of Dinah by Shechem, but on the rape of Shechem by the brothers of Dinah'. Hence Coats entitles his interpretation as 'Rape of Shechem'. The rapist becomes the raped one and the rape of Dinah becomes an act of love. Coats transforms the biblical narrative substantially.

Once in Ancient Israel: Historical Considerations
Some scholars refer to the historical circumstances in ancient Israel to explain Genesis 34.[25] Danna Nolan Fewell and David Gunn claim that Shechem acts appropriately within the 'narrow limits of [Israelite] society'.[26] He offers marriage which would give Dinah a respected status. Therefore, 'if sympathy is being accumulated, it seems to us to be sympathy for Shechem'. Fewell and Gunn characterize their reading as feminist because they do not identify Dinah as 'a helpless girl to be rescued' but as 'a young woman who could have made her own choices—limited though they might have been—had she been asked'. Although both scholars acknowledge that 'to advocate a woman's marrying her rapist might itself seem to be dangerous and androcentric advocacy', they argue that 'the story world' offers no 'other liberating alternatives'.[27]

25. The historical argument is problematic for three reasons. First, scholars have questioned the historical reliability of the Hebrew Bible as a source for reconstructing ancient Israel's history, e.g. Philip R. Davies, *In Search of 'Ancient Israel'* (Sheffield: JSOT Press, 1992); and Keith Whitelam, *The Invention of Ancient Israel: The Silencing of Palestinian History* (London: Routledge, 1996). Secondly, a detailed and extensive treatment on the issue of rape does not exist for ancient Israel, so that scholarly explanations remain selective and incomplete. Thirdly, the date and the literary location of this narrative within the Jacob cycle (Gen. 25.19–35.22) are very much disputed. Many scholars believe that Gen. 34 was added to the Jacob cycle, e.g. Eduard Nielsen, *Shechem: A Tradition-Historical Investigation* (Copenhagen: Gad, 1955); for an examination of Gen. 34 within the Jacob cycle, see Peter L. Lockwood, 'Jacob's Other Twin: Reading the Rape of Dinah in Context', *Lutheran Theological Journal* 29 (1995), pp. 98-105; cf. also Walter Brueggemann, *Genesis: A Bible Commentary for Teaching and Preaching* (Atlanta: John Knox Press, 1982), p. 274: 'Historically, we can say little about the narrative.'
26. Danna Nolan Fewell and David M. Gunn, 'Tipping the Balance: Sternberg's Reader and the Rape of Dinah', *JBL* 110.2 (1991), pp. 193-211.
27. For a critique of their view, see Meir Sternberg, 'Biblical Poetics and

Irmtraud Fischer likewise considers the marriage proposal an exon-
erating factor in ancient Israel. Subordinating the narrative to laws in
Exod. 22.15-16 and Deut. 22.23-27, she argues that Shechem tries at
least to restore the legal requirements after the rape. Thus Shechem
does not 'brutally' use his power against the other tribe. He has intercourse with Dinah before marrying her; this is the problem of Genesis
34.

> By raping, he [Shechem] disregards law and custom and especially the
> personal integrity of the woman. However, the young man tries to
> restore them by officially negotiating a marriage and by accepting all
> conditions.[28]

For Fischer, the narrator does not consider rape the problem of Genesis
34. Rather, the narrative exemplifies the fact that marriage negotiations
of the family of Sarah and Abraham are often deceptive. When foreign
men approach the women of this family, the foreigners and not the
'patriarchs' are endangered.

Gerhard von Rad also uses a historical approach. He proposes that
Genesis 34 be read as a reflection of ancient Israelite tribal history:

> The narrative seems to go back to the time when Israelite tribes were not
> yet settled in Palestine but on their way thither in search of new pas-
> tures...By some catastrophe they were pushed out of the territory around
> Shechem and other tribes could settle there later. The essential intention
> of the narrative in its final form is to present this prehistorical conflict of
> Simeon and Levi. But like many sagas it has changed the political
> proceedings into a conflict of fewer single persons and accordingly illus-
> trated it on the level of the personal and universally human.[29]

Reconstructing tribal history, von Rad regards the characters as per-
sonifications of the different tribes and groups in Canaan. Rape
becomes an unspecified 'catastrophe'. The particular features disappear
for the sake of larger historical considerations.

Sometimes reference to ancient Near Eastern texts places Genesis 34

Sexual Politics: From Reading to Counterreading', *JBL* 111.3 (1992), pp. 463-88;
Paul Noble, '"Balanced" Reading of the Rape of Dinah: Some Exegetical and
Methodological Observations', *BibInt* 4 (1996), pp. 173-204.

28. Irmtraud Fischer, *Die Erzeltern Israels: Feministische-theologische Studien
zu Genesis 12-36* (Berlin: W. de Gruyter, 1994), p. 233. All translations are mine
unless indicated otherwise.

29. Gerhard von Rad, *Genesis: A Commentary* (London: SCM Press, 3rd rev.
edn, 1972), p. 335.

into a historical framework. Nicholas Wyatt compares the biblical story with such texts and classifies it as a relic of an archetypal marriage rite similar to 'the basic plot of premarital love present in Ugaritic and Akkadian texts'.[30] To fit the comparison, Wyatt must change the vocabulary of Gen. 34.2. He proposes to switch the stem of '*nh* from the piel to the qal, so that the verb translates as 'to make love'. This suggestion enables Wyatt to maintain that 'the essence of the affair between Shechem and Dinah turns out to be substantially that of the other ancient Near Eastern form'. Changed into a premarital love story, Genesis 34 remains, however, unique in one aspect. The account includes the 'untimely death of one of the partners'. And so Wyatt claims that this narrative 'is hardly a tale of love requited and brought to fruition: it is *au contraire* a tale that ends in tragedy'. Subordinating the biblical account to ancient Near Eastern texts, Wyatt reconstructs a story about a sacred marriage ritual. Unfortunately, in this version the bridegroom dies.

An Original Love Story: Source-Critical Observations
Source criticism provides another avenue to discuss the rape. Dividing Genesis 34 into two literary sources, scholars differentiate between an early love story and a later edition. The original love story does not include the rape.

Ita Sheres reads Genesis 34 'in its unredacted, reconstructed state'.[31] This original form of the story does not contain the rape 'since structurally and linguistically it is difficult to accept his [Shechem's] "rape" of Dinah'. Sheres hypothesizes that in the original story the heroine Dinah goes out to seek a husband, finds him in Shechem, and becomes his legitimate wife. Based on the original story, the final edition contains the elements that portray Shechem sympathetically. And so Sheres claims that 'Shechem is the only person in the tale sympathetic to Dinah'. He is depicted as 'a man in love'.

> If one is to find male compassion in the story, one has to turn to Shechem, 'the stranger', who after the rape falls in love with Dinah and realizes that he must 'console the girl' before proceeding with official, ritualized courtship. Excluding all the other difficulties that this peculiar

30. Nicholas Wyatt, 'The Story of Dinah and Shechem', *Ugarit-Forschungen* 22 (1990), pp. 433-58.
31. Ita Sheres, *Dinah's Rebellion: A Biblical Parable for our Time* (New York: Crossroad, 1990). This and the following quotes are from pp. 3-18 and 105-37.

> order of events suggests, it is fair to observe (as the text *unambiguously*
> does) that the only man sympathetic to Dinah is Shechem, the presumed
> villain of the piece. In fact, it can be easily argued that Shechem's
> attitude is not only the *most human* but also the *most credible*: how else
> could he have expected to live with Dinah, whom he had raped, as his
> wife?

Sheres considers Shechem as the 'most human' and the 'most credible' character.[32] The editors attempt to change this view of the original story. They 'put the final stamp on the portrait of Dinah as well as on those of all the other men and women in the text; and the specific manner in which Dinah appears in the text is due mainly to their ideological convictions', Sheres argues. Adding the rape and the 'bloody confrontation' between the Shechemites and the two Israelite tribes, the redactors place the blame on Dinah because 'she undertook the forbidden [by the redactors] act of "going out to see the women of the land".' According to Sheres's reconstruction, rape becomes a consequence of 'her [Dinah's] *unthoughtful* behavior and [is] an *instant* punishment for disobeying the rules spelled out by the men of the tribe'.[33]

Erhard Blum posits two sources. The original source emphasizes the innocence of Shechem and 'the unreasonableness of the revenge of Simeon and Levi'. This source promotes a 'pro-Shechemite position' which the later editor changes. In the earlier version, according to Blum, 'the narrator does not tire of stressing the sincerity of Shechem's courtship for Dinah: v. 3 in the account of the narrator: his love for Dinah; v. 4: his intention to pay any bride price; v. 19 an interjection: Shechem's devotion to fulfill the condition'. Hence Blum insists: 'It is beyond question that *after* his deed Shechem meets his duty in every respect. After all he desires to marry Dinah and he even agrees to pay an excessive bride price.'[34] For Blum, the original narrator denounces clearly the brothers by juxtaposing Shechem's love to the fraternal vengeance. Only a later Judaic secondary tradition softens the image of the brothers. Similar to other source critics, Blum construes an original love story that questions the proportion of the fraternal revenge to Shechem's 'passion'.

32. Judith S. Antonelli calls Sheres' characterization of Shechem 'as the good guy' 'a strange twist of logic', cf. her book *In the Image of God: A Feminist Commentary on the Torah* (Northval, NJ: Jason Aronson, 1995), p. 94.

33. Sheres, *Dinah's Rebellion*, pp. 8 and 17 (emphasis added).

34. Erhard Blum, *Die Komposition der Vätergeschichte* (Neukirchen–Vluyn: Neukirchener Verlag, 1984), pp. 210-29.

Seeking 'to reconstruct the original source', Yair Zakovitch articulates how source criticism explains Genesis 34. He observes: 'The sequence of actions at the beginning of the story is difficult: Shechem lay with the girl and ravished her (v. 2), and only afterward became infatuated with her and sought to persuade her (v. 3).'[35] The original story presented 'Shechem's innocent attraction to Dinah and Jacob's sons' treacherous exploitation of the situation in order to plunder the city'. It did not contain 'the rape element', claims Zakovitch. Because of the anachronism in v. 7, the awkward syntax regarding the 'defiling of Dinah' in vv. 13 and 27 and the 'real tension over which of the brothers attacked the city of Shechem' in vv. 25-31, later editors added vv. 2b, 5, 7ab, 13a, 13b, 17, 25a, 25b, 27, 30 and 31. Editors also assimilated the original story to two biblical texts: the story of the rape of Tamar (2 Sam. 13) and Jacob's curse of his two sons (Gen. 49:5-7). The assimilation of Genesis 34 to these texts results in a contrived story in which the rape explains the fraternal violence.

Insider versus Outsider: An Anthropological Comparison

Some scholars use an anthropological argument. They maintain that fear of the Canaanite neighbors motivates a narrative which struggles between integration and exclusion. Lyn M. Bechtel proposes such an interpretation. She suggests that Genesis 34 reflects the dispute within Israel. As a group-oriented society Israel was divided as to whether to interact with non-Israelites and to cross tribal boundaries or not.[36] The characters represent the different positions. Personified by Dinah and Jacob, one faction wants to interact with outsiders; personified by the brothers, 'the militant folks', the other faction, votes for separation and group 'purity'. The writers of Genesis 34 oppose the excluding position, Bechtel believes: 'The story seems to be challenging this attitude [of the brothers] by showing the potential danger in which it places the group.'

Bechtel explains that in a group-oriented society like ancient Israel individuals lived and worked to serve the good of the group. In such a society the differentiation between 'us' and 'them' was essential.

---

35. The quotes are from Yair Zakovitch, 'Assimilation in Biblical Narratives', in Jeffrey H. Tigay (ed.), *Empirical Models for Biblical Criticism* (Philadelphia: University of Pennsylvania Press, 1985), pp. 175-93.

36. Lyn M. Bechtel, 'What If Dinah Is Not Raped? (Genesis 34)', *JSOT* 62 (June 1994), pp. 19-36. The following quotations are from this essay.

'Closely knit' boundaries had to be maintained. The activities of individuals strengthened the boundaries. Marriage was a group affair and sexual intercourse perpetuated the values of the family and clan. Sexual intercourse became shameful when it lacked family or community bonding. Dinah and Shechem, however, are 'two unbonded people' when they have 'intercourse'. The question is therefore not whether rape occurred but whether the 'sexual intercourse' between Dinah and Shechem was shameful.

Referring to texts like Deut. 22.23-29, Bechtel maintains that Shechem does not threaten the social bonding of the community. He tries to win the approval from the other group. He proposes marriage and offers many goods. This behavior indicates to Bechtel that the intercourse between Dinah and Shechem is not shameful. Bechtel claims, 'The text stresses that these are honorable men [Shechem and his father Hamor]' and that 'the overall action of Shechem...is one of honor'. And so she concludes: 'Throughout the text there is no indication that Dinah is raped. The description of Shechem's behavior and attitude does not fit that of a rapist...All of this diminishes the likelihood that rape was seen to have occurred.'

Excusing Shechem, Bechtel considers the brothers as the villains. Stuck in an exclusionary group-oriented behavior that threatens to destroy the whole group, the brothers retreat to unjustifiable vengeance. Similar to scholars who use other hermeneutical approaches, Bechtel explains: 'Ironically, if there is a rape in this story, it is Simeon and Levi who "rape" the Shechemites'.[37] Again, the killing turns to rape and the rape into acceptable sexual intercourse.

Walter Brueggemann similarly promotes Genesis 34 as a discussion on xenophobia. For him, the theme is 'Israelite accommodation to non-Israelites in the land...a much disputed issue in Israel'.[38] And so 'the liaison of Dinah and Shechem' refers to the interaction between Canaanites and Israelites which Brueggemann considers to be the result of a 'seduction'. Israel, however, considers 'intermarriage' as 'perversion'. Therefore, 'the report on Shechem is obviously given from a polemical Israelite perspective'. Judging the brothers, Brueggemann

---

37. For a detailed criticism of Bechtel's reading, see my dissertation 'Rape Plots', pp. 127-30; see also the brief critique of Harold C. Washington, 'Violence and the Construction of Gender in the Hebrew Bible: A New Historicist Approach', *BibInt* 5.4 (1997), pp. 324-63 (357).

38. Brueggemann, *Genesis*, pp. 274-80.

states that 'this narrative evidences the unsophisticated and irrational response of a passion unencumbered by reflection'. The brothers are not interested in 'accommodation, cooperation, or even ratification'. Vengeance dominates them. 'Fixed on the narrow sexual issue', they are 'blind to the larger economic issues, blind to the dangers they have created, blind to the possibilities of cooperation, and blind even to the ways they have compromised their own religion in their thirst for vengeance and gain'. Understandably for Brueggemann, Jacob despairs over his sons. The father's attempt to achieve a 'more pragmatic settlement' with Shechem makes more sense to Brueggemann than the fraternal response. And so he regrets that even Jacob could not prevail against the 'more sectarian and destructive settlement' of his sons.

Ethical Responsibilities for the Interpretation of Genesis 34 from a Feminist Perspective

'It is…important to avoid complicity with the rape cultures, ancient and contemporary, that would have us deny that the crime is violent or blame the victims of sexual assault,' Harold C. Washington demands recently.[39] The previous examination, however, demonstrates that interpretations of Genesis 34 contain numerous assumptions complicit with a contemporary belittlement of rape. Scholars suggest that the rapist 'really' loved Dinah. They find rape less harmful in ancient Israel. They maintain that in ancient Israel a marriage could redeem the rape, that the story reflects a tribal conflict with Canaanite neighbors or that similar to other ancient Near Eastern texts Genesis 34 narrates a sacred marriage ritual. Further, interpreters identify an original love story and relegate the rape to a later edition. They explain the events with the dynamics of group-oriented societies in which sexual intercourse is only problematic when it threatens the community.

Biblical cultural critics propose that 'real readers' are always located, interested, and socially and historically conditioned. As such, their interpretations reflect cultural assumptions of their time. If this suggestion is correct, interpretations of Genesis 34 mirror a culture that minimizes rape, sympathizes with a rapist and blames victim-survivors. Although feminists have worked to change these perceptions for over 25 years, interpretations of Genesis 34 continue to perpetrate androcentric views. Unfortunately, scholars do not investigate their assumptions

39. Washington, 'Violence', p. 359.

critically, even when they call their readings feminist. Supporting the marriage proposal of Shechem, they do not criticize the rapist or his deed.

The interpretations and the critique of this article reflect a division in contemporary society. A majority undervalues the injustice perpetrated by rape and considers other factors as more important. A minority, the feminist view, sides with raped victim-survivors and stresses the evil of rape. This split appears most clearly when rape occurs in complex circumstances like those in Genesis 34. Recently a similarly complex story occurred in Peru.[40] On 12 March 1997 the *New York Times* reported:

> Lima, Peru. Late one night more than three months ago, a group of drunken men in their 20s raped a 17-year old girl who was on her way home from work in the crime-ridden Villa El Salvador district of Lima. After the young woman told her family about the assault, her father and brother tracked down the three rapists, who lived in their neighborhood. Her father wanted to kill them, said the young woman, who told her story on condition that she be identified only by her first name, Maria Elena. Her brother wanted to beat them. She wanted to press charges. But when one of the rapists offered to marry her, her family put pressure on her to accept, and she finally yielded after being threatened by the men who had raped her.[41]

As in Genesis 34, a young woman is raped and the rapist offered to marry her. Whereas the brothers of Dinah rejected the marriage proposal, the family of Maria Elena pressured her to accept. The penal codes of Peru and 14 other Latin American countries exonerate a rapist if he offers to marry the raped victim-survivor and she accepts. Some penal codes exonerate the rapist even if the raped victim-survivor rejects the offer. The newspaper quoted Peruvians saying that 'marriage is the right and proper thing to do after a rape' because 'a raped woman is a used item. No one wants her.'

Peruvian women's rights groups are outraged about the legal situation in their country. They are fighting for the removal of the law because it is degrading to women and legally unsound. The president of

---

40. I chose this example because the story is similar to Gen. 34. Numerous national rape stories within the United States are reported regularly, see, e.g., *New York Times*, 14 August 1996; 21 May 1997; 10 June 1997; 17 September 1997; 26 February 1998.

41. 'Justice in Peru: Victim Gets Rapist for a Husband', *New York Times* (12 March 1997), pp. A1, A12.

the congressional committee on women and Harvard-trained lawyer, Beatriz Merino Lucero comments:

> To believe in 1997 that it is intelligent and moral for a rapist to marry his victim as a mechanism for pardon shows me that some of my colleagues in Congress don't fundamentally understand what rape is. If we know that rape is the worst act of violence against a woman, that it attacks her most intimate sense of security and places her in a situation of disadvantage, how can we assume that a woman in this state can have a life with the person who abused her?[42]

The example from Peru demonstrates the contemporary division on the issue of rape. Feminists and their organizations define rape as 'the worst act of violence against a woman'. Others believe that rape devalues the victim-survivor. The previous analysis demonstrates that biblical scholars have participated in this debate, siding with the non-feminist view.

Only a few exceptions exist, such as the interpretation of Alice A. Keefe. Her reading focuses on the rape in Genesis 34 considering it as 'a way of speaking of its [Israel's] struggle to retain a distinctive and separate cultural identity'.[43] The rape 'serves as an expression of Israel's vulnerability to being dominated, taken over and absorbed by the other peoples, particularly by urban Canaanite culture'. Keefe regards Dinah as a metaphoric character through whom Israel imagined itself as a violated woman. Rape was a literary element necessary for Israelite authors to imagine a future of wholeness. Although an understanding of rape as a 'metaphor' for Israel's vulnerability is problematic, Keefe acknowledges the rape as the central event in Genesis 34. Most interpretations, however, do not. They also ignore the 'flesh-and-blood' consequences of their interpretations. One scholar expresses his concern about this lack. Responding to Fewell and Gunn who support the marriage between Dinah and Shechem, Meir Sternberg exclaims: 'Tell it not to rapists, publish it not in the streets' because 'some would call it [their interpretation] a license to rape.'[44]

If, then, interpretations, 'no matter how rational, systematic, and scientific',[45] connect to the cultural assumptions of their day, what are the

42. *New York Times*, 'Justice', p. A12.
43. Alice A. Keefe, 'Rape of Women/Wars of Men', *Semeia* 61 (1993), pp. 79-97 (94).
44. Meir Sternberg, 'Biblical Poetics', pp. 476, 474.
45. Aichele and Phillips, 'Introduction', p. 15.

ethical responsibilities for interpreting Genesis 34? Certainly progres-
sive Bible readers cannot afford to read this narrative and disregard the
prevalence of rape in contemporary society. If biblical cultural critics
observe correctly that the Bible shapes culture and culture shapes the
Bible, interpreters cannot reinterpret, minimize or ignore the rape of
Dinah. They have to take the rape seriously and express their clear dis-
approval of the rapist. At stake are the ethics of biblical studies in a
culture that has often used the Bible to support injustice and discrimination. Biblical cultural studies challenge such usage and offer opportunity to read the Bible in an ethically responsible way.

JEREMIAH AS FEMALE IMPERSONATOR:
ROLES OF DIFFERENCE IN GENDER PERCEPTION
AND GENDER PERCEPTIVITY

Angela Bauer

Discourse on impersonation, gender bending, gender boundaries and gender performativity in feminist and queer theory has revolved around constructions of *desire*.[1] While such perspectives may yield intriguing readings of all kinds of texts, including biblical ones, I am interested here in addressing gender boundaries and their crossings in the Bible, pondering *identification*(s) of/by gender in terms of perception and perceptivity. Rather than with *object choice*, I am concerned with the choice of *subject*. What causes a reader to hear 'female' or 'male' voices in a text? What clues do the gender identifications of the implied author(s) and the implied reader(s) suggest for the gendering of voices?[2] What does the construction of difference(s) of/by the reader contribute to the analytic process of reading/listening/hearing?

To attempt some answers to these questions I shall look at a couple of instances in the book of Jeremiah where the male prophet speaks in what some (including myself) have identified as a female voice.

Jeremiah 4.19-21

The poem Jer. 4.19-21 introduces the reader(s) of the book of Jeremiah

1.   See, e.g., Judith Butler, *Gender Trouble: Feminism and the Subversion of Identity* (New York: Routledge, 1990); *Bodies that Matter: On the Discursive Limits of 'Sex'* (New York: Routledge, 1993); Marjorie Garber, *Vested Interests: Cross-Dressing and Cultural Anxiety* (New York: Routledge, 1992); Eve Kosofsky Sedgwick, *Epistemology of the Closet* (Berkeley: University of California Press, 1990).
2.   For methodological considerations, see Athalya Brenner and Fokkelien van Dijk-Hemmes, *On Gendering Texts: Female and Male Voices in the Hebrew Bible* (Leiden: E.J. Brill, 1993).

to the image of woman in labor. In first-person speech the prophet laments:

19 מעי מעי אחולה [אוחילה]
קירות לבי
המה־לי לבי
לא אחריש
כי קול שופר שמעתי [שמעת] נפשי
תרועת מלחמה:
20 שבר על־שבר נקרא

כי שדדה כל־הארץ
פתאם שדדו אהלי
רגע יריעתי:
21 עד־מתי אראה־נס
אשמעה קול שופר: ס

19 My-belly! My-belly! I-writhe-in-labor![3]
Walls of-my-heart![4]
In-uproar-is for-me my-heart.
Not can-I-keep-silent.
For the-sound of-the-trumpet I-hear[5] with-my-whole-being,
the-signal of-war.
20 'Shattering upon shattering!' is-shouted.[6]
For devastated-is all the-earth,
suddenly devastated-are my-tents,[7]
in-a-moment[8] my-curtains.
21 How long must-I-see the-signal,[9]
must-I-hear the-sound of-the-trumpet? (4.19-21)

3. Reading with LXX and Vulg. the *kethib*, חול cohortative, 'I writhe in labor', rather than the *qere*, יחל hiphil, 'let me wait'.
4. LXX reads αἰσθητήρια, 'feelings'. Holladay proposes 'with hesitation' as an emendation, reading הֲקֵירוֹתָ, 'you are chilled', to match verbal structure; see William L. Holladay, *Jeremiah 1* (Hermeneia; Philadelphia: Fortress Press, 1986), p. 142. The necessity of this move, however, eludes me.
5. Reading with the *kethib*; the *qere* has 2 fem. sg.
6. LXX and Vulg. read קרא I, 'to call' (also Rudolph, Holladay, McKane *et al.*); Pesh. and Targ. read קרא II, 'to meet' (also Duhm, Volz, Bright, Carroll *et al.*).
7. LXX and Pesh. read sg. for MT pl.
8. LXX reads διεσπάσθησαν, 'are torn'.
9. LXX reads φεύγοντας, 'fugitives'; similarly Vulg. and Pesh.

Speaking with the voice of a woman in travail, the prophet identifies with Jerusalem. Jeremiah in labor pain takes on a female persona.[10] The signs and sounds of destruction elicit an intensity of feeling that is embodied in the labor pangs of a woman. The prophet in first-person speech (אחולה) cries in an agony unique to the female. *My belly! My belly! I writhe in labor! Walls of my heart! In uproar is for me my heart. Not can I keep silent. For the sound of the trumpet I hear with my whole being, the signal of war.* The people (earlier identified as 'Daughter My People') and the prophet Jeremiah have merged to cry out in light of impending devastation.

A chiastic structure encloses this devastation at its center (4.20). *'Shattering upon shattering!' is shouted. For devastated is all the earth, suddenly devastated are my tents, in a moment my curtains.* The rhetorical structure surrounds the destruction with signals of war (תרועת מלחמה [4.19]; and נס [4.21]), and frames it by the sound of the trumpet (קול שופר [4.19]; קול שופר [4.21]). Repetitions of words and sounds punctuate this outcry: שבר שבר (4.20); שדדו שדדה (4.20); as the entire lament mirrors such intensity: מעי מעי (4.19); לבי לבי (4.19). Lamenting in first-person speech, the prophet impersonated as a woman in travail embodies the pain caused by the devastation.

Standard Bible translations veil the gendered voice of the lament ascribing generic pain to 'anguish' (NRSV, RSV, NIV) or 'suffering' (JPS). Commentators are divided about the identity of the speaker of the lament. Duhm, Rudolph, Bright, Thompson, Berridge, Holladay and Brueggemann read 4.19-21 as Jeremiah's speech.[11] Yet they do not acknowledge the female character of the prophet's voice here. By contrast, Volz and Carroll identify the speaker as the land and the city

10. Cf. Barbara Bakke Kaiser, 'Poet as "Female Impersonator": The Image of Daughter Zion as Speaker in Biblical Poems of Suffering', *JR* 67 (1987), pp. 164-82; esp. pp. 166-68 and pp. 172-73.

11. Bernhard Duhm, *Das Buch Jeremia* (KHCAT, 11; Tübingen: J.C.B. Mohr, 1901), pp. 52-53; Wilhelm Rudolph, *Jeremia* (HAT, 1.12; Tübingen: J.C.B. Mohr, 3rd edn, 1968), p. 33; John Bright, *Jeremiah* (AB, 21; Garden City, NY: Doubleday, 1965), p. 34; John A. Thompson, *The Book of Jeremiah* (NICOT; Grand Rapids: Eerdmans, 1980), pp. 227-28; John McLean Berridge, *Prophet, People, and the Word of Yahweh* (BST, 4; Zürich: EVZ, 1970), p. 169; Holladay, *Jeremiah 1*, pp. 160-63; Walter Brueggemann, *To Pluck Up, to Tear Down: A Commentary on the Book of Jeremiah 1–25* (ITC; Grand Rapids: Eerdmans, 1988), pp. 54-55.

Jerusalem, thus taking different account of the female imagery.[12] Polk, who carefully argues for Jeremiah as the speaker,[13] admits to the possibility of hearing the resonance of Jerusalem's voice in the voice of the prophet, thus blending the personae of prophet and city.[14] It is Barbara Bakke Kaiser, however, who to my knowledge is the first to identify the phenomenon of Jeremiah lamenting in a female voice in this passage as impersonation.[15] It is to her that I owe the title of this paper. She observes that labor pain, an agony unique to the female, characterizes the prophet's state when lamenting in light of the impending destruction.

Within the book of Jeremiah, crisis has urged identification. At the point of impending destruction, the male prophet chooses to identify with the people as female. Does the destruction of national boundaries find a mirror in the breaking down of gender boundaries? Are gender boundaries 'destroyed'—if only for a moment—with the impending destruction of the city? Or is the conflation of land, city and female voice of the prophet yet another instance of how the female body functions as a metonym for the social body as it is disrupted in war?[16]

What makes me read this text as a female voice? While I maintain an understanding of gender as performative and thus socially constructed, and conversely, as socially constructed and thus performative, I need to acknowledge the paradox that the gendering of the voice in Jer. 4.19-21 as female is dependent on the biological bases of gender identification. We can be sure that in the Ancient Near East, or more specifically in Judah in the late seventh century and early sixth century BCE, constructions of gender were different from constructions of gender in the late twentieth century CE in the US and in Europe, or more specifically for me in the urban centers of the US north-east coast and in the western part of Germany today. This banal observation has rather complex ramifications for our topic. As all reading is in part projection, what are the particularities of our gender identifications that we project onto the

12. Paul Volz, *Der Prophet Jeremia* (KAT; Leipzig: A. Deichert, 1922), p. 56; Robert P. Carroll, *Jeremiah: A Commentary* (OTL; Philadelphia: Westminster Press, 1986), p. 167.

13. Timothy Polk, *The Prophetic Persona: Jeremiah and the Language of the Self* (JSOTSup, 32); Sheffield: JSOT Press, 1984), pp. 45-53.

14. Polk, *Prophetic Persona*, p. 69.

15. Cf. n. 10 above. For another instance, see the reading of Jer. 20.7 below.

16. Cf. Alice Keefe, 'Rapes of Women/Wars of Men', *Semeia* 61 (1993), pp. 79-97.

texts we read? How is our gendering and/or de-gendering of ancient texts grounded in gender perception(s) shaped by contemporary constructions of gender?

The image of a woman in labor pain traverses any of these differences of gender perception and gender perceptivity—childbirth then and now is ascribed to female gender identifications. It would, however, most probably not be without my specific location as a gendered reader, which has allowed me to participate in the discourses on gender in the les/bi/gay/transgender communities in Hamburg, New York and now Boston, that I identify Jeremiah as female impersonator.

Jeremiah 20.7

Another passage in the book of Jeremiah that suggests to me such an identification of the prophet as female impersonator is Jer. 20.7. There in the last of Jeremiah's 'confessions' (20.7-13 [18]), the prophet again takes on a female persona. Jeremiah describes encountering the deity as an experience of rape.

7 פתיתני יהוה ואפת
חזקתני ותוכל
הייתי לשחוק כל־היום
כלה לעג לי:

7   You-seduced-me, YHWH,   and-I-was-seduced;
    you-raped-me/overpowered-me,   and-you-prevailed.
    I-have-become a-laughingstock the whole day,
    all-of-it mocks me (20.7).

The prophet addresses the deity and relates an experience of sexual violation. The expressions פתיתני, 'you seduced me', and חזקתני, 'you raped me/overpowered me', embody a forceful accusation. The root פתה in the piel carries sexual innuendo.[17] The word describes the seducing of a virgin in Exod. 22.15. It refers to YHWH's seductive activity in Hos. 2.16. It is also used in Judg. 14.15 and 16.5 for what the daughter of the Philistines and later Delilah are asked to do to Samson—in a reversal of sorts. A related root is employed for YHWH's action of raping the daughters of Zion in Isa. 3.17. Violence is its context also in other instances (e.g. Prov. 16.29; 1 Kgs 22.20-22).

17. Cf. M. Sæbø, 'Art. פתה *pth* verleitbar sein', *THAT*, II, cols. 495-98; esp. 497.

The parallel חזק in the hiphil underscores this meaning of seduction and rape. Conveying sexual violence, it is used in Deut. 22.25 to describe the forcing of a woman to have intercourse. In 2 Sam. 13.11, 14 it describes the rape of Tamar. Thus, the vocabulary invites a reading of Jer. 20.7 as the prophet's experience of sexual violence at the hands of the deity. Jeremiah identifying as female accuses YHWH of seduction and rape. The prophet's pain is further compounded by the laughter and mocking of the people.

Scholars have been divided over the interpretation of this verse. Prior to Heschel's reading that proposes seduction and rape to capture Jeremiah's relationship to God in 20.7,[18] commentators such as Hitzig, Duhm, Baumgartner, Volz and Rudolph find the language of enticement at best peculiar.[19] Since Heschel, there have been those who repudiate sexual connotations as unlikely, though possible. Clines and Gunn argue for persuasion rather than enticement as an alternative interpretation, thereby reducing the passage to a rhetorical conflict.[20] While Polk joins Clines and Gunn in understanding פתה piel as 'persuaded', Lewin finds 'a sense of ambiguity' in translating 'entice'.[21] Carroll considers an image of sexual violation 'too grotesque' though possible.[22] Likewise Diamond, O'Connor and Smith note that seduction is a possible meaning, but deem such an interpretation unlikely.[23]

---

18. See Abraham J. Heschel, *The Prophets* (2 vols.; New York: Harper & Row, 1962), I, pp. 113-14.

19. Cf., e.g., Ferdinand Hitzig, *Der Prophet Jeremia* (KEHAT, 3; Leipzig: S. Hirzel, 1866), p. 152; Duhm, *Jeremia*, p. 164; Walter Baumgartner, *Die Klagegedichte des Jeremia* (BZAW, 32; Giessen: A. Töpelmann, 1917), pp. 63-64; Volz, *Der Prophet Jeremia*, pp. 206-207; Rudolph, *Jeremia*, pp. 130-31.

20. David J.A. Clines and David M. Gunn, ' "You Tried to Persuade Me" and "Violence! Outrage!" in Jeremiah XX 7-8', *VT* 28 (1978), pp. 20-27 esp. p. 21.

21. Polk, *Prophetic Persona*, p. 161; Ellen Davis Lewin, 'Arguing for Authority: A Rhetorical Study of Jeremiah 1.4-19 and 20.7-18', *JSOT* 32 (1985), pp. 105-19 esp. p. 113.

22. Carroll, *Jeremiah*, pp. 398-99.

23. A.R. Diamond, *The Confessions of Jeremiah in Context* (JSOTSup, 45; Sheffield: JSOT Press, 1987), p. 110; Kathleen O'Connor modifies her assessment claiming that poets choose words for their connotations thus allowing for an inclusion of sexual nuances; Kathleen M. O'Connor, *The Confessions of Jeremiah: Their Interpretation and Role in Chapters 1–25* (SBLDS, 94; Atlanta: Scholars Press, 1988), pp. 70-71; see also Mark S. Smith, *The Laments of Jeremiah and Their Contexts: A Literary and Redactional Study of Jeremiah 11–20* (SBLMS, 42;

Other scholars, however, continue to explore the language of seduction and sexual violence. Berridge cites Exod. 22.15 as 'evidence that פתה is legal vocabulary for seduction', and points to Deut. 22.25 as an instance for 'the use of חזק (Hiphil) to indicate the forcing of a woman'. He concludes 'that v. 7a employs the language of seduction and violation'.[24] With this understanding Fishbane, Thompson, Crenshaw, Holladay, McKane and Brueggemann agree.[25] They acknowledge that this verse characterizes an experience of Jeremiah as being seduced and raped by the deity. Some of these scholars have also begun to wrestle with the theological implications of such a reading. For instance, Heschel ponders the complexity of the divine–human relationship;[26] Berridge observes that YHWH here violates God's Torah.[27] Recalling the marriage metaphor, Thompson suggests marital violence.[28] Holladay admits that such language of sexual violence by the deity 'raises grave theological issues' without identifying and/or exploring them further.[29]

As for the book, Jeremiah continues to wrestle with the vocation that has made this prophet the outcast and enemy of the people. He/she agonizes over his/her identification with his/her people and his/her relationship with God (who is gendered both male and female, depending on the particular encounter).

In regard to gender identification, to be sure, rape per se does not imply a female voice. It is the constructions of sexual violence within the book of Jeremiah as well as in the Bible at large and beyond, that suggest a male-female gender dualism here. The use of the husband-wife metaphor in Jeremiah, Hosea and Ezekiel is but one instance of this dynamic of gender hierarchy which assumes gender identification

Atlanta: Scholars Press, 1990), p. 24.

24. Berridge, *Prophet, People, and the Word of Yahweh*, pp. 151-55.

25. Michael Fishbane, 'Jeremiah 20.7-12/Loneliness and Anguish', in *Text and Texture* (New York: Schocken Books, 1979), p. 94; Thompson, *The Book of Jeremiah*, p. 459; James L. Crenshaw, 'Seduction and Rape: The Confessions of Jeremiah', in *A Whirlpool of Torment* (OBT, 12; Philadelphia: Fortress Press, 1984), pp. 38-39; Holladay, *Jeremiah 1*, pp. 552-53; William McKane, *Jeremiah* (2 vols.; ICC; Edinburgh: T. & T. Clark, 1986–96), I, p. 470; Brueggemann, *To Pluck Up, To Tear Down*, p. 174.

26. Heschel, *The Prophets*, p. 114.

27. Berridge, *Prophet, People, and the Word of Yahweh*, p. 154.

28. Thompson, *The Book of Jeremiah*, p. 459.

29. Holladay, *Jeremiah 1*, pp. 552-53.

of the superior as male and the inferior as female. Other instances of porno-prophetics both in the book of Jeremiah (e.g. Jer. 2.20-25, 33-34; 3.1-5; 4.30-31; 13.20-27; *et al.*) and in other prophetic literature (e.g. Isa. 3.16-24; 47.1-3; Ezek. 16.35-42; 23.9-10, 22-35; Hos. 2.4-5, 11-12; Nah. 3.5-6; *et al.*) support this reading.[30] Further, the experiential insights of living as a woman in a sexist and homophobic society today strongly suggest to me such identification of gendered voices.[31]

The sound of a female voice in Jer. 4.19-21 and Jer. 20.7 lets the prophet appear as a female impersonator. Significantly, the two female experiences with which the gender-bending Jeremiah identifies are both women's boundary experiences between life and death: childbirth and sexual violence. Jeremiah laments as a woman in labor (Jer. 4.19-21), experiencing the pain of a mother giving birth. Then, the prophet describes his encounter with YHWH as an experience of rape (Jer. 20.7).

The metaphors of childbirth and of sexual violence against women are the female images most frequently used elsewhere in the book of Jeremiah.[32] Both experiences of labor pain and rape, when they refer to the people as female, imply judgment. Woman's pain in childbirth (e.g. Jer. 4.30-31; 13.21; 22.20-23; cf. 30.6) and her suffering of sexual vio-lence (e.g. Jer. 2.20-25, 33-34; 3.1-5; 4.30-31; 13.20-27; 15.8-9; 22.20-

---

30. For recent feminist interpretations, see Athalya Brenner, 'On Prophetic Propaganda and the Politics of "Love": The Case of Jeremiah', in Athalya Brenner (ed.), *A Feminist Companion to the Latter Prophets* (The Feminist Companion to the Bible, 8; Sheffield: Sheffield Academic Press, 1995, pp. 256-74; 'On "Jeremiah" and the Poetics of (Prophetic?) Pornography', in Brenner and van Dijk-Hemmes, *On Gendering Texts*, pp. 178-93; 'Pornoprophetics Revisited: Some Additional Reflections', *JSOT* 70 (1996), pp. 63-86; J. Cheryl Exum, 'Prophetic Pornography', in *Plotted, Shot, and Painted: Cultural Representations of Biblical Women* (Gender, Culture, Theory, 3; Sheffield: Sheffield Academic Press, 1996), pp. 101-28; Pamela Gordon and Harold C. Washington, 'Rape as a Military Metaphor in the Hebrew Bible', in Brenner (ed.), *A Feminist Companion to the Latter Prophets*, pp. 308-25; F. Rachel Magdalene, 'Ancient Near Eastern Treaty Curses and the Ultimate Texts of Terror: A Study of Divine Sexual Abuse in the Prophetic Corpus', in Brenner (ed.), *Feminist Companion to the Latter Prophets*, pp. 326-52.

31. The experiential insights of living as a white person in a racist society raise further questions as to the complex connections between gender and race, which need to be addressed elsewhere.

32. See Angela Bauer, *Gender in the Book of Jeremiah: A Feminist-Literary Reading* (Studies in Biblical Literature, 5; New York: Peter Lang, forthcoming).

23) function to characterize the people's fate of destruction and exile. In contrast to the prophet, the people's experiences as female are reduced to the death-threatening part: they focus on the pain of child-bearing without giving birth (4.31; 13.21; 22.23), and sexual violation as 'deserved punishment'. It is, however, at this point of irreversible judgment that the prophet's identification with the people as female stops. Note that it is the form of lament/confession rather than judgment oracles that provides the context for the female impersonator. Jeremiah has the option to move beyond the lament for which he uses a female voice toward implicit acceptance of his vocation as prophet through his actions.

So what to make of this chorus of female and male voices of the presumably male prophet? For this reader three observations surface. One, as for the gender identification of the prophet, the images of the prophet as mother in labor pain and as rape victim mirror the liminality of women's realities. On one hand, the prophet's taking on a female persona constitutes a subversion of gender dualisms. It does not conform to gender attributions and expectations, neither in the seventh/sixth century BCE nor today. Thus Jeremiah as female impersonator destabilizes the status quo. Yet, on the other hand, the male prophet's female persona reinforces female gender stereotypes. The emphasis on and thus validation of gendered boundary experiences of childbirth and sexual violence does not allow space for nor value women's experiences in all their particularities and differences. The male prophet has the choice of dis-identification from his female persona. Jeremiah can decide to cease acting as a female impersonator. In that, the performative character of gender plays into the stabilization of the status quo of gender dynamics of domination and submission.

Two, my own gender constructions and performances have provided the foil for this reading of Jeremiah. As for the implied male reader as well as for the actual readers with gender identifications different from my own, I can only speculate and/or listen/be attentive to the differences and nuances of their readings.

Three, the fluidity of constructed and performative gender identity allows for construing gender-fluid texts in reading Jeremiah, in reading the Bible, in reading ourselves and society. The next task may be to explore how the reading of trans/gendered texts and the gendering of texts are related to the construction of (de-gendered) gender justice and the trans/gendering of justice.

A FEMINIST HERMENEUTIC OF 1 CORINTHIANS

Luise Schottroff

Introduction

This essay on 1 Corinthians is related to my work on the recently published *Kompendium Feministische Bibelauslegung* (Compendium of
Feminist Interpretations of the Bible), a volume, nearly 1000 pages in
length, of feminist commentary on the Bible and some extra-biblical
texts within the German context (Schottroff and Wacker 1998). More
than 50 authors contributed to this project, which was inspired by two
North American works: *The Woman's Bible Commentary* (Newsom
and Ringe 1992) and *Searching the Scriptures* (Schüssler Fiorenza
1994).

In my task of reflecting on a feminist hermeneutics of the Pauline
letters, and especially 1 Corinthians, I am particularly indebted to the
fundamental work of Antoinette Clark Wire. Her interest is in reconstructing the history and theology of the Corinthian women prophets by
means of a critical analysis of Pauline rhetoric. For an understanding of
the Jewish context of Pauline *halakhah* the work of Peter Tomson has
offered me some valuable aids, despite its failure to offer a critical
analysis of the relationship between the sexes.

In the development of a specifically feminist hermeneutics of 1
Corinthians, I believe there are four crucial questions:

1. What concept am I using to describe the relationship between
    the writer of the letter and the community? How is it founded
    on the texts and the method I am using?
2. How are my views regarding Pauline expressions of opinion
    on the position of women within creation and society related
    to Christian anti-Semitism?
3. What concepts of sexuality and asceticism am I using?
4. How do I deal with the Pauline self-contradiction between a

liberating gospel and Paul's teachings that are oppressive to women?

Here I will treat Question 1 at length and add some briefer remarks on Questions 2, 3 and 4.

Question 1

The traditional concept of Christian exegesis regarding Paul's relationship to the Christian communities of his own time can best be understood in terms of the understanding of the apostolic office. I will make an ideal distinction between two types of interpretations and illustrate them from the recent history of interpretation in Germany. Rudolf Bultmann understood the apostolic office (according to Paul's ideas, with which he implicitly identifies) as the highest office (with appeal to 1 Cor. 12.28; see Bultmann 1954: 157). Those who have the office of apostle have the right to distinguish between true faith and error in the communities they have founded. They thus claim and exercise a teaching authority and also have the authority to care for order within their communities (Bultmann 1954: 452, with reference to Paul).

Ernst Käsemann, in contrast, sees Christian communities as democratically organized. All the members of the community are laity, and as such they are priests and have office. The apostle is not fundamentally different from others, but is merely the outstanding representative of the universal priesthood (Käsemann 1964: 248). Only gradually and in contradiction to this democratic community organization did hierarchies emerge in early Christianity ('early Catholicism'). According to Käsemann, when Paul seeks order in the communities and puts a stop to the enthusiasts' activities he does not do so on the basis of a special office, but as an exercise of the universal priesthood. In spite of the contrast in these two interpretations of the apostolic office the following presumptions are a matter of course for both authors: the apostle is a systematic theologian, a figure with whom the interpreter (and the Protestant pastor) can identify, a male who, with respect to his opponents, is always right.

Antoinette Wire has reversed the traditional concepts of the relationship between Paul and the community. Her goal is to acknowledge Pauline rhetoric as an instrument of domination, 'to expose the text where it is an instrument of oppression' (Wire 1994: 159). Paul appears as a speaker and writer whose intention is to persuade by rhetorical means and to cause his opinion to prevail against both that of his competitors and of the community itself. In contrast, the community, and in particular the women prophets within it, have a correct relationship among themselves, 'not competitive but communal'. Antoinette Wire does not read Paul any longer with the presupposition that he is always right (Wire 1990: 10): when his rhetoric is analyzed he becomes subject to criticism as unpersuasive, oppressive, competition-oriented and even power-hungry. By contrast, the 'opponents', that is, the groups within the community that oppose him, appear as bearers of divine wisdom and prophecy who through their faith are already experiencing joy and resurrection. Paul, since he himself has suffered a loss of status because of his Christian faith, demands of others, and women in particular, that they also practice self-denial, abstinence, humility and delay of resurrection until after death (instead of experiencing resurrection during their lifetime).

I would like to propose another model alongside these and consider their common connections as well as their differences. My starting point is the socio-historical question: How do I understand the early Christian communities in their internal social structure and their immersion in society? I view Jewish communities in the Diaspora as comparable structures; they were at this time to be found throughout the Roman Empire. The Christian communities were constructed analogously to these Jewish communities. During the first century CE both the Christian and Jewish communities experienced social and political persecution because they were regarded as politically dangerous (especially because of their messianism). On the one hand, their conscious and deliberate choice of a lifestyle according to Torah (which I also see as true of Christian communities) was attractive to people from the Gentile nations, but, on the other hand, people who lived in this way, whether Christian or Jewish, were plagued by powerful social authorities in the cities; they were denounced and frequently prosecuted or driven out.

The internal structure of the Christian communities can be discerned from a number of mutually confirming statements they make about themselves. These people understand their relationship as that of sisters and brothers with the same father and mother: namely God. Their familial relationship is to remain deliberately free of dominance and differs in this way from the socially prescribed patriarchal family and the larger society (see Mk 10.42-45 par.). Paul attempts to describe the structure of relations that should be present in all types of relationships as 'agape', which excludes a hierarchy of charismata (1 Cor. 13).

Christian attempts to establish a structure of relationships free of dominance were often possible only at the price of conflicts; sometimes they did not succeed. Paul seems not to have been the only one who saw God's world as the end of all relations of domination (1 Cor. 15.28), but at the same time regarded the domination of men over women as a natural law, the unchangeable expression of the creative will of God (1 Cor. 11.2-16). I read the internal structure of the community as an unperfected experiment with dominance-free structures, but not as a perfect early Christian world.

In attempting to understand Paul's relationship to the communities I cannot begin with a model that positions him as a unique figure, for example as one exercising an exalted office in relationship to the community. Then—and this is how it goes in traditional interpretations— Paul would be a special case, the bearer of an office for which there was no analogy at this early period (but only in the later hierarchy of bishops from the middle of the second century onwards). Although the traditional exegesis speaks of 'apostles' in the plural, the thought is always of Paul and his uniquely prominent role. I must, however, posit that the Pauline letters are expressions of the opinion of a member of a community. They are not, either in their own claims or in the expectations of other members of the community, anything more than the expressions of opinion by other members of the community. The list in 1 Cor. 12.28 is simply that: a list, not an order of merit. In this thesis, which rests on the non-hierarchical structure of the gifts of the Spirit, I am supported by the observations of Peter Tomson, who has located Pauline expressions of opinion, in terms of their content, within rabbinic *halakhic* discussion (Tomson 1990). That is, Paul sees himself as a teacher of Torah, someone whose opinions on practical questions do not stand alone and who is not in possession of special authority. Every other teacher of Torah (male or female) may possibly represent a different opinion with the same authority. His positions on the questions of circumcision or whether women are the image of God (on this see Boyarin 1995) are undoubtedly extreme positions within Jewish discussions in his time, but they have their *Sitz im Leben* in those discussions.

It was only through Western systematic-theological hermeneutics that awareness of the *halakhic* structure of Pauline letters and their Jewish *Sitz im Leben* was lost. And it was only through the later

establishment of hierarchical church offices that Pauline authority
became an authority with absolute claims, and that the image of Paul
and 'his opponents' arose. The idea that Paul was always right did not
exist either in his own head or in those of his addressees, as he certainly
must have known. He fights, he argues, he employs rhetorical tools
most certainly in awareness of the limited nature of his authority.

Hence I understand the Pauline letters as capturing certain moments
within a multivocal process of discussion about the interpretation of
Torah in one's own life. And I read the Pauline letters in large part as
collective documents in which the voices of many women and men
from the communities can also be heard. For example, Paul did not
invent all the images of hope that he employs; he delivers to us the language of hope that was the source of life for many Jewish and Christian
people of his time.

In this portrayal of the relationship between Paul and the communities I am in continuity with Wire's image of the women prophets in
Corinth, but not with her picture of Paul. Antoinette Wire's Paul is the
Paul of traditional exegesis: a churchman with claims to authority and a
message that is often oppressive. I agree in part with Ernst Käsemann's
picture of Paul, with his image of the priesthood of all believers in early
Christianity, but not with his picture of the 'opponents' of Paul and
certainly not with his antithesis between Law and Gospel. In terms of
such a concept of the relationship between Paul and the communities it
is a feminist task not only to seek the history of women, but also to read
the Pauline texts anew and in a different way from that of traditional
exegesis. In this task the international discussion of Paul is only at its
beginning.

Question 2

The association of the subject of women with anti-Semitism in traditional and feminist interpretations of Paul has been given model analyses by Marlene Crüsemann and Daniel Boyarin. The structure of anti-
Jewish discussion is such that rabbinic Judaism is regarded as a
monolithic block of teaching and scriptural interpretation that is
oppressive to women. Pauline texts are then either exculpated because
of their Jewish background (as a Jew, Paul did not know any better) or
formally justified as pro-Jewish (feminist attempts to locate the liberation of women in early Christianity are unserious scholarship because

Paul thought like a Jew). Or else 1 Cor. 14.34-35 is disqualified as Jewish and non-Pauline, and Paul and early Christianity, in contrast, are justified as pro-woman and un-Jewish. This is the model that, especially in the beginnings of German feminist exegesis, was all too readily adopted from traditional exegesis. In all these models of argumentation the authors work with a few quotations from the rabbinic writings, sometimes only one. No attention is paid to the context of the quotation (see Crüsemann 1996: 211). Sometimes a Jewish-rabbinic position is stated without any support (e.g. when Paul says that only the man is the image of God this is assumed to be a Jewish interpretation of Gen. 1.27: see Boyarin 1995: 4).

For this question nothing can help us but the study of rabbinic sources and the work done on them by Jewish scholars. To put it another way, we need a fundamental hermeneutics of suspicion regarding Christian assertions about (rabbinic) Judaism. It is indispensable at the same time to place early Christianity within the context of the Roman-Hellenistic world and the ancient church.

Question 3

Fundamental to a feminist hermeneutics of Paul is that the interpreters are aware of the significance of sexuality for Paul. The Christian tradition from which I come was anti-sexuality and considered the repression of sexuality a sign of successful Christian identity. This idea about Christian attitudes toward sexuality is transferred to Paul in traditional exegesis: Christian marriage is good and the norm for human social existence. Still better is sexual asceticism, although of course it represents a special and exceptional way. Nevertheless, it was the source of a negative view of sexuality. Even though marriage remains the model for society, the idea remains that it is not the place for sexual joy, but serves the purpose of controlling and restraining sexuality. Read in these terms, the women in Corinth who wanted to leave their marriages, to live their married lives without sex, or who, as betrothed women like Thecla desired to live as heroes of self-denial, appear to be rejecting sexuality as dirty and dangerous. Even when Christian virgins appear as autonomous women in feminist historical writing the negative Christian picture of sexuality is often retained. Through sexual ascesis the women acquire freedom from patriarchal marriage and its controls. What needs to be questioned, therefore, is the concept of sexuality with which I read this tradition. Undoubtedly we know very little about the sexual practices of women living outside of marriage; what we do know is the clearly positive theological evaluation of the body, including the female body. Here we may cite not only the preaching of Paul in the legends of the Acts of Thecla, but also the historical Paul: bodies are temples of God, the place of God's dwelling. The resurrection changes the body, but the people of the resurrection are bodies in their social and personal identity (1 Cor. 15). Against this background the traditional Christian negative concept of sexuality, whether it is welcomed or rejected, becomes shaky. Perhaps in a few more years we will know more about the early Christian history of affirmation of sexuality and joy in it as a God-given creative power.

Question 4

Ilse von Stach was a writer of the 1920s who is, unfortunately, little known today. She wrote a play entitled *The Women in Corinth*. In this play Elefteria appears as protagonist. With other women she celebrates a Spirit-filled worship service. A messenger arrives with a papyrus roll, the letter of Paul to the Corinthian community. He interrupts Elefteria's song of praise: 'Let the woman be silent in the assembly. Because of her lesser sex the woman should cover herself before God...' Elefteria breaks off the worship service. During the night she reads the whole of Paul's letter and passes through a shifting series of emotions. She reads, 'the lesser things of the world God has chosen' and hears it as a gospel for herself and all women. She reads, 'do you not know that you are the temple of God...(and) that God's Spirit dwells in your bodies?' and hears it as a word of liberation for her womanly body. Then comes the 'wanderer through time', a kind of personified hermeneutical suspicion, who asks, 'And are you, then, quite sure, woman, that this question about the Spirit of God applies to you, even to you?' The command to silence in 1 Cor. 14.34-35 throws her into confusion. She prays to Christ, 'You freed a person who could not speak. You said to his tongue: "*Ephphata*, be opened". Say "*ephphata*" to my tongue as well'.

We cannot resolve Paul's self-contradictions from a feminist perspective. He regards the oppression of women as God's will and natural law. He writes this manifesto of women's oppression in 1 Cor. 11.2-16 in the literary context of chapters in which he rejects hierarchies among the members of the body of Christ with a great many arguments (1 Cor.

12–14). We can only describe this self-contradiction and by no means dissolve it. Ilse von Stach overcomes the self-contradiction of Paul and those of Christianity only in a prayer to Christ. But in doing so she surpasses any fundamentalistic misunderstanding of the Scriptures. She leaves Paul behind when necessary and speaks directly to God. Her prayer has no less authority than the liberating tradition that is to be found in Paul as well: We have all received the same Spirit from God (1 Cor. 12.4-11).

BIBLIOGRAPHY

Boyarin, Daniel
    1995   'Paul, the Law, and Jewish Women', Conference paper, SBL Annual Meeting (Philadelphia, PA, 19 November).
Bultmann, Rudolph
    1954   *Theologie des Neuen Testaments* (Tübingen: J.C.B. Mohr).
Crüsemann, Marlene
    1996   'Unrettbar Frauenfeindlich: Der Kampf um das Wort von Frauen in 1 Kor 14, (33b)34-35 im Spiegel antijudaistischer Elemente der Auslegung', in Luise Schottroff and Marie-Theres Wacker (eds.), *Von der Wurzel getragen: Christlich-feministische Exegese in Auseinandersetzung mit Antijudaismus* (Leiden: E.J. Brill): 199-223.
Käsemann, Ernst
    1964   *Exegetische Versuche und Besinnungen 2* (Göttingen: Vandenhoeck & Ruprecht).
Newsom, Carol A., and Sharon H. Ringe (eds.)
    1992   *The Women's Bible Commentary* (Louisville, KY: Westminster/John Knox Press).
Schottroff, Luise, and Marie-Theres Wacker (eds.),
    1998   *Kompendium feministische Bibelauslegung* (Gütersloh: Chr. Kaiser Verlag).
Schüssler Fiorenza, Elisabeth (ed.)
    1994   *Searching the Scriptures 2: A Feminist Commentary* (New York: Crossroad).
Stach, Ilse von
    1928   Die Frauen von Korinth', *Hochland* 26 (2): 141-63.
Tomson, Peter J.
    1990   *Paul and the Jewish Law: Halakha in the Letters of the Apostle to the Gentiles* (Minneapolis: Fortress Press).
Wire, Antoinette Clark
    1990   *The Corinthian Women Prophets: A Reconstruction Through Paul's Rhetoric* (Minneapolis: Fortress Press).
    1994   '1 Corinthians', in Fiorenza 1994: 153-95.

III

INNOVATIONS:
EXPANDING THE BOUNDARIES OF BIBLICAL SCHOLARSHIP

THIS IS *MY* STORY, THIS IS *MY* SONG...:
A FEMINIST CLAIM ON SCRIPTURE, IDEOLOGY
AND INTERPRETATION

Margaret B. Adam

A few propositions:

> Texts don't have ideologies.
>
> The author's intention does not determine the text's meaning.
>
> A text's author, its historical social context or its interpretation to date do not determine the text's ideology.
>
> A text cannot oblige its interpreters to think in any particular way.
>
> The Bible does not contain patriarchal (or any other) ideology.

These are some of the provocative claims and suggestions made in SBL papers recently, expanding on and applying to biblical interpretation the earlier work of philosopher Jeffrey Stout[1] and other postmodern literary theorists. In 1992, Stephen Fowl addressed the Ideological Criticism Group with a paper entitled 'Texts Don't Have Ideologies', wherein he examines possibilities for richer interpretation when we move beyond the assumption that texts possess ideologies implanted by authors' intentions and contexts. A.K.M. Adam continued the discussion in 1994, in the Literary Aspects Group, with an explanation of why Matthew is not inherently anti-Semitic.[2] Reactions in the world of

---

1. Jeffrey Stout, 'What is the Meaning of a Text?' *New Literary History* 14 (1982) pp. 1-12.

2. Stephen Fowl's paper is now published in *BibInt* 3.1 (1995), pp. 15-33. A.K.M. Adam's paper, 'Matthew's Readers, Ideology, and Power', is published in the *SBL 1994 Seminar Papers*. (For related material, see also, S. Fowl, 'The Ethics of Interpretation, or What's Left Over after the Elimination of Meaning', in D.J.A. Clines, S.E. Fowl and S.E. Porter [eds.], *The Bible in Three Dimensions* [JSOTSup, 87; Sheffield: JSOT Press, 1990], pp. 379-98; A.K.M. Adam, 'Twisting to Destruction: A Memorandum on the Ethics of Interpretation', *Perspectives in*

biblical criticism to Fowl's and Adam's rather mild-mannered assertions range from irritated frustration to furious denial. Feminist and
conventional biblical interpreters alike seem wary of the texts-don't-
have-ideologies propositions.

One might be tempted to seize the moment and hail this shared dis-
content as a rallying point for feminist biblical interpreters[3] and those
who are still waiting for the fad of feminism to pass. One might. But let
us not.

Instead, I propose that the claim that texts are not determined by
ideology nor bound to ideology can be a powerful position for feminist
biblical theology. By positing that interpretation is ideologically *colored* by interpreters and their situations rather than ideologically
determined by the texts 'themselves', feminists can read Scripture
as our own. We can [re]name text as the site of revelation and practice, rather than as the container of meaning. And, we can claim all
of Scripture[4] as ours, without apology and without justification by

Religious Studies 23 [1996], pp. 215-22; and A.K.M. Adam, *What Is Postmodern
Biblical Criticism?* [Minneapolis: Fortress Press, 1995].) Both Fowl and Adam
offer clear, engaging and persuasive explanations of the texts-don't-have-ideologies
position and some ramifications for biblical interpretation. I am indebted to their
work thus far, and I hope in this essay to explore still further applications in feminist biblical interpretation.

    3.   I am not prepared here to offer a definitive definition of 'feminist biblical
interpretation' or even of 'feminist', but I am hoping that the reader can continue to
allow this signifier to do at least some of the work it might. As we begin to imagine
a post-patriarchal world, we are only just beginning to discover and name women
as subject. It is my hope that we are working toward a day when 'feminist' can be
more than a position of resistance, when categories of 'woman' and 'feminine/
feminist' are determined in an economy of power which names women as subject.
Meanwhile, for the purposes of this paper, I use 'feminist' as it is frequently used in
the field, with the request that we not move too hastily to exclude from its realm
women whose race, educational or economic bracket often keep them from participation in the discussion of what counts as feminist.

    4.   When I refer to Scripture, I am referring to that which is (however vari-
ously) canonically accepted to be Scripture. I am eager to encourage the exploration
of canonical boundaries and the appreciation of extra-canonical texts, recognizing
that the process of canonization itself has always been a practice of ideological
interpretation. In particular, I would recommend an understanding of 'non-canonical' texts (old and new) as *supplemental*, adding to and enhancing our readings of
canonical texts. However, I am also determined to claim my position as a part of
the church and in continuity with all those who have heard and told and retold our
scriptural story. To decline to accept the body of Scripture as a whole would be to

conventionally and patriarchally authorized historical method.

But what about the patriarchal nature of Scripture? If texts don't have ideology, if Scripture doesn't *have* patriarchy, then who is responsible for the patriarchal ideology we sense when we read and hear Scripture? Are we, as feminists, patriarchal ourselves just because we perceive Scripture that way? In a sense the answer is 'yes', since it would be hard for any functioning members of our (still patriarchal) society to read otherwise. This is how ideology works, not as an item which can be located *in* a text or anywhere else, but as a characteristic of relationships. Just as Foucault counters the notion that power is owned by some people and not by others, explaining that, instead, power is a function of relationships between people; and just as we know that gravity doesn't reside *in* objects but is a force that attracts; so, too, with ideology. Ideology doesn't live *in* some interpretations or arguments, and there are no ideology-free zones; ideology is an aspect of the relationships we have with each other and with scripture. Hence the patriarchy we sense in Scripture is a function of our participation in a world dominated by patriarchally colored relationships. *Of course* we will read and understand texts on the terms of the world we inhabit, and in the context of our expectations and practices. However, as we try to resist and problematize dominant ideologies, then our expectations and practices are in the process of changing. As we imagine relationships other than abusively oppressive ones, we try to live such relationships in our lives, and we will be able to read Scripture (and other texts) with such right relationships understood as possible.

This does not guarantee that if we try to be post-patriarchal, or at least to have problematized patriarchy, then we will be able immediately to read the Bible as free of patriarchal relationships. While an immensely wide range of interpretations is always possible, it does seem likely that the seminal text of a patriarchal people will appear patriarchal to those marginalized folks who identify the group as patriarchal. And, certainly, labelling presentations of stories as 'patriarchal' is one aspect of feminist interpretation. The problem is that that step, which may seem so liberating (freeing women from the oppression of the story by critiquing the story's and the story-tellers' ideologies), plays into the hands of patriarchal authority. It is a move which dumps responsibility for interpretation, and actions justified by such interpretations, on the text's ideology.

reinforce the otherness of my voice as a Christian claiming her texts.

But this is a sleight of hand designed to distract us, and it is a deceptive move. Texts, all by themselves, don't read, preach, teach, enlighten, indoctrinate, brainwash, incite, provoke, reform, inspire or repress. Neither do texts function as agents, *compelling* people to kill, discriminate, oppress, rape, nurture, clothe, embrace, build up or create anew. *People* interpret texts as justifications for these actions, according to their ideological contexts and practices. A text is not inextricably bound to one and only one interpretation, a point that the number of publications in the field of biblical studies amply illustrates. Our practices and our ideological baggage, which help to form our readings, are not set in stone either. The ideological ways we live, the ideological habits of how we go about our practices can change. Neither our actions, our interpretative practices nor the texts we interpret are equivalent to or bound by particular ideologies. Texts don't have ideologies. If we accept the premise that Scripture is to be equated with a particular, inappropriate, ideology then we hand over interpretative authority, readership, and voice to one group of interpreters and deny the rest of us any participation in the Word of God.

But, one might argue, people have used scriptural texts patriarchally so consistently and for so long; how can we make any sense of the Bible otherwise, and, if we could, who would pay attention? Don't eons of association between text and interpretation constitute a binding relationship between that text and its familiar ideological presentations?

Here it is important to note that recognizing patriarchal interpretation and presentation is different from accepting an essential patriarchal content. It is one thing to acknowledge a history of accepted ideological meaning; it is another to continue to accept that interpretation as the only one possible. We know all too well, for example, that texts don't *contain* humor. 'Jokes' are not necessarily jokes or even funny, simply because an author or reader asserts so. What makes a so-called joke funny is a combination of factors, including shared position, practices and perspective. The 'same' words can come across as very unfunny when the joker and the audience don't share enough presuppositions. People's emphatic reactions to 'jokes' are so varied as to point out the problematic: 'That's not funny, that's rude!' and 'How can you be offended, it was a joke!' are statements which can be and are often made about the same remark. Even something which might be generally recognized as a joke can also be recognized as very unfunny. Women workers in an office might recognize a sexist memo as an apparent joke that makes some of their male co-workers laugh, while at the same time these women can know that the 'joke' is not in the least funny to them, but offensive and demeaning. If the women object, their co-workers might typically respond, 'Lighten up, it's only a joke!' Such a response reflects the men's assumption that the 'joke's' allegedly humorous meaning is contained in the memo's text. These amused workers are not likely to recognize the determinative influence of their own interpretative position and practices.

In order to combat this form of sexual harassment in the workplace, the offended women would need to move away from a focus on the text in question (away from an attempt to determine whether or not it is 'really funny') to a focus on the practices of the male co-workers, whose laughter, manner and use of a text were offensive to the women workers. By shifting the discussion to questions of practices, the offended women can problematize 'textual' authority (which simply pits one interpretation against another), and claim their own authority as interpreters of text and practice.[5]

Likewise, as feminist biblical interpreters, we might be wise to attend to the practices and contexts that inform our understanding of Scripture. The social climate which helps determine how funny a joke sounds also helps determine the ideology of our interpretations. The basis on which we might oppose a patriarchal interpretation of Scripture is not one of accuracy, historical or otherwise. Similarly, the basis on which we propose an alternative interpretation is not that the Bible, *accurately understood*, contains the 'good stuff' which authorizes our (more sensible) interpretations and allows us to say, 'See! We are authorized by the text itself. It's right there *in* the Bible!' The 'good stuff'—the feminist, womanist, *mujerista*, liberationist, revivalist ideologies which empower us—is not *in* the Bible any more than patriarchy is; our ideologies are an aspect of how we know God, Scripture, and each other. The authority with which we interpret Scripture is the authority of our

---

5.   US Senator Jesse Helms's 1994 'joke' about President Clinton's likely reception at a military base in Fayetteville, NC, is a good example of how jokes can be understood. In an initial statement, Helms suggested that Clinton might need a bodyguard when he visited the NC troops, referring obliquely to the troops' presumed animosity toward their president. When it became clear that these words were taken as offensive and even threatening, Helms later claimed that the fault was with the press corps for not having accurately represented his remarks as humorous, meant as a joke. This clarification failed to appease those who were not amused.

own positions as women created in God's image, as recipients of and participants in God's creating Word.[6]

Scripture doesn't contain meaning distinct from our Spirit-visited engagement with interpretation and practice. How we read it, with whom, and what we do about it, are all essential factors in sense-making. Scripture is not a magic lamp which releases the genie-meaning when the hero (the certified biblical authority) rubs it right. Scripture is a place where we open ourselves to God. We come, as always, with all of our ideological habits; and God meets us, our ideologies, and the text, all jumbled up together.[7] The sense that we make of this crowded meeting is what we call 'interpreting Scripture', our ongoing work of telling the story rightly.

Although we might like to downplay our role (and God's) in interpretation by labeling at least some texts as inescapably ideologically bound, two problems remain. First, every passage, even the (apparently) most repulsive and the most clearly redemptive can be interpreted in a variety of ways, leaving us to shift our focus from essential meaning to discernment and authority of interpretation issues ('Whose judgment is more sensible and why?', 'Whose interpretation carries more weight?'). Secondly, even when we are interpreting passages in the 'same' way as each other, our multitudinous interpretative practices belie the 'sameness' of our interpretations. We might give alms readily to beggars or decline for their 'better interest'; we might resist all violent action or we might fight to defend those in danger; we might eschew entirely the accumulation of wealth and belongings or we might give amply and broadly from our thoughtfully invested resources. Whatever the particulars of our daily practices are, these very actions and habits will inform the ways we interpret—and the ways our interpretations are understood by others. Since the same text can elicit apparently infinitely various and variously enacted interpretations, then the text cannot determine the ideological cast of our interpretations.[8]

6.   While I would want to distinguish my position from one which advocates an essential woman-experience, we have only just begun to hear and learn from women's experiences. In this I am more sympathetic to Luce Irigaray than to those who would criticize her for her alleged essentialism.

7.   Some examples of ideological habits might include the foods we eat—and don't—and how and with whom; where and with whom we live; and how and with whom we spend our money and time.

8.   It might be possible to argue that, given particular interpretative contexts, each passage affords a limited range of interpretations to choose from, but since we

This leads us to consider the *process* of interpretation and the weight we place on particular schools and habits of interpretation. Dominant interpretative practices reflect dominant ideological worlds. When we try to justify our scriptural interpretation with historical critical research practice, we reproduce in our readings the ideological assumptions associated with that particular approach to interpretation. This is by no means to say that historical-critical method has nothing to offer us as feminist theologians. Certainly there has been and we hope there always will be engaging feminist historical research which offers helpful insights for making sense of biblical texts. There are, however, significant questions before us which historical criticism alone cannot answer, including, 'Where do we find the authority and justification for our interpretations?' and, 'If the Bible does not contain good news any more than it contains bad news, why do we even read Scripture?'[9]

I suggest that there really is no good reason for us to read the Bible as Scripture unless we claim it and construe it as our own text.[10] Each

won't be able to agree on a closed set of possible options, we don't gain anything with that move.

9. Kwok Pui-lan offers these additional problems: 'The historical-critical method is perhaps the most suitable praxis for white, male, and middle-class academics, because they alone can afford to be "impartial", which literally means "non-committed". Oppressed women and men of all colors find that the historical-critical method alone cannot help them to address the burning questions they face. Illiterate women in the Third World churches care more about daily survival than any critical method. For Third World and African-American biblical scholars, the method is helpful, yet too limiting, because it does not allow certain questions to be raised or certain perspectives to be entertained. Renita J. Weems, an African-American scholar of the Hebrew Scriptures, powerfully points out that the negative result of the historical-critical method has been "to undermine marginalized reading communities by insisting that their questions and experiences are superfluous to Scripture and their interpretations illegitimate, because of their failure to remain objective"', 'Racism and Ethnocentrism in Feminist Biblical Interpretation', in Elisabeth Schüssler Fiorenza (ed.), *Searching the Scriptures. I. A Feminist Introduction* (New York: Crossroad, 1993), p. 103. (Cf. also Weems from 'Reading *Her Way* through the Struggle: African American Women and the Bible', in C.H. Felder [ed.], *Stony the Road We Trod* [Minneapolis: Fortress Press, 1991], p. 66.)

10. We could, of course, read it as the set of sacred texts of another's religion, in a comparative, rhetorical, historical, anthropological, psychological or sociological exercise, but that would not be a specifically theological project. And although it is certainly possible to read *Scripture* rhetorically (or historically, anthropologically, etc.), the warrants for such interpretations would be theological rather than rhetorical (etc.).

of us, even and especially those of us who are women, is a part of God's creation and, therefore, a part of God's creating. Likewise, we are, each of us and all of us, creators and creations of God's word and presence in our lives. Even though women and others have been marginalized in countless ways, we can still lay claim to Scripture's story of God-with-us. God is present with us, each of us, as we read and tell and practice that story.

If this is true, one of the challenges for feminist theology, then, is to sing out loudly and clearly that Scripture does not authorize its own interpretations all by itself. We know that we need not only the Torah, but the Mishnah and the Talmud and ongoing interpretative scholarship as well. The cloyingly familiar children's hymn notwithstanding, we do not know that Jesus loves us simply because the Bible tells us so. Contrary to the Reformation notion that Scripture itself is its own interpreter, Scripture does *nothing* all by itself. And yet much of feminist biblical scholarship continues this habit of trying to justify interpretation by referring to the text itself. Major voices in feminist biblical studies have called for us to read Scripture critically, drawing on the rich insights of women's experiences, and to discover and bring to light previously hidden or obscured meaning in the texts.

One recent and comprehensive example of this approach is *Searching the Scriptures*. II. *A Feminist Commentary*, edited by Elisabeth Schüssler Fiorenza (New York: Crossroad, 1994), which offers expansive and exciting resources for reading the Bible as feminists. And yet, I would argue, the goal of this project, 'an increase in historical-religious knowledge and imagination' (p. 9) is at least as problematic as it is empowering. The contributors to this commentary volume consistently use the rhetoric and authorizing practices of the academy-approved historical-critical methods, even when they propose unconventional readings. Although these interpreters are feminists and although their presentations significantly counter much of conventional scholarship, the *Searching the Scriptures* project perpetuates the premise that Scriptures contain meaning, waiting for historical, sociological, political textual archaeologists to uncover the true meanings. *Searching the Scriptures* is an invaluable work, both in what it provides and in what it inspires in interpretations yet to come. It is, however, no less ideologically colored than any other commentary—a fact which could be its greatest strength, if only the authors were proud enough to locate interpretative authority in their own midst rather than in Scripture 'itself'.

If we consider texts neither as containers for meaning nor as containers for meaning-justification, where then do we find the authority to make sense of and defend our biblical interpretations? The same place we always have—from our interpretative communities. For most of us, our interpretative communities are not limited to the worlds of published biblical commentaries (of whatever approach), sermons, hymnody or popular culture. Although certainly our participation in each of these contexts may be productive, much of the time these traditionally authoritative text-constituting sites are not affirming, nurturing or even sensible to many aspects of our lives. If we are exclusively historical critics, then we might want to authorize our interpretative moves solely on the terms of that community. If we are cloistered, ultramontane Roman Catholics, then we will look solely to the magisterium for our authority. If we are, single-mindedly, cultural anthropologists, disassociated from participation in a God-with-us story, then we will follow the analytical procedures appropriate to that field. But if we are, most of us, members of an eclectic passel of communities, then our multiple and particular community relationships will inform and authorize our interpretations.

I like to think of our community involvements along the lines of the Venn diagrams I remember drawing in elementary school when we learned about sets. Different circles (often differently colored circles) represent various sets; the circles overlap, a little or a lot, depending on the extent to which the sets' contents overlap. Few if any of us live in just one of these 'set' circles. Our lives are made up of associations with, commitments to, and shared experiences with others in many sets, many circles, all of which overlap at least to the extent that we are a common denominator. Furthermore, our relationship circles are multidimensional and convoluted. The visual aid possibilities are fascinating if complicated. I know that my own life drawn on these terms would be something of a Venn diagram nightmare. And, indeed, many of us inhabit conflicting communities, whose interpretative differences seem insoluble.

However many sets we inhabit or even just visit occasionally, we need to learn to recognize the wisdom (and folly?) of the communities in which we live and with which we are connected. If we understand ourselves as God's people, then our practices are our responses to

God's presence with us. In this case, we need to grant our multiplicities of communities at least as much interpretative authority as those professional interpreters who claim authority as their own. As women, we need to learn to name our community connections as sites for authoritative scriptural interpretation. And, as women who interpret the Bible, we might do well to expand our basis for authoritative interpretation beyond the terms established for us by our fathers and brothers in the field. Our many various overlapping and shared experiences as daughters, as sisters, as mothers, as intimate friends and lovers, as abused children and wives, as homeless and as privileged, as harassed employees, as struggling professionals, as ignored or overlooked biblical scholars and theologians, as church school teachers and pastors, as oppressed and as oppressing, as creators and nurturers, as the butt of jokes, as objects of derision and as objects of dehumanizing veneration—all these, and many more, combine to make the communities of our interpretation. A small group or even a vast historical band of male and male-identified Bible experts can not (any longer) convince us that their interpretative practices carry enough authority to outweigh the truth of our own experiences of God-with-us in Scripture and practice.

We are, however, still participants in and perpetrators of our patriarchal economy of words and meaning. It is all too easy for us to adopt a sort of fundamentalist stance that bonds conventional male-identified ideologies with Scripture. Those of us who know and profess God as She are still ever tempted to explain that practice from within the context of historical-critical method, even if such method is not how God makes Herself known to us in our lives. And there is a temptation, particularly for white American mainstream Protestant feminists, to accept a patriarchal version of Scripture and then feel moved to reject the whole package. It is, on the face of things, a most sensible move. I would guess that one of the most common thoughts to cross the minds (and lips) of those of us who still try to participate in conventional church worship life is, 'How can I and why should I participate in a church whose Scriptures seem to deny my very presence?'

One answer might lie in another challenge to feminist theology: Luce Irigaray's call for us to find the divine feminine and the feminine divine. Irigaray wonders why feminist biblical scholarship has focused its attentions on equal access to church leadership (from remembering and retelling women's roles in early church history to taking on 'equal' roles in contemporary church hierarchy) rather than working to

discover feminine divine identity. As she writes in 'Equal to Whom?',
her critical review of Elisabeth Schüssler Fiorenza's *In Memory of Her*,
'sociology quickly bores me when I'm expecting the divine'.[11] Instead
Irigaray urges us to explore, claim and celebrate the possibilities of
woman as subject, as defining gender, as divinity.[12] If we are truly
divine women—and not simply 'equal' counterparts to God-made-
men—then our experiences, our revelations, our interpretations, and
our scriptural claims will be divinely inspired. We may never be able to
authorize our interpretations in terms comprehensible to those whose
practices don't acknowledge our presence as subject, as story-tellers,
but I'm not sure why we should try. If we are prepared to accept
women as created in God's image, as potentially and even presently
divine, then the justification for our interpretative explorations and the
authority for our ideological readings will be powerfully present in our
practices, relationships and communities—the places and times and
ways in which God is with us in our lives.

Opening up the interpretative field to radically untraditional interpretations and interpretative methods does not mean that we are now
doomed to wallow in an anarchical mire of chaotic interpretation.[13] As
we have already discussed, we always do interpretation in contexts and
in conversations with others—the rest of God's creation. An interpretative move will only go as far as a body of interpreters can carry it. A
reading of the Delilah and Samson story which names cosmetology as
the essential practice for the fulfillment of the Covenant will only work
as long as there are people willing to preach and practice such an
interpretation. And it is likely that these holy hairdressers would be the
recipients of much advice about the wisdom of their position. We have

11. Luce Irigaray, 'Equal to Whom?', *differences* 1 (1989), pp. 59-76.

12. 'Equal to Whom?' and 'Divine Women', in her *Sexes and Genealogies*
(trans. Gillian C. Gill; New York: Columbia University Press, 1993) pp. 57-72.

13. One might observe that even while arguing otherwise, within this essay I
speak of texts (other articles, papers, books) as if they have meaning and as if their
authors have intentions. Of course I do. I'm not advocating an Alice-in-
Wonderland approach to communication and interpretation, whereby, as Humpty
Dumpty asserts, words can mean whatever I please. I certainly hope that readers
will understand something akin to what I intended when I wrote these words in
these combinations. At the same time, I don't presume to assume that there are no
other possible interpretations or that all others will necessarily understand what I
am thinking at the time of writing. And I would expect and even hope that this
essay, in another context, might come across very differently indeed.

ample evidence throughout the ages of how this has worked. Interpretation and interpretative practices have always changed, in conjunction with and in response to shifting contexts.[14] The challenge to us as feminist biblical theologians is to participate more actively in that process of change.

If we were to accept that texts contain ideologies, then we would feel bound either to accept others' assertions about what the texts contain or to bicker with others about which texts actually convey which meanings. But since we know that particular ideologies are not pre-installed in Scripture—that the relationship between ideologies, texts, readers, contexts and practices is complex and fluid—we can go about the business of engaging with the texts as makes sense to us and our practices. This may very well mean that some scriptural passages are not coherent to us. In direct defiance of a powerful modern premise that univocal meaning is not only possible but desirable, I propose that we free ourselves to name some passages exactly as we know them: as anomalous. Instead of labeling a problematic pericope as ideologically impaired, and thereby relinquishing it to others for their own purposes, we can still claim the text and name it as ours—even as we label it an anomaly according to our biblical theological story.[15]

One frequently cited example is Eph. 5.22, 'Wives, be subject to your husbands as you are to the Lord'. What sense can we make of a passage which seems to tell us that God requires women to be subordinate to their husbands? Generally, we recognize only a few options. We can accept the authority of those who would embrace the very

14. Cf. Cain Felder's discussion of the treatment of Gen. 9.18-27, 'the so-called curse of Ham', in *Stony the Road We Trod*, pp. 129-32, and the 'process of sacralization wherein cultural and historical phenomena are recast as theological truths with vested interest for particular groups' (p. 130).

15. The institution of rock music offers us many examples along these lines. The overall appeal of classic singles appears not to have been affected by the inclusion of lyrics which are undeniably nonsensical. The Beatle's song, 'I am the Walrus' is one case in point: 'I am the eggman, they are the eggmen—I am the walrus GOO GOO GOO JOOB' (*Magical Mystery Tour*, Apple Records, 1967). The same music world offers another practice which effectively resists the notion that texts contain ideology, that of creative 'covers'. When one group 'covers', sings their own version of, another group's song, the differences in gender, position, attitude, audience and arrangement can offer a radically altered ideological presentation of the supposedly 'same' song, such as when a gay men's chorus sings a rendition of 'My Guy'.

interpretation we find so painful ('Yes, you're right folks, this passage *is* about the necessary subordination of women...'). We can argue about why the text is even in the canon ('Well, these household codes weren't really written by Paul,[16] and whoever wrote it was certainly so overwhelmed by his patriarchal historical context, so motivated by political agendas, as to be dismissible now...'). Or, we can try to soften the impact of the text by noting that a few lines later the author asks husbands to love their wives as they do their own bodies ('This is, of course, a radical concept for the day, so this must actually be a *feminist* move...'). If we denounce the text as essentially offensive, relinquish it as unnecessary or downplay its problematic aspects, in each case we are handing over the interpretative authority to others. We give up our own position *at* the text, the site of revelation and ideological practice.

Instead we might observe that all the interpretations of this passage we have heard so far just don't make sense given what we know about our story of God-with-us, our biblical theology. Perhaps someday we will be able to make more sense of it. For now, we can name it as a *placeholder* for future interpretations we might recognize in another time, when our contexts and experiences are different. Meanwhile, we would do well to remember that all Scripture readers make discernments about which passages they draw on more heavily than others. Rather than hiding our interpretative discernments, let's be so bold as to make them intentionally and explicitly. It seems clear that Eph. 5.22 is inconsistent with many other New Testament passages that recount the primacy of communal, grace-filled interaction over hierarchical social convention.[17] As discerning, feminist, divine women, we will,

16. Elaine Pagels, in Ch. 1 of *Adam, Eve, and the Serpent* (New York, Vintage Books, 1988), argues the deutero-Pauline letters were (among other things) attempts by community leaders to present a more moderate Paul and to counter the radical stories of Thecla and Mygdonia, women for whom 'Pauline' asceticism and celibacy meant (socially threatening) empowerment.

17. E.g. Mt. 6.24 eliminates the possibility of serving two masters (for our purposes, husband and God); Mk 3.33-35 reconstructs family relationships in terms of doing the will of God rather than biology or household; Jn 4 tells of the Samaritan woman at the well whose five (or six) spouses have not been husbands in Jesus' eyes, regardless of custom; 1 Cor. 12.12-31 names the members of the church all as necessary members of one body; Gal. 5.13-15 exhorts, 'For you were called to freedom, brothers and sisters; only do not use your freedom as an opportunity for self-indulgence, but through love become slaves to one another. For the whole law is summed up in a single commandment, "You shall love your neighbor as your-

therefore, give more weight to the latter body of texts than to the problematic one when fleshing out our theology of how to be godly women.

When we make such a move, we are claiming our authority as members of a living text-community, rather than justifying our interpretation by referring to the text alone. We are naming ourselves as faithful and ideologically embodied readers, rather than sidestepping the responsibility of interpretation. And, most significantly, we are making room for the promise of the Spirit's presence and activity in our interpretative lives, even beyond our present receptive and constructive capacities. Meanwhile, our efforts to reimagine and reconstruct practices of right relationships in a post-patriarchal world may open up possibilities for new interpretative life in what now appears to be infertile ground.

Not only *can* feminists read the Bible as our own, not bound by pre-installed ideology, we *have* done so and do so now (although we might be well served to explore why the academy seems more comfortable *documenting* such activity than practising it in biblical scholarship). One example is the vast wealth of womanist biblical interpretation, which flows from the 'aural hermeneutic' of African American women[18] who claim the Bible as liberating, as empowering, as their own, and as not only accessible through the ideological presentation of their oppressors and their brothers. Judith Plaskow, in *Standing Again at Sinai: Judaism from a Feminist Perspective* lays the groundwork for reclaiming Jewish memory through recreations and reworkings of liturgy and ritual in communities which are Jewish *and* feminist.[19] The Solentiname community's interpretative dialogues model how Scripture can speak to and through a people when their hear and retell the story as their own.[20] Kwok Pui-lan offers yet another example in a homily put together by Asian Women about Jesus healing the

self". If, however, you bite and devour one another, take care that you are not consumed by one another'; and 1 Pet. 4.8-11 spells out, 'Above all, maintain constant love for one another, for love covers a multitude of sins. Be hospitable to one another without complaining. Like good stewards of the manifold grace of God, serve one another with whatever gift each of you has received. Whoever speaks must do so as one speaking the very words of God; whoever serves must do so with the strength that God supplies...'

18. Weems, 'Reading *Her Way* through the Struggle', see n. 9 above.

19. *Standing Again at Sinai: Judaism from a Feminist Perspective* (San Francisco: Harper & Row, 1990).

20. Ernesto Cardenal, *The Gospel in Solentiname* (4 vols.; Maryknoll, NY: Orbis Books, 1976).

Canaanite woman's daughter. The homily names the Canaanite woman
as particular poor, struggling, courageous women and gives voice to
their cries through their stories and the Canaanite woman's story.[21]
Mary McClintock Fulkerson offers a view of some Pentecostal women
in a community and context which is apparently patriarchally offensive
in its scriptural interpretation and practice, women who have managed
nonetheless to construct a practical hermeneutic of resistance and
power through the Scripture they claim.[22] Marchienne Rientra's
Swallow's Nest is a presentation of psalms for women's worship, which
names God as feminine throughout, thereby asserting the authority of
women's experiences of God in women's community over the conventional wisdom of scholarly translation and historical context.[23] The
possibilities are, of course, boundless.

When we are the readers, we can claim for our own the responsibility
and power of telling our scriptural story. Remembering the powerful
heritage of our faithful forebears whose example as Scripture-claimers
lights our path, we can hold on to the possibilities of revelation through
our engagement with Scripture. As it is not only our own agency which
determines meaning, but God's Spirit as well, let us not presume that
the Spirit can work through Scripture only in those ways we, and
others, have already imagined. Instead, let us engage our collective
hermeneutical capabilities actively, drawing on our experiences of
God-with-us and guided by the community practices of those, past and
present, in whom we recognize the Spirit's activity. Let us discover and
sing our story of God-with-us, the scriptural story which reflects and
informs our ideologies, practices, and revelations. This is *our* story; this
is *our* song.[24]

21. *The Asia Journal of Theology*, 1.1 (1987) pp. 90-95. This homily is also
reprinted in Ursula King (ed.), *Feminist Theology from the Third World*
(Maryknoll, NY: Orbis Books, 1994), pp. 236-42.

22. *Changing the Subject: Women's Discourses and Feminist Theology*
(Minneapolis: Augsburg–Fortress, 1994).

23. *Swallow's Nest: A Feminine Reading of the Psalms* (Grand Rapids:
Eerdmans, 1992).

24. Profound appreciation to the Critical Theology Group and especially SPU
95, for helping to birth, discipline and nurture earlier drafts of this essay into its
present form.

'CREATIVE REVERENCE':
A WOMANIST HERMENEUTICS OF IMAGINATION
IN MAUDE IRWIN OWENS'S 'BATHESDA OF SINNERS RUN'

J.A. Craig Edwards

'I...put my ear down close upon...[the Bible], in great hopes that it would say something to me; but I was very sorry, and greatly disappointed, when I found that it would not speak. This thought immediately presented itself to me, that every body and every thing despised me because I was black.'[1] This passage from James Gronniosaw's *Narrative* (1770)—cited by Henry Louis Gates, Jr, as the foundation text of the African-American literary tradition[2]—suggests the defining function of the Bible in African-American literary history. The first encounter of this early African-American writer with the central text of white Western culture (the Bible) convinced Gronniosaw that he would be (de)valued in Western culture because of the blackness of his skin.

Gates also describes five additional African-American texts which repeat this originary scene: John Marrant's *Narrative* (1785), Quobna Ottobah Cugoano's *Thoughts and Sentiments* (1787), Olaudah Equiano's *Narrative* (1789), John Jea's *Life* (1815) and Rebecca Jackson's *Gifts of Power* (1830).[3] Gates refers to such symbolic scenes, in which illiterate slaves first see someone read aloud from the Bible and mistakenly believe the book can talk, as the 'trope of the Talking Book'. Based upon the repeated occurrences of this trope, Gates argues that for the past two hundred years the black literary tradition has been

---

1.   J.A. Gronniosaw, *A Narrative of the Most Remarkable Particulars in the Life of James Albert Ukawsaw Gronniosaw, An African Prince, As Related by Himself* (1770) (N.p.: Hazard, 1840), p. 8.

2.   H.L. Gates, Jr, *The Signifying Monkey: A Theory of African-American Literary Criticism* (New York: Oxford University Press, 1988), p. 136.

3.   All dates in this list represent the first time a given work was published except for Jackson's work which was written between 1830 and 1832 but not published until 1981.

engaged in revising the original identification of blackness with a despised voicelessness and absence. He believes that this oppressive view of blackness was internalized at the beginning of the tradition by Gronniosaw when he became convinced that the central text of white Western culture, the Bible, refused to talk to him because he was black.[4]

From the beginning of African-American literary history, then, the Bible has been interlocked both with white culture's negative stereotypes of blacks as well as with black writers' literary revisions of those stereotypes.[5] Gates argues that the trope of the Talking Book died out after the first century of black literary history. His final example of this trope, however, is from a black *woman's* text, Rebecca Cox Jackson's *Gifts of Power*. Jackson's revision of this trope, according to Gates, 'is cast within a sexual opposition between male and female. Whereas her antecedents used the trope to define the initial sense of difference between slave and free, African and European, Jackson's revision charts the liberation of a (black) woman from a (black) man over the letter of the text...Jackson freed herself of her brother's domination of her literacy and her ability to interpret', using the trope of the Talking Book.[6] I would argue, therefore, that in spite of Gates's assertion, Jackson's usage of the trope represents not the death of this biblical tradition, but its transformation. With Rebecca Cox Jackson the trope of the Talking Book is newly engendered and continues to be used in different, less literal ways by black women. Maude Irwin Owens is one such black woman whose troping of the biblical text for purposes of self-definition will be the focus of this study.

This revisionary, self-defining usage of the Bible by black women has not simply been illuminated by black literary scholars, but also by black feminist religious scholars. Cheryl Townsend Gilkes, for example, is a womanist[7] sociologist of religion who has coined the term 'creative reverence' for the self-defining, creative revisions of the Bible

---

4. Gates, *Signifying Monkey*, pp. 136-37.

5. This interlocking theory is the underlying thesis of Ch. 4 of *Signifying Monkey*.

6. Gates, *Signifying Monkey*, p. 241.

7. 'Womanist' is the term which Alice Walker coined to refer to 'a black feminist or feminist of color'. For a much fuller definition, see A. Walker, Preface, in *In Search of Our Mothers' Gardens: Womanist Prose* (San Diego: Harcourt Brace Jovanovich, 1983), pp. xi-xii (xi).

found in African-American art.[8] Gilkes locates one such example of creative reverence in the African-American gospel song 'Father to the Fatherless'. She notes that through the art of music black women actively revised the text of Ps. 68.5. In this song, the empowering phrases 'sister to the sisterless' and 'mother to the motherless' have been added to the biblical assertion which defines God as 'father to the fatherless'. Through these revisions of the biblical text, those black women who sang this song clearly identify themselves as the daughters and sisters of a God who is defined as both male *and female*. Although Gilkes has noted a few other instances of this self-defining, revisionary usage of the Bible in black art, Elisabeth Schüssler Fiorenza is the white feminist religious scholar who has written at greatest length about how such revisionary approaches to the Bible might contribute to a feminist theory of biblical interpretation.

Fiorenza explains her feminist hermeneutic in *But She Said*. She argues that a liberational strategy of biblical interpretation must be comprised of a hermeneutics of suspicion, remembrance, proclamation and imagination. 'A *hermeneutics of suspicion* seeks to explore the liberating or oppressive values and visions inscribed in the text by identifying [and being suspicious of] the androcentric-patriarchal character and dynamics of the [biblical] text and its interpretations.'[9] Fiorenza's hermeneutics of remembrance seeks to recover all possible remnants of women's lives and history from this suspiciously patriarchal text and to rearrange or re-member them into a different, less patriarchal body of texts.[10] Her hermeneutics of proclamation 'insists that texts [both interpretations of the Bible and the Bible itself] which [do not seek to remember, but] seek to reinscribe patriarchal relations of domination and exploitation must not be affirmed and appropriated…as the word of God but…exposed as the words of men'.[11] Finally, Fiorenza's hermeneutics of imagination calls for creative redramatizations of androcentric-patriarchal texts from a feminist point of view.

Fiorenza further asserts the importance of situating her four-part

---

8. C.T. Gilkes, '"Mother to the Motherless, Father to the Fatherless": Power, Gender and Community in an Afrocentric Biblical Tradition', *Semeia* 47 (1989), pp. 57-85 (77).

9. E. Schüssler Fiorenza, *But She Said: Feminist Practices of Biblical Interpretation* (Boston: Beacon Press, 1992), p. 57.

10. Fiorenza, *But She Said*, p. 54.

11. Fiorenza, *But She Said*, p. 54.

hermeneutic within the 'logic of democracy'[12] which seeks to bring justice to a system marked by kyriocentric (or 'master-centered') forms of gender, racial, ethnic, class and age oppression. Fiorenza, therefore, clearly intends her hermeneutical theory to be applied not only to gender, but also to racial oppression. And it is particularly Fiorenza's hermeneutics of imagination as it relates to gender and racial oppression which may be roughly equated with Gilkes's 'creative reverence'.

Fiorenza gives this extended definition of her hermeneutics of imagination in Chapter 2 of *But She Said*:

> A *hermeneutics...of imagination* seeks to actualize and dramatize biblical texts differently [from their original kyriocentric or 'master-centered' construction]...Creative re-imagination employs all our creative powers to celebrate and make present the suffering, struggles, and victories of our biblical foresisters and foremothers. It utilizes all kinds of artistic media to elaborate and enhance the textual remnants of liberating visions. It retells biblical stories from a different perspective and amplifies the emancipatory voices suppressed in biblical texts. It elaborates on the role of marginal figures and makes their silences speak.[13]

In this essay, therefore, I would like to present Maude Irwin Owens's short story 'Bathesda of Sinners Run' (*sic*) as a brilliantly engendered and racialized example of what Gilkes calls 'creative reverence' and Fiorenza a 'hermeneutics...of imagination'. I wish to suggest that in 1928—over 60 years before Gilkes and Fiorenza published their theories—Maude Irwin Owens published a short story which actually practices 'the hermeneutics of imagination' and 'creative reverence'. Published in the NAACP's *Crisis* magazine, Owens's 'Bathesda of Sinners Run' is an elaboration on the Pool of Bethesda story (Jn 5.2-9) in which the silent, marginalized, healing pool is personified as a black woman who 'speaks' with a powerfully healing touch.

In 'Bathesda of Sinners Run', Owens tells the story of a mulatta, named Bathesda Creek, who is the seventh in a line of black women. All six of her foremothers have been slaves, have been products of rape by white masters, have been deeply religious, and have had a miraculous gift of healing and of alleviating pain. Bathesda, however, is the first of her family born after Emancipation; and, apparently, because she refuses to participate in the hypocritical religion of her community, she has not inherited the miraculous gift of healing pain. Bathesda is

---

12. Fiorenza, *But She Said*, p. 120.
13. Fiorenza, *But She Said*, pp. 54-55.

extremely talented with her hands, both as an artist and as a folk doctor. The sanctimonious women in her community are jealous of her abilities and of all the suitors this beautiful mulatta attracts. These women decide with sickening self-righteousness that she needs to be taught a lesson by flogging. When these persecutors drag Bathesda up a hill, however, and attempt to pin her to a tree, they are frightened away as the tree seems miraculously to crash to the ground. Two loggers appear and explain that they were felling this same tree when one of them injured his arm and they had to seek a bandage. Bathesda, however, embraces a much more spiritual explanation for this tree-experience. She sees the similarities between her own ordeal and that of the persecuted Jesus. It is on this hilltop, at the foot of this tree that Bathesda works out her 'own destiny in the Lord, in…[her] own way'.[14] Bathesda 'finds religion', and she immediately receives the gift of healing pain which she quickly practices on the dumbfounded white, male lumberjack.

In addition to this literary story about the spiritual rebirth of a black woman, Owens also clearly intended this piece to be read as a hermeneutical work in a way which directly anticipates Fiorenza and Gilkes. Owens's first imaginative revision of the biblical text occurs in the first word of her title. 'B*a*thesda' is a revision of the spelling of the biblical place name 'B*e*thesda'. The Greek word transliterated in the King James Version as 'Bethesda' is itself probably a revision (or variant) of the Hebrew word 'Beth-zatha' which (interestingly enough) may be translated as 'House of Olives'.[15] Owens's Bathesda, we learn, is the last daughter of a 'house' of olive-skinned mulattas. From the outset, therefore, Owens's creative reimagination of biblical spelling suggests a revision of a traditional, kyriocentric stereotype of black women. One of the stereotypes slaveholders had used to justify the selling of children away from their mothers was that African Americans were subhuman animals, who had no sense of family or maternal bonds. Owens's revisionary spelling of Bathesda, 'House of Olives', may imply her counter-assertion: the olive-skinned woman clearly *does* possess a historical sense of a family or 'House of Olives'.

Owens foregrounds her hermeneutics of imagination even more explicitly in the first sentence of her text. This opening statement not

---

14. M.I. Owens, 'Bathesda of Sinners Run', *The Crisis* 35 (1928), pp. 77-79, 121-22, 141-42 (78).

15. K.W. Clark, 'Beth-zatha', in *IDB*, I, p. 404.

only announces to the reader Owens's revisionary intent, but also identifies her revisionary practice as biblical: 'It was like reading the books of Chronicles, to read in the Thornton family history of the attending succession of slave women that formed the single line of Bathesda's ancestry.'[16] By comparing her own book of Bathesda to the books of Chronicles, Owens enhances the validity of her own biblical redramatization, which is clearly motivated by gender and racial politics. She cites a sacred precedent in Chronicles, a doubly biblical revision of Samuel and Kings, which many scholars have argued was motivated by religious politics.[17] The books of Chronicles, of course, are 'doubly biblical' in that they both revise biblical texts and they are themselves included in the biblical canon. Owens implies, therefore, from the outset that the Bible itself both anticipates and validates her politically motivated hermeneutics of imagination.

The biblical texts which Owens seeks to reimagine in 'Bathesda of Sinners Run' comprise portions of the beginning, middle and end of Jesus' life. It is crucial here to think of Jesus as a white male. For, although he was a Jew in the Roman Empire and, therefore, a member of an oppressed political group, it is more important to an understanding of Owens's work to focus on his membership in the almost universally dominant white, male culture.

The beginning of Jesus' story, as it is presented in the Gospel of Matthew, is comprised of his genealogy. Although this genealogy is not exclusively patriarchal, it is nevertheless a patrilineage which claims to trace Jesus' ancestry through 42 generations of men while mentioning only four women (Tamar, Rahab, Ruth and Bathsheba). As Fiorenza's theory might suggest, Owens apparently saw in those biblical foremothers four 'marginalized figures' whose stories needed to be retold from a 'different perspective' which would amplify 'the emancipatory voices suppressed in' the Gospel text. Owens, therefore, begins her redramatization of the life of a miraculous healer with the genealogy of a black woman, Bathesda, which begins with the founder of her line, Jezebel: 'So Jezebel became the mother of Georgie; who begat Abigail; whose brat was Callie; whose offspring was Ruth; whose child was Viney; whose daughter was Anne; and twenty years after slavery, came Bathesda.'[18] Bathesda is the first of this line who is not a slave and not

16. Owens, 'Bathesda', p. 77.
17. E.g. see R.H. Pfeiffer, 'Chronicles', in *IDB*, I, p. 580.
18. Owens, 'Bathesda', p. 77.

a child of white, male rape. Bathesda's mother freely chose to marry Bathesda's father, a man named Enoch Creek whom the text describes as 'a fusion of Creek Indian, Negro and white'.[19] Consequently, in Owens's liberated vision of the place of the woman in a crucial genealogy, Bathesda is liberated from the generations of white, male sexual aggression. She is the first woman in her line who is not the direct product of illegitimate white patriarchy.

Furthermore, Bathesda's matrilineal genealogy, in sharp contrast to Jesus', is exclusively matriarchal: Owens names only women as she traces out seven generations. Ironically, Owens uses the very manners and customs of the sexist and racist South as her excuse for writing Bathesda's white patrilineage out of her text. Owens wryly declares, 'The paternal side of the issue was always politely ignored in strict accordance with the manners and customs of the South'.[20] The numerous ways in which Bathesda will not simply parallel, but also displace, Jesus begin to accumulate in this passage. In Owens's creative reimagining, it is the black woman—not the white man—who has a female ancestor by the name of Ruth. It is Bathesda's mother—not Jesus' grandmother—whose name was Anne. And instead of the white man being the True Vine, the black woman is the true daughter of Viney.

Owens's redramatization of the end of Jesus' story similarly displaces the white, male Jesus with the black, female Bathesda. It is the black woman at the end of 'Sinners Run' who is dragged 'up...[a] hill'[21] which Bathesda herself compares to 'Calvary'.[22] And it is the black female healer who is redeemed by being pinned to a tree.

At the beginning of her story, therefore, Owens employs the hermeneutics of imagination to retell the genealogy of the great healer and at the end to recreate the redemptive crucifixion. Owens's redramatization of a text from the middle of Jesus' life is perhaps even more powerful. The Gospel of John handles Jesus' 'genealogy' much differently than does Matthew. Perhaps it was John's identification of Jesus with the Word (Jn 1.1-14), which Owens had in mind when she applied her hermeneutics of imagination to John's Pool of Bethesda story. Owens apparently saw in this Gospel story what Fiorenza would later call a 'textual remnant' which reminded Owens of her own vision of

19. Owens, 'Bathesda', p. 77.
20. Owens, 'Bathesda', p. 77.
21. Owens, 'Bathesda', p. 122.
22. Owens, 'Bathesda', p. 142.

black women's history in America. Owens (like many other black women writers) believed that African-American women have special healing powers for their own community. These womanist writers have also asserted that white patriarchal culture has repeatedly sought to suppress, marginalize or displace black women's powerful healing abilities with the white phallocentric word. Owens must have seen in this biblical text, therefore, a parallel instance in which a dark 'pool' (a feminine noun in the Greek), which traditionally healed by a touch, became a 'marginal figure', displaced by the white man's word. Owens's hermeneutics of imagination redramatizes this patriarchal text. She personifies the dark Bethesda Pool as a dark-skinned woman, Bathesda Creek. She restores the pool's marginalized tradition (of healing with a touch) to a central role in her re-membered text. Additionally, Owens's redramatization transforms Jesus, the white, male carpenter with omnipotent speech, into two white male loggers, who become impotent in speech.

Before studying Owens's liberational revisions of this story, let us re-examine the displacement of the dark pool's healing touch by the white man's healing word in the original King James translation of John's narrative (the translation which Owens would have heard):

> Now there is at Jerusalem by the sheep market a pool, which is called in the Hebrew tongue *Bethesda*, having five porches. In these lay a great multitude of impotent folk, of blind, halt, withered, waiting for the moving of the water. For an angel went down at a certain season into the pool, and troubled [or touched] the water: Whosoever then first after the troubling of the water stepped in [or was touched by the pool] was made whole of whatsoever disease he had. And a certain man was there, which had an infirmity thirty and eight years. When Jesus saw him lie, and knew that he had been now a long time in that case, *he saith* unto him, Wilt thou be made whole? The impotent man answered him, Sir, I have no man, when the water is troubled, to put me into the pool: but while I am coming, another steppeth down [and is touched] before me. Jesus *saith* unto him, Rise, take up thy bed, and walk. And immediately the man was made whole, and took up his bed, and walked (Jn 5.2-9, emphasis added).

In her revision of this biblical story, Owens makes present the suffering, struggles and healing victories of black women by re-imagining this marginalized, silenced pool as a black woman who powerfully heals with a touch while white men stand by speechless.

The climactic scene of Owens's hermeneutical text actually com-

bines the Pool of Bathesda story with the Calvary narrative. In the
original biblical story, being nailed to Calvary's tree and declaring 'It is
finished' (Jn 19.30), further empowered the white male Word, so that
he could say, 'Verily, verily I say unto you, He that heareth *my word*...
hath everlasting life, and shall not come into condemnation; but is
passed from death unto life' (Jn 5.24; emphasis added). In this androcentric text, the white male has the verbal power not only to heal the
body, but also the soul. Owens, however, silences this omnipotent
Logos in her recreated text. She replaces him with a black woman who,
by being pinned to a tree, gains the power to heal both body and pain
by her touch.

This climactic passage describes Bathesda both healing the body and
miraculously removing the pain of the white, male logger by her touch:

> [Bathesda] unwrapped the crude bandage [from the logger's injured
> arm], wiped away the stench of liniment, cupped her two hands about
> the swollen arm and gazed upward—her thin lips moving almost imper-
> ceptibly while the men stood transfixed.
>
> She finally withdrew her hands, clenched them into tight fists and then
> shook them open and away from her, as if throwing off the contamina-
> tion of alien flesh [Saying,] 'Now...it is well!'[23]

During the act of healing, the Logos/loggers are silent: the almighty
male word is replaced by the female touch and, at first, by the black
woman's lips moving silently, 'almost imperceptibly' and, finally, by
the black woman's full-throated declaration, 'It is well!' Furthermore,
the white men stand 'transfixed'. One imagines them with open and
empty mouths. When these men do find their voices, their words can
only confirm the healing power of the black woman's touch. The
injured logger declares, 'Bill! Honest to John! She's right! The dad-
burned misery has gone completely, and look! The swellin' is goin'
down right before my very eyes!'[24] His partner responds, '"Good God!
'tis a miracle we've just witnessed! The woman's a saint." And he
hastily crossed himself, while the other man tested his healed arm by
swinging an ax.'[25]

After this climactic scene, Owens unmistakably links the marginalized pool in the biblical text to her protagonist, a muddy-brown female
healer:

23. Owens, 'Bathesda', p. 122.
24. Owens, 'Bathesda', p. 122, 141.
25. Owens, 'Bathesda', p. 141-42.

Bathesda went down the hill with wide masculine strides—the light winds causing her snagged skirt and white apron to billow and flurry. Her eyes were two *muddy pools* of tears. She was testifying...

And she went home with a new power—with understanding, tolerance and forgiveness; to be one of her people; to take care of...[and heal her people]; and the fragrant drops of rain pelted [or touched] her in gentle benediction.[26]

As early as the Harlem Renaissance, therefore, black women like Maude Irwin Owens were already actualizing and dramatizing biblical texts differently from their original kyriocentric constructions.

Cheryl Townsend Gilkes's assertions about the empowering force of creatively redramatizing biblical texts can certainly be applied to Owens's work:

Since...[black women's] creative reverence involved fitting a patriarchal text to a world view full of bilineal descent and strong slave women, most of whom became mothers, there are important lessons to be found for the biblical feminist who seeks to remain faithful to the Bible as a foundation—an authoritative foundation—for faith, while rejecting a death dealing social order—the social order of contemporary patriarchy.[27]

Owens clearly has used a creatively reverent approach to a patriarchal text from the Bible in order to reassert her faith in the black woman's tactile power to heal.

Similarly, Owens seems to have anticipated Fiorenza's hermeneutics of imagination. Fiorenza urges us to employ 'all our creative powers to celebrate and make present the suffering, struggles, and victories of our biblical foresisters and foremothers'.[28] Owens's creative re-imagination already employs all her creative powers to celebrate and make present the suffering of slavery, the struggle to work out one's own destiny in the Lord in one's own way, and the victorious discovery of tactile healing powers experienced both by her biblical and African-American 'foremothers'. Fiorenza demands the use of 'all kinds of artistic media to elaborate and enhance the textual remnants of liberating visions'.[29] Owens has already used both the artistic medium of the word and of the picture—she both wrote and illustrated her short story—to elaborate

26. Owens, 'Bathesda', p. 142, emphasis added.
27. Gilkes, 'Mother to the Motherless', p. 77.
28. Fiorenza, *But She Said*, pp. 54-55.
29. Fiorenza, *But She Said*, p. 55.

and enhance the textual remnants of the Pool of Bathesda story. Fiorenza calls us to retell 'biblical stories from a different perspective and amplif[y]...the emancipatory voices suppressed in biblical texts'.[30] Owens has already re-membered the biblical story of Jesus from a black woman's perspective and amplified the emancipatory voices suppressed in the biblical texts. Finally, Fiorenza charges us to elaborate 'on the role of marginal figures and make...their silences speak'.[31] Here we have seen that in her brilliant short story Owens amazingly anticipates Fiorenza's charge when she elaborates on the role of the marginalized, muddy pool of Bathesda and makes her silences 'speak' through a liberated, healing touch.

30. Fiorenza, *But She Said*, p. 55.
31. Fiorenza, *But She Said*, p. 55.

PATRIARCHY'S MIDDLE MANAGERS: ANOTHER HANDMAID'S TALE

Susan Lochrie Graham

Date: 24 Oct 1...
From: ....epas.utor....[1]
Reply to: WIT-L@AOL.COM
To: Multiple recipients of list WIT-L<WIT-L@AOL.COM>
Subject: Scholarship and subjectivity

<Forwarded from CC>
Michael Novak, especially in his book *Belief and Unbelief* talks about the notion of 'intelligent subjectivity', which names a way of under-standing that transcends the traditional dichotomies of subjectivity and objectivity—here we are back where we started with that problem, but I think he may provide a way out—as a process beginning in conscious awareness of one's own experience and standpoint, though I understand this process in a somewhat different way than he does.[2] Within the ethos of eros and empathy, the scholar remains firmly rooted in her or his own body, life experience, history, values, judgments and interests. She or he names the interests that inspired and to some extent shaped her research.

Empathy flows from eros, the drive to connect, and is aided by imagination, which enables us to make connections between our own experiences and those of others. Imagination also enables us to see and understand difference, the otherness of the Other. All the standard tools of scholarly research, including criticism, historical research, analysis, careful attention to data, statistical research, theory, concern for truth, and so on, are brought to bear upon the task of understanding the sub-ject matter in this second moment of disciplined research. In this second moment our work will not differ dramatically from what we

---

1.   sgraham@epas.utoronto.ca
2.   Cf. Farnham, Impact.

have been trained to do under the standards of the ethos of objectivity. What will differ is that we keep in mind the limits of our ability to be objective, while at the same time keeping in mind that we can be far more than simply subjective.

The third moment of scholarship is judgment. After completing research and analysis, the scholar returns to her or his now-expanded standpoint. In an act of judgment, she or he incorporates the insights gained from research and analysis into her or his expanded standpoint or perspective. The scholar acknowledges that the judgments she or he makes are finite, limited by the body, history, life experiences, values and judgments of their author. But again this does not mean that judgments are narrowly personal, or merely polemical, as the ethos of objectivity would label them. Nor hopefully are they uncritically ethnocentric or imperialistic. Rather, the scholar recognizes that her or his standpoint has been enlarged by her or his research, by entering into the disciplined analysis of a text or historical period, and so on. The scholar also recognizes her or his grounding in the community of scholars, a community of discourse, within which she or he shares and receives criticism on both the research and analysis and the judgments made. The scholar avoids solipsism and polemic not by attempting to become objective, but by ever expanding the range of her or his empathy, her or his grounding in an ever expanding community of knowledge and scholarship, which in turn expands her or his standpoint.

<Forwarded from PQ>
I appreciate what Carol is trying to do, which I take to be placing objective, historical research in a larger and more subjective context. I think you said once that our task as scholars is to deconstruct the ethos of objectivity, and this is a kind of deconstructive move, although that's a loose use of the term. But I wonder if your idealist view of 'the scholar' isn't problematic. Who is included? And then who is the new Other? It's like the uncritical use of first-person plurals. Language like that makes us forget—there I'm doing it myself—that identities are constructed socially.

<Forwarded from TF>
That is what I was getting at when I said that identity is created in social systems, in which all participate. There is something about 'heterosexual society' which produces so-called homosexuals.

<Forwarded from TF>
On 24 October PQ wrote,

>And so there is something about men which produces women? ;-)

Yes, but not in the sense that you mean. Systems need their Other to define their boundaries. Take the question of sexual preferences, for example. Any system pretending to exclusiveness, like heterosexuality, use scapegoats. By definition heterosexuality denies homosexuality; but it both requires and suppresses the scapegoat. Her function is to be the unthinkable alternative, the non-choice of heterosexuality; to validate it by being a mistake; to preserve the system, the ideological construct and its material, institutionalized forms. To be wrong, so the other can be right; to be bad, so the other can be good; to be unnatural, so the other can be natural; to be different.[3] An oppressed group performs the negative function of supporting the oppressive; but it also acts, in its liberatory movement, to transform those relations. Everybody knows this on some level, or nobody would need either to deny it or to partici-pate in it: nobody would need to struggle around it. Difference would have no function in oppression; oppression would have to be different. For oppression uses difference—especially differences that can be made to seem natural, according to whatever social—and by that I mean, scientific or religious—constructs we use to delineate a 'law'.

<Forwarded from CC>
I agree with Tucker.

It's taken as a given, something that everybody knows, that women are 'naturally' more emotional than men, say, or more nurturing or whatever, and that this given sets our agenda and determines the results of our research. Then, when we seek employment in the university as feminist scholars, the first and easiest way to discredit our work is to call it personal or political, therefore not objective, therefore not schol-arly, therefore no tenure. Because of the very real economic pressures we face, many of us have chosen to hide the personal and social rele-vance and meaning of our work behind the mask of a dispassionate, objective voice. 'I'm not interested in finding the meaning of my life through my work, or in changing the world through it', we say. 'I'm only interested in analyzing the meter and form of Sappho's poetry.' Even as we adopt this strategy, we know that our work has the capacity

---

3.   *Future of Difference.*

to give meaning to our lives and to transform the world, but we hope that the powers of the academy will not notice this, or at least will not think us unscholarly because our work has this capacity. Of course they do notice, and they *do* find our work threatening.

<Forwarded from GG>
NB wrote

> >But the threat seems to lie in the fact that as feminist scholar I am also
> >and unavoidably an activist.[4] The attempts by women to do different
> >research differently are challenges to the patriarchy. All parts of the
> >enterprise are significant—the attempts by women to participate as
> >equals in the academic enterprise, their different subjects, and their
> >specific, feminist perspectives or preferences in research strategies. My
> >academic work *as such* now represents an attack on androcentrism in
> >intellectual matters, whether or not I do anything that might be
> >explicitly regarded as feminist.

Of course, and the difference between the first wave of feminism and this second wave is precisely in the existence of feminist scholarship, of a large and diverse and vital body of work that constitutes a significant oppositional force. It is here that we've presented fundamental challenges to the structures and institutions of society and to the structure of knowledge itself. There was no equivalent to this in the first wave of feminism. In this, critical theory has been an invaluable tool, because it has provided means to dismantle epistemological categories and reveal systems as systems, as conventional rather than 'natural'. This means that feminist scholarship is extremely important; we have a real mission. Our task as teachers and scholars is to develop critical and political consciousness in those who are coming of age in a world dominated by Republicans and reaction and cynicism and fear.

<Forwarded from CC>
Maybe not Republicans so much nowadays:-)
   In my field, because the battle to legitimate religious studies within the universities has so recently been fought, the feminist critique of the ethos of objectivity touches nerves that are extremely sensitive. This sensitivity may also explain why major departments of religious studies have been slow to hire feminist scholars whose work challenges the ethos of objectivity.

   4.   Tomm 1989—on political science.

<Forwarded from CC>
On 25 October PQ wrote

>The objectivity–subjectivity dualism seems still to be the place where
>the argument over feminist method is situated.

I think that it is a false dualism, but one implicit in the notion of the
ethos of objectivity. It is a dualism that posits rationality, objectivity,
dispassion and analysis on one side, and irrationality, subjectivity,
passion and chaos on the other. The ethos of objectivity is of course
found in the scientific method, in which the researcher aspires to dispassionate, disinterested, 'scientific' analysis and control of data.

<Forwarded from TF>
I want to emphasize that this dynamic takes place in a historical context, in which we are all implicated. None of us wants to participate in
the 'the social function' of oppression.

   To speak of a social function is to speak of a systemic process which,
as is true of any system, has structures and procedures that, by certain
criteria, benefit some at the expense of others, and an ideology that
obscures this dynamic. The survival of women, like other marginal
groups, has required—even as we rebel—our participation in our own
oppression. I think we have to locate and refuse the means by which we
participate, to render them socially dysfunctional—to recognize in the
dialectic of oppression, that subversive transformation in which we
each play a different and crucial part.

<Forwarded from EE>
It's an important political step, to acknowledge our place in discourse,
and to acknowledge that we have *not* been absent during the 2000 years
of patriarchal metaphysics, not merely helpless and suppressed but, for
many reasons and in many ways, collaborators. Liking, trusting, working with other women, blows up the law that says women can be con-
quered, as they always have been, by division. To take responsibility
for my participation means that perhaps for the first time I can make a
real difference: that I can avoid the trap of merely reproducing only
with female personnel, the same old stories of power.[5]

<Forwarded from PQ>
What is continuing to happen is that feminists working in the patriar-

5.   *Changing Subjects.*

chal structures typical of the institutions that employ most of us are kind of middle managers, facilitators for programs over which we have no ultimate control, doing the lower-level jobs, teaching the required courses and so on. In my field, most of the undergraduate students are female, as are the graduate assistants who teach them, while the majority of the senior professors are male. But because of the teaching done by graduate students, who have to accept these poorly paid jobs as an unacknowledged condition for getting the degree, those who are in privileged positions have the time to do their research and speaking and publishing, which then reinforces their position. And it's not so much the people as the system that enables this to happen.

<Forwarded from JAF>
We've had a system failure here this weekend, so I'm just getting into this.

I agree with whoever said that the powers that be are agents of power-systems with which we often collaborate, even when we think we are in opposition. That's an important point.

<Forwarded from GG>
I'd like to have Elizabeth's optimism. But the signals reach us, directly and indirectly, through cajolery, flattery, warning, implicit and explicit—if we heed them we are rewarded, if we resist, we are dropped; and they are so subtle and persuasive that we may bend to them without noticing, without noticing how they have bent us out of shape.

<Forwarded from JAF>
Feminism, as much or more than any other social movement, has had to grapple with the question of difference, especially sexual difference. Feminism wants at once to deny difference—I'm just like you—and to proclaim it—but women are different from men—an insoluble dilemma.[6] But if feminism has given us choices that are painful, opening up more room for difference, it has also given us more ways to connect. French theory too has given us ways of celebrating difference, of resisting appropriation, even while it cautions us to modesty about our gains.

6. Also in Greene.

<Forwarded from EE>
We can't resist the kind of pressure Gayle is talking about alone,
though. That's why groups like this one are so important. A soloist
feminist is a contradiction in terms, although this contradiction is one
fostered eagerly enough by the patriarchal establishment within the
university and outside it. Gayle mentioned flattery in her last post.
Among the many familiar gambits of patriarchy for preserving its hierarchical exclusions, one of the most seductive, apparently, is the patriarchal compliment 'You're different', which translates, 'You're like us,
not like them.' I think that a feminist—that is, a woman who likes other
women with all that entails politically—is not comfortable with this
praise in any explicit or implicit version. She is uncomfortable being
'the woman' in the senior ranks, on the job list, the panel, the committee. To accept the patriarchal compliment 'You're different', is to
accept a posture of competition with other women of that kind that
perennially has undermined women's solidarity. It always has worked,
and it still seems to work, like a charm. A feminist is a woman who can
resist the many temptations to fall into competition with other women
for favored slave status.

<Forwarded from CM>
It is difficult to force an established administration, by definition hostile
to subversive change, to welcome the very vital forces that threaten its
foundation. Academic careers have their competitive and constrictive
aspects. If feminism at its best promotes the libidinal economy—the
forces or value for life—at the expense of the political economy—the
drive for power—it will have a hard time finding a place in an institution as rigidly structured as the university. Hence the radical critique of
academic feminism, which holds that if you use language accessible to
the 'intellectual community', you cannot possibly speak as a woman.[7]

<Forwarded from GG>
To say 'I', to get personal, is a way of centering ourselves, grounding
ourselves; to articulate the relation of that 'I' to the social and political
forces that have shaped us is a way of making that 'I' more than personal, of re-envisioning the personal as political—it is a way of saying
'I' while also saying 'we'.[8]

7. Cf. Difference—this is useful.
8. Changing subjects. Get this!

I'd also emphasize that personal criticism, rather than a practice pitted against theory and reinforcing the usual binarisms like personal against public, female against male, concrete against abstract, and so on, may be imbricated in theory in a way which broadens the notion of theory. So, far from turning in on itself in a response which is trivial, self-indulgent, merely personal, such writing is engaged.

<Forwarded from EE>
I know that if I'm not part of the solution, I'm part of the problem. If I do not collaborate in my own suppression, I cannot really be suppressed; but I cannot stop collaborating and assume a constructive role until I acknowledge my actual constructions, look at them, and see whether they are any good. To take that latter, critical step, I need other women because only they share my problem, my discursive identity, my particular woman's 'I'. That's how I see speaking as a woman. In one way, it's subjective, but in another way it's a shared voice. I think that Gayle is right about that.

<Forwarded from GG>
We—feminists in academia—inhabit an environment that is unbelievably hostile to what we do, as I'm sure Tucker especially would agree. This has got to be remembered, and it can hardly be overstated. Feminist criticism grew up and was shaped by institutions dominated by men and dedicated to a tradition that has never served our interests; and in many ways, it shows. What has happened with women in academia is a microcosm of what has happened with women in society—and it is what always happens, historically: a few women are let in so that there are a few women in visible positions who can be pointed to as evidence that women have made it; meanwhile the majority of women are left where they always were. This means that much of what has succeeded in academia has been allowed to succeed because it's the kind of feminism institutions can live with. A theoretical discourse that's preoccupied by increasingly subtle deconstructions of subjectivity and experience is unlikely to be much concerned with changing people or experience; it's no accident that this is the going thing. So what it comes down to, again, is power, who's at the center, who's King of the Mountain. The problem is not with 'theory' per se or with theory at all, but with the enlistment of theory in this scramble for power and position.

<Forwarded from GG>
On 26 October PQ wrote

>   >Are you saying that we need to move away from theory, even though
>   >that seems to be where we have the best chance for making inroads in
>   >the power structures?

The question is, once we've 'got theory', what do we do with it? What's it for? Who's it for? In the early days of feminism I remember a lot of talk about the dangers of cooptation; I don't hear a lot of that kind of talk any more, now when the disconnection of theory from the political and its connection to the star system endangers us more than ever. As hooks suggests, we live in a culture that promotes narcissism, that encourages it because it deflects attention away from our capacity to form political commitments that address issues rather than identity. And so we often seem more engaged by who was speaking/writing than by what they were saying. That cult of personality has severely limited the feminist movement. Stardom is about hierarchy, self, career, commodification. It is not about dialogue or action or collectivity or the political, except in the most strategic, self-serving sense.

<Forwarded from AK>
There is a real danger of losing sight of our political responsibilities in our own personal grab for power. To write chapters decrying the sexual stereotyping of women in our literature, while closing our eyes to the sexual harassment of our women students and colleagues; or to display Katherine Hepburn and Rosalind Russell in our courses on 'The Image of the Independent Career Woman in Film', while managing not to notice the paucity of female administrators on our own campus; or to study the women who helped make universal enfranchisement a political reality, while keeping silent about our activist colleagues who are denied promotion or tenure—and these are just some examples that I've seen—this destroys both the spirit and the meaning of what we are about. It puts us, however unwittingly, in the service of those who laid the minefield in the first place. In my view, it is a fine thing for many of us, individually, to have traversed the minefield; but that happy circumstance will only prove of lasting importance if, together, we expose it for what it is—I mean, the male fear of sharing power and significance with women—and deactivate its components.[9]

9.   Cf. Showalter 1985.

<Forwarded from PQ>

What Annette says is all well and good, but how do you imagine doing that? We seem to live in a zero-sum-balance world, where a gain for you is a loss for me, where if a woman gets a share in the power and influence, if a woman gets a senior appointment, for example, it has to be at the expense of some man.

<Forwarded from CC>

On 27 October NA wrote

> >Never mind male fears—I have my own. If male critics begin to accept
> >what we are doing, I fear that this acceptance will lead to our being
> >locked into a new prison. If a woman's reading of a novel is perceived
> >as insufficiently 'womanly', will her fresh perceptions be tabooed
> >as our feminist ones were in the old days? Separatism is always a
> >double-edged sword; women are praised for having qualities that
> >are then forced on them, and if 'reading as a woman' becomes an
> >institutionalized enterprise, I fear that its hegemony will crush our
> >power to read as it has been crushed so often before.[10]

That's why I wanted to propose an alternative model for scholarship, one that can be related to the female experience of connection, and to try to sidestep the problem of separation, with what I have called 'the ethos of eros and empathy'. As I said, one of the goals of our scholarship is empathy, a form of understanding that reaches out to the otherness of the other, which is rooted in a desire to understand the world form a different point of view.

<Forwarded from NA>

I have another fear: I fear that the embrace of patriarchy means our own disappearance. Some men have written of their conversion as if feminism were an act of grace freely given to them: lauding their own illumination, they fail to cite the names of any actual, female feminist critics. This shyness about acknowledging female authority probably springs from an attempt to reproduce the evangelical feminist voice, but when they abandon conventional scholarly decorum to embrace life studies, they abandon the female lives that inspired our writing, and then their own, in the first place...our experiences are continually

10. Benstock 1987.

threatened by absorption in the self-proclamation of male truth. The
next generation's Anon. may be ourselves.[11]

<Forwarded from EE>
That kind of 'feminism' raises problems of definition. If a feminist is a
woman who likes other women, as I've argued before, it follows that
feminism is a negotiation between women, among women. A man, for
example, cannot be a feminist, however supportive he may be of a
woman's personal and professional development, for the simple reason
that no man is culturally constructed as a woman and thus no man is
qualified to engage in this particular dynamic between women. This
point may be worth making in an academic context where some men,
having seen the power of feminism, are here and there hopping on the
bandwagon as if a couple of articles with woman-friendly topics could
make them feminists.

<Forwarded from PQ>
On 28 October TF wrote,

> >We need to remember that our civilization is built on systemic woman-
> >hating, and is maintained by systemic denial of the fact. Like the
> >parasitic dependency of the ruling class upon those it exploits, the
> >dependency of 'men' upon 'women' is a great secret of history. To
> >keep it, same-sex social/sexual relations—which provide the evidence
> >to disprove the 'necessity' of exploiting dependency relations of gender
> >difference—are made taboo. At the same time, difference is used as a
> >tool for maintaining divisions in the hierarchies of power. It follows
> >that 'History, capital H'—the male record of civilization—has been a
> >socially masculine construct, by definition hiding, containing and
> >refuting female power function. History silences and requires silence.

So the question is, how do we do history so that these hierarchies of
power can be undone? How do we read historical documents as feminists so that women are no longer silenced?

<Forwarded from AK>
I think that what we have really come to mean when we speak of com-
petence in reading historical texts is the ability to recognize literary
conventions which have survived through time—so as to remain opera-
tional in the mind of the reader—and, where these are lacking, the

11. Yes!

ability to translate—or perhaps transform?—the text's ciphers into more current and recognizable shapes. But we never really reconstruct the past in its own terms. In my field, what we gain when we read the 'classics', is an approximation of an already fictively imputed past made available, through our interpretative strategies, for present concerns. I would say, incidentally, that the kind of history Carol works with in her second stage is also fictively imputed, although there is a different relationship to actual past events in that case that has caused scholarship to privilege 'objective' analysis.

What distinguishes feminists in this regard is their desire to alter and extend what we take as historically relevant from out of that vast storehouse of our literary inheritance and, further, feminists' recognition of the storehouse for what it really is: a resource for remodeling our history, past, present and future.

If what the larger women's movement looks for in the future is a transformation of the structures of primarily male power which now order our society, then the feminist critic demands that we understand the ways in which those structures have been—and continue to be—reified by our texts and by our criticism. Thus, along with other 'radical' critics and critical schools, though our focus remains the power of the word to both structure and mirror human experience, our overriding commitment is to a radical alteration—an improvement, we hope—in the nature of that experience.

Historical Notes

Being a partial transcript of the proceedings of the Seventeenth Symposium on Gileadean Studies, held as part of the International Historical Association Convention, which took place at Memorial University North, St. Anthony-L'Anse-aux-Meadows, 8–11 June, 2245.

Chair: Professor Joe Sundown, Department of Caucasian Anthropology, and Director of the Centre for Religious Sociology, University of Labrador at Nain.

Keynote Speaker: Professor Sumit Rana, Director, Twentieth and Twenty-first Century Archives, Cambridge University, England.

...and this afternoon there will be a trip to the World Heritage Site at

L'Anse-aux-Meadows by replica ships of the Viking period in Northern Europe. Those of you who are athletically inclined may participate in the actual sailing of the vessels, although of course they all have professional crews. You will all need warm clothes and rain gear. 'Sou'westers' designed to resemble the sort used by late twentieth-century fishermen in Newfoundland will be provided, and if you wish to keep yours, you may purchase them as souvenirs.

I am also asked to remind you that the annual dinner of the Historical Association will be held here in St. Anthony this evening, and that a few tickets are still available at the Registration Desk.

Those of you who attended our first session this morning need no introduction to Professor Sumit Rana. The document which Professor Rana presented to us is one of the more exciting new discoveries at the Niagara Falls dig, and we look forward to the analysis of it. If you did not receive a copy, you can load it from one of the transfer disks on the table by the back door. There will be time for questions after Professor Rana's talk.

Professor Rana.

Rana:
Thank you. I'm very pleased to be able to share the results of the preliminary work I have done on this document, one of the very few documents of this sort to have survived from the time immediately preceding the Early Gileadean Period. As you know, these are a collection of what appear to have been an archived thread of related messages. The discussion seems to have occurred shortly after a meeting which we believe took place in the late years of the twentieth century, probably in one of the large cities of what was then the northern United States. We have found what we believe to be a recording of a presentation at this meeting, done on audiocassette of the type that was still widely available until the early years of the twenty-first century, but unfortunately the tape was badly damaged. My colleague, Dr Merlin, and I, using historical tools, are attempting to reconstruct the paper which was the occasion for the email discussion, but that work has only just begun, and is hampered by the lack of extant documentation typical of this period. Fortunately my predecessor, Professor J.D. Pieixoto, and his colleague Dr Knotly Wade had reconstructed a machine capable of playing this sort of recording, which made possible the publication of what they called 'The Handmaid's Tale', a taped diary which comes

from the Early Gileadean Period, probably about a decade after the material we are considering today. Although the recording of the academic presentation is so far undecipherable, the cassette was found together with a computer diskette in a 3.5 inch format widely used in the last decade of the century, onto which the email messages had been downloaded in apparent chronological order. The headings had been deleted, so the dates and details of the addresses are unfortunately unavailable. Along with the diskette, we discovered an annotated hard copy, with the messages in a slightly different order, which has enabled us to be relatively sure of the logical order of the discussion, as it was understood by the owner of the diskette.

The paper was preserved by a fluke, having been slipped into a plastic bag with a seal at the top which prevented water damage. One of the most important additions provided by this document are the handwritten notes in the margins of the transcript, which we have included in your material as footnotes. These were written in a clear hand, apparently with a 'ball-point' pen, an instrument widely used before computerized notebooks became common. This, incidentally, is one of the factors that leads us to date the document early. The ink in this instrument reacted with the paper to become for all intents and purposes indelible. Because of the high acid content of the paper, it has become very fragile. Our museum technicians have just completed transferring the document to special sleeves which enable us to work with the separate sheets without damaging them further.

The discovery of the materials in Niagara Falls, on what was the Canadian side of the border, is consonant with our previous theories about the underground movement of dissidents in the transition period and the beginning of the Early Gileadean Period. The email address at the top of the document has been damaged, but it appears to be include 'epas', which we have identified as part of the address used at the University of Toronto at the time. The list owner, whose name is not legible, may have been a Canadian resident, and it is possible that the 'sgraham' whose address is written in the margin at the top of the document, in your Note 1, was in fact the list owner. We have attempted to identify this person, whom we suppose to have been a woman, but there is no trace of any female academic of the time with that patronymic, although the name is common enough. The person who collected and downloaded these messages probably made the marginal notes, and perhaps is also one of the participants in the discussion, although there is no indication which one he or she might be.

Dating the document remains our principal question. The conference which preceded this discussion must have taken place fairly early. Some, if not all, of the writers appear to be women, which would have been impossible once the Constitution had been suspended, and the quick abrogation of Compubank privileges would naturally have prevented travel for most women after the first few months of the Early Gileadean regime. Other than what is preserved for us in documents such as 'The Handmaid's Tale', we have very little information about the transition time, since the Gileadean regime periodically purged its own computer records, and records of this sort from the pre-Gileadean era were destroyed because of the danger they were thought to pose to public order. For reconstructing the history of private life of that time, we ordinarily have little more to go on than the genealogical records preserved in the computers at Salt Lake City. By the way, I cannot emphasize too strongly what a treasure we have found in these materials. It is perhaps humbling for us to realize that women who were born three hundred years ago were participating in activities not so far removed from ours today.

None of the women in the discussion seems to have had any premonition of the political upheavals to come. One might question their political astuteness, of course. They discuss their political roles at great length, but have completely missed the tenor of their time. Late in the '90s this error would have been unthinkably naive. Changes in property law and banking practices had probably come into effect by that time, as had limitations on women's access to electronic networks. Marginal notes in our text with dates appear to be references to publications related to the subject at hand; in two cases, 'Showalter 1985' and 'Benstock 1987', these dates are helpful in determining the *terminus post quem* for our manuscript. A date in the early '90s is enough after the 1987 date in the notes to allow for adequate dissemination of Benstock's book, if indeed that is what Note 9 means. And it is early enough to account for women's participation at this level in the universities, their freedom to attend conferences and to use electronic mail services.

One other reference may also corroborate our conclusions. 'Gayle G.' refers to 'a world dominated by Republicans', among other things. The word refers to one of two main political parties in the United States. They had been in power for most of three decades in the late century, losing a presidential election only twice in that time. The first case, the election of Jimmy Carter, occurred well before this time; however, the Republicans lost a presidential election in late 1992. 'Carol C.'s response, 'Maybe not so much Republicans nowadays,' may be a reference to this election. The party was overwhelmingly returned to power in the mid-term Congressional elections of 1994 and of course in 1996, in spite of Bill Clinton's re-election to the Presidency. If our interpretation is correct, then the conference and our document probably date between 1993 and 1995 or 96 at the latest.

The origin of the materials which have been discovered, then, appears to be a late-twentieth-century conference and electronic discussion, probably in the years just preceding the President's Day Massacre. The writers are identified by letters, which we have assumed are the initials of their names. It appears to have been the policy of the list to use initials only in email addresses, unfortunately. This may have been for convenience, or it may indicate that certain participants in email discussions were beginning to feel that partial anonymity was desirable. In the course of the discussion, some of the speakers referred to others by their first, or to use an expression of the time, their Christian names. Most of the names generally refer to females. We suppose that all the writers, with one exception, are women. The evidence is unclear regarding the exception, identified as 'TF'; unfortunately, the name, Tucker, is not gender specific. However, 'Tucker F.'s self-inclusion at one point, saying 'The survival of women...has required...our participation in our own oppression', would seem to indicate strongly that all the participants are female. Since the writers appear to be a self-selected group of academics, and since universities required teaching staff to publish, we have hope of being able to identify the writers further, particularly if they had done any serious research which might have been published in journals which also included the work of men, and which therefore were not all destroyed.

Thus our preliminary conclusions are that the writers are probably female. We turn next to the content of the discussion in order to analyze the social situation of the individuals involved. The speakers refer to themselves as academics, although they may not have been professors. However, women involved in teaching in universities even at lower levels would have been part of an elite class. We suppose they were not paid as highly as men in similar positions, as 'PQ's comments indicate, but their salaries would probably have enabled them to support themselves independently of better-paid spouses. This is one element in our hypothesis that these women were not married. Again, I want to stress that our research is just beginning, but I want to sketch the lines of reasoning that we are following.

As I said, we are attempting to reconstruct the content of the presentation that preceded this discussion. Several factors indicate that 'Carol C.' was the presenter. Hers is the first forwarded message in the document. We believe that the presentation concerned what she called the 'ethos of empathy', an idea on which she expands here. 'PQ', in her response to 'Carol C.' quotes her, saying 'you said in your presentation'. Since there is no other explanation of this phrase, it must refer to a presentation familiar to all the participants in the discussion. It is likely that the presentation dealt with the problem of the inclusion of personal and subjective reflections in academic discourse. The 'ethos of empathy' provides us with one possible way this project was conceived at the time, although there were doubtless others. Of course, with the inception of the early Gileadean regime, the problem was eliminated by removing women from academic positions. There is some evidence from this document that there were men who considered themselves 'feminists': these people might have been able to remain in their posts, so long as it was not known that they questioned the Doctrine of Objectivity. Oaths were not required immediately, of course, but unorthodox books and articles were rarely published, even in the first years of the Early Gileadean Period. So 'NA's fears that male feminists would cause the disappearance of 'actual, female feminist critics', as she says, were ungrounded, although ironically her conclusion, 'The next generation's Anon. may be ourselves', was in fact correct.

There are ten different individuals contributing to the discussion. In the early years of electronic discussion groups, the format allowed for what appears to be open responses from a variety of points of view, with some questions and answers and some points made in an attempt to build on what other writers have said. Although the 'forwarded from' messages indicate that the list was moderated, the moderator was apparently not censoring the messages. This sort of unstructured discussion may reflect the attempts of women in the pre-Gileadean and early Gileadean periods to develop a way to 'democratize' and 'feminize' academic discourse. One of the concerns voiced by several of the participants is that women find their identity and voice. We may find that concern difficult to understand. I want to point you particularly to the comment by 'Carol C.', who asserts that women in the university system were under considerable pressure to adopt a rational and objective method of working, contrary to their 'feminist' desires for a revolution in method. One wonders what would have happened had they succeeded.

One of the speakers has provided a clear definition of the term 'feminist', which has been a difficult problem for historians. Nearly all of the written work which could be classified as 'feminist' was destroyed by the Early Gileadean regime, for obvious reasons. In this case, 'EE', or 'Elizabeth', defines a feminist as 'a woman who likes other women with all that entails politically', and by definition she excludes males who might have been sympathetic to women's causes. This definition gives us another reason to believe that 'TF' is probably a woman. The group as a whole is suspicious of men. None of them appears to have been married, but in spite of 'Tucker F.'s interest in using homosexuality as an analytical category, 'liking other women' does not seem to necessarily imply a sexual preference, although further work is still needed in this area. What is entailed politically, as far as we can tell, is a change in the power structures within the universities. If this movement had succeeded, universities might well have lost their status as institutions where knowledge is produced, and we might have lost the tools needed to advance human learning, indeed, even to understand documents like this one. The repression of North American feminists, of course, had wide-reaching effects, not only in North America, but ultimately worldwide, for which we today remain grateful.

Although all the speakers consider themselves feminist, they apparently worked in different fields. The complete title of the list is lost, and we have only the acronym, WIT-L, to go on. Because the list participants all appear to be female, we suspect that the title begins 'Women in,' but the field designated by T, if that is the case, remains a puzzle. 'Carol C.' appears to have been a historian interested in ancient Greek culture; she seems to have been familiar with 'religious studies', and she refers to 'Sappho'. 'AK', or 'Annette', indicates that her area is 'classics', which we take to be either Greek or Latin literature from about the fifth century BCE to the second or third century of the Common Era. She is interested in the conventions of 'historical texts', which supports this view. On the other hand, the examples she uses for the dangers of losing sight of the political implications of feminist action, particularly her mention of the course title, 'The Image of the Independent Career Woman in Film', seem to contradict this conclusion. It is unlikely that such a course appeared in the listings of any classics department of the time, even though there appears to have been a good deal of interest in what was called 'media studies', which were often cross-listed with more traditional disciplines. 'NA' refers to the reading of novels, indicating that her area may have been one of the modern literatures, but it is a slender bit of evidence. As for the others, while they seem to have been part of the broad area called the 'humanities', it is difficult to be more specific at this point.

The interest in 'theory' evidenced in a number of comments might suggest philosophy as a field, although in the late twentieth century, scholars in a number of different departments, particularly what they then called 'modern languages', also claimed 'theory' for their own fields. The 'subtle deconstructions' to which 'Gayle G.' refers is an allusion to a minor philosophical school of the time which was part of 'post-structuralist' thought. It was especially influential during the '80s, after which it quickly dropped out of fashion. I might recommend to those of you who find this question interesting, that we have in our Archives at Oxford a first edition of Alice's critique of post-structuralism, dated 1996, if you would like to pursue the matter further. It was probably the book that marked the beginning of the end of the movement, although the political turmoil which followed soon after its publication resulted in a sharper break than would normally have been the case. I'm sorry to report to Professor Sundown, because I know that this is a special interest of his, that there is no trace of religious thought in the manuscript, aside from 'Carol C.'s passing reference to religious studies as her field. Neither feminist nor post-structuralist thought seems to have had much interest in religion, if this document is any indication.

One of the recurring themes of both movements appears to be dichotomy, a 'binarism' in 'Gayle G.'s terms, which was apparently a theoretical term. Much of the conversation about dualism, in which the meaning of a term is said to be defined in terms of its opposite, is a feminist borrowing of a linguistic technique of analysis. This may help with the references to 'difference'. Political implications were extrapolated from linguistics in a questionable logical move, but it is clear from the emotional tone of this document that these feminists, at any rate, were not troubled by the niceties of logic. There is a surprising amount of 'feeling language' in this academic document; I refer especially to NA's repeated use of the verb 'fear'.

The content of the discussion is of primarily antiquarian interest, and in the time remaining, I want simply to discuss some of the more obscure references. There are a number of allusions that we have tried to trace, with more or less success. Michael Novak's book is well known to specialists of the period, of course. 'hooks' is unknown. The lack of capitalization in the name may not be a typographical error; there is a precedent in the poet e.e. cummings. 'hooks', however, does not appear to be a poet, and so the spelling may indicate that we need to look for another interpretation. Most of you are well versed in the twentieth century, so I suppose you recognize the names of two of the better-known film actresses of the time, Katherine Hepburn and Rosalind Russell. The marginal notes make reference to books and articles that seem to be related to the discussion. 'Tomm' appears with what may be a title; the reference may be to an article in a collection. There are some ambiguities in the notes that we have not yet been able to clarify. 'Changing subjects' appears twice, once capitalized and underlined, once with the further annotation, 'Get this!' This may be a title, with a reminder to acquire the book; or it may be a note that the discussion is taking a different direction, while 'get this' was a colloquial expression sometimes used at the time to indicate surprise and disbelief. The context of the note indicates that the first explanation is probably better; but if 'Changing subjects' refers to a book, we have not yet been able to trace it. It may be a feminist publication, of course, in which case, it would no longer be extant. The notes include a comment that 'difference' is useful, where again we are not sure if this is a reference to the concept of difference touched on in the discussion, or if it is a second reference to the *Future of Difference* found in Note 3. To this point, we have only checked references in English; if any of the books or writers was published internationally, there is a chance that we will be able to find the reference.

I see that I have run a few minutes over time, so I'll stop here, and I apologize if you will be late for the last sessions today. Thank you for your interest and patience. I welcome any questions you may have.

INTEXTS

Atwood, Margaret
    1986   *The Handmaid's Tale* (New York: Ballantine).
Auerbach, Nina
    1987   'Engorging the Patriarchy', in Shari Benstock (ed.), *Feminist Issues in Literary Scholarship* (Bloomington: Indiana University Press): 150-60.
Benstock, Shari (ed.)
    1987   *Feminist Issues in Literary Scholarship* (Bloomington: Indiana University Press).
Black, Naomi
    1989   'The Child Is Father to the Man: The Impact of Feminism on Canadian Political Science', in Tomm 1989: 225-43.
Christ, Carol P.
    1987   'Toward a Paradigm Shift in the Academy and Religious Studies', in Christie Farnham (ed). *The Impact of Feminist Research in the Academy* (Bloomington: Indiana University Press): 53-75.
Eisenstein, Hester, and Alice Jardine (eds.)
    1987   *The Future of Difference* (New Brunswick, NJ: Rutgers University Press).
Ermath, Elizabeth
    1993   'On Having a Personal Voice', in Greene and Kahn 1993: 226-39.
Farley, Tucker Pamela
    1987   'Lesbianism and the Social Function of Taboo', in Eisenstein and Jardine 1987: 267-73.
Farnham, Christie (ed.)
    1987   *The Impact of Feminist Research in the Academy* (Bloomington: Indiana University Press).
Fleiger, Jerry Aline
    1993   'Growing up Theoretical: Across the Divide', in Greene and Kahn 1993: 253-66.
Greene, Gayle
    1993   'Looking at History', in Greene and Kahn 1993: 4-27.
Greene, Gayle, and Coppelia Kahn (eds).
    1993   *Changing Subjects: The Making of Feminist Literary Criticism* (New York: Routledge).
Kolodny, Annette
    1985   'Dancing Through the Minefield: Some Observations on the Theory, Practice, and Politics of Feminist Literary Criticism', in Elaine Showalter (ed.), *The New Feminist Criticism* (New York: Pantheon): 144-67.
Makward, Christiane
    1987   'To Be or Not to Be...a Feminist Speaker', in Eisenstein and Jardine 1987: 95-105.
Novak, Michael
    1986   *Belief and Unbelief: Philosophy of Self-Knowledge* (Lanham, MD: University Press of America).

Quelle, Prim
     1999   *The Impossible Possibilities* (New York: Vanity).
Showalter, Elaine (ed.)
     1985   *The New Feminist Criticism* (New York: Pantheon).
Tomm, Winnie (ed.)
     1989   *The Effects of Feminist Approaches on Research Methodologies*
                 (Waterloo, ON: Wilfrid Laurier University Press).

WHAT DIFFERENCE DOES DIFFERENCE MAKE IN FEMINIST HERMENEUTICS? A PERSONAL ESSAY

Cheryl A. Kirk-Duggan

Introduction

This essay explores how different contexts and conversations make a difference in the interpretation of biblical texts. People read and hear texts that include their own reality as well as texts that exclude their own reality. Cultural experiences shape how scholars representing diverse feminist, womanist and *mujerista* biblical theological hermeneutics interpret texts. Indeed, the various constituencies and the communities from which these scholars emerge also hear and read texts differently. In the following, after reflecting on what scholars and other reader/listeners bring to the moment of interpretation and to conversations about texts, I raise questions about interpreting Isaiah 50 and Phil. 2.6-11. These questions emerged in response to the contributions of Athalya Brenner, Cheryl Townsend Gilkes, Jean M. Kim and Sharon Ringe to the 1994 SBL Feminist Theological Hermeneutics of the Bible session titled, 'What Difference Does Difference Make in Feminist Hermeneutics?'

When people gather to dialogue, they bring their offerings, expertise, passions and, ideally, a willingness to be dialogue partners. Dialogue makes clear that different backgrounds, assumptions and social locations shape interpreters' reading and hearing of texts. My own socio-cultural, hermeneutical location is that of professor, preacher, performer, poet, writer, Christian Womanist, musician, athlete and creative spirit who sees the good, is compassionate about justice issues, and tempers life with humor and the prophetic. My life experience is multi-culturally ecumenical: I am an ordained Christian Methodist Episcopal minister, married to an Irish Roman Catholic, with a Presbyterian Master of Divinity degree and a Baptist PhD. I have had Jewish roommates, I participate in Jewish and African-American dialogue, and

I have mentored Asian women. As a graduate student, I had the challenge of teaching music and black studies courses in coed, undergraduate classes at a large university. Armed with my Master of Music degree, I taught performance and pedagogical courses in music at a historically black college in the Southwest. PhD in hand, I had the opportunity of teaching biblical, theological and ethics courses at an all-women's liberal arts Baptist college.

Currently I have the call and joy of being a professor and administrator in a consortial, ecumenical, seminary and university setting, where I teach, preach, perform, conduct research, write, listen, travel and meet diverse people from varied walks of life. In this setting I work to promote interest in the religious experiences of women, to develop programs, and to raise funds to support them. For five years I was privileged to be part of the 'Wimmin in Purple' group, four passionate prayer warriors in Austin, Texas who supported each other in the parish, higher education and life itself. Since 1984 I have maintained a close connection with an ecumenical, interracial, socio-economically diverse Bible study and prayer group of over 15 families. This spiritual group is an extended community of praise, compassion, love and support through life changes of weddings, births, deaths, anniversaries, job changes, geographical shifts, and all that flows in between. All of these experiences have taught me to see and joyfully acknowledge difference and diversity. As my geographical context has shifted and broadened, taking me from the US South and Southwest to the Northeast, Southeast and now the West, my ability to hear difference with integrity, curiosity, humor and appreciation has grown and matured. I hear many voices.

My childhood taught me to hear other voices. Intellectually I began to recognize the existence of these voices from elementary school geography, history and civics. I learned not to disparage these voices because I grew up in a unique home, where I was taught that there is always someone who can do something better than you and always someone whom you can surpass. This was not a lesson of inferiority or superiority, but of reality checks. Such lessons of appreciation let me see differences without being jealous, envious or fearful. As my father was the first African-American deputy sheriff in the state of Louisiana since Reconstruction, and thanks to the dialogue that my parents had together, there was no sense of oppression in our home. We knew the reality of racism, but we were not taught to hate nor to fear. The support I felt from my parents, and their ability to give me the room to think creatively always provided a sense of welcoming difference. For me, this meant that I was a citizen of the world. This freedom instilled a curiosity and passion about many issues, from social justice to the arts, always hearing many, many voices. This hearing has significantly influenced the manner in which I hear Scripture.

Life experiences and educational journeys influence the assumptions one brings, the questions that emerge and the lessons one gleans from a particular scriptural text. Interpreters hold assumptions concerning issues as varied as the validity and historicity of the text, the text's authority, and which voices in the text the reader inclines to identify with or to reject. Whether one approaches the biblical text for purposes of personal reflection, for teaching and/or preaching, for a journal article, as part of a textbook, or as part of a commentary, certain expectations and presuppositions will influence the reader's encounter with the text.

The growing participation of female scholars and non-white scholars of both genders in the academy has heightened awareness of the complexity of hermeneutical strategies and the myriad biases couched within traditional exegesis. A hermeneutics of suspicion allows one to approach the text with doubts and the freedom to question traditional readings. A confrontational hermeneutic of displacement enables one to uncover clear images and provocative ideas. A hermeneutic built on a melodic/rhythmic socio-cultural and aural motif brings one to an imaginative, integrative, committed, usable discourse. A hermeneutic of disclosure can expose problematic church dogmas, their authoritarianism and in some cases their culturally contingent, non-liberating models of God or Jesus. A hermeneutics of liturgical and dialogical encounter can offer an empirical/experiential, dialectical reading out of a communal context of solidarity amid suffering. A hermeneutics of righteous indignation, grounded in analysis of the roles of women and of female imagery in the Bible, heightens one's consciousness about the subtlety of oppression, the ways that biblical women's roles and women-oriented metaphors have often been used to punish, demean and control women, and the incredibly inadequate recognition and respect for the day-to-day power that women exercised in the past and still do today.

A hermeneutic of liberation allows for difference and for challenging alleged norms, while at the same time denying the oppressed the opportunity to remain victims. In Alice Walker's *The Color Purple* (Walker

1982), there is violence and oppression due to race and gender, but the novel celebrates Celie and Mr.— (the metamorphosed Albert) as persons who transcend the accepted norms of oppressed and oppressed/ oppressor respectively, to become transformed persons who have agency, dignity and compassion for each other. New liberation models that accord freedom with responsibility can build spirits of optimism, empowerment and beauty. Hermeneutics based on women's experience celebrates the realities of life and acknowledges that many biblical texts engender anger, disparagement, hopelessness, disenfranchisement, ugliness, pain and manipulation. Some of these texts remain problematic, while other texts allow an option for a redemptive, liberative praxis. The importance of difference and diversity in biblical interpretation becomes clear when we attend to the ways that oppressed women hear and wrestle with particular biblical images or metaphors. A good example is the servant imagery in Isaiah 50 and Phil. 2.6-11.

The Servant of Isaiah 50

Acknowledging a certain discontinuity between Isa. 50.1-3 and the third 'Servant Song' of Second Isaiah that follows (50.4-11), I will not here explore further the question of the origins and development of Isaiah 50. Focusing on the term 'servant', however, raises questions about both the ancient and contemporary meaning of this motif. Isaiah 50, moreover, is problematic not only for its servant imagery, but also because Isaiah 50 uses divorce as a metaphor related to redemption of Israel.

A consideration of the servant imagery begins with the question: what does it mean to be a servant? Who is the servant? Whom does that servant obey, wait on, and at what cost? Is the term 'servant' synonymous with 'slave'? How does the context of exile shape the discourse, given Second Isaiah's exilic setting? How do the historic events of the Holocaust, the slavery of those in the African Diaspora, the trail of tears resulting from the slaughter of Native American peoples, the Nanking massacre, the terror bombings of Coventry and Dresden, and the fact that there have been more homicides and murders due to internal and external wars in the twentieth century than at any other time in the recorded history of the world—how do these realities shape a contemporary reading of Isaiah 50? How does the present-day sex-slavery trade, where children, women and men are stolen or coerced into prostitution affect one's interpretation of Isaiah 50? Given the ongoing oppression of women in the workplace and the reality of domestic violence in the home, how does one read Isaiah 50? What is the effect upon readers of Isaiah of the generally unspoken sexual harassment perpetrated on women who have worked as domestic servants, as wet nurses, maids, housekeepers and nannies at the hands of their employers?

In the Hebrew Bible the noun *'ebed*, 'servant', or 'slave', derives from the verb *'abad,* 'to work, serve, labor.' Though an *'ebed* may be accorded certain rights and positions of trust, the term nonetheless designates a person in the position of a vassal, a bondsman or bondswoman. The word may apply to someone who is restricted, forced into labor, kept in servitude, made servile or subordinate, for example, in the military, as a political subject, or as a worshipper of God. In Isaiah 39–66, the term *'ebed* occurs 31 times, in the singular and the plural, as a messianic designation in reference to the national and spiritual people of Israel, a people of promise (Harris, Archer, Waltke 1980: II, 639-40; BDB: 712-14; Holladay 1971: 261-62).

To translate *'ebed* as 'slave' or as 'servant' has profound political and pedagogical implications. Either choice can be correct and both offer potential for rich conversation and reflection. The choice of either term and the impact upon interpreter and audience says a great deal about both the interpreter/reader's location and the treatment of the speaker(s) in the Isaian text. In the cultural and political environments of US institutions, religious and secular, such a translation decision cannot be made lightly. Numerous factors, personal and communal, influence how contemporary interpreters/hearers experience the term 'servant' and understand the reality of slavery. These might include knowledge and experience of history; ethnicity and the social advantage or disadvantage that pertains to it; academic study and the privilege it accords; various other social locations of dominance or marginality; contexts of personal growth, employment at a university, denominational seminary, church or synagogue; and vocation or creative focus as a biblical scholar, literary critic, theologian, ethicist, historian, sociologist, minister, priest or rabbi. Factors such as these will both expand and limit the interpretative possibilities of the reader of Isaiah 50.

As one of the four so-called Servant Songs (Isa. 42.1-4; 49.1-6; 50.4-11; and 52.13–53.12), Isaiah 50 is part of a canon within a canon. In this subcollection, God first introduces God's servant in Isa. 42.1-4. Some scholars posit that the servant is an individual, others argue that the context and language indicate that the servant is Israel. Isa. 49.1-6 recounts, in the servant's voice, the divine call of the servant Israel from the womb and the servant's sense of failure, followed by an account of the servant's commission to restore Israel. Following a divine rhetorical query in Isa. 50.1-3, the servant speaks in 50.4-11 of the servant's mission and response to suffering. The fourth Servant Song begins by announcing the appearance, vicarious suffering and ultimate success and exaltation of the servant, Israel (52.13-15). There follows a confessional lament of the nations (53.1-9); and the song concludes by resuming the themes of the first Servant Song, recalling God's purpose in the servant's life, the servant's mission and final vindication (53.10-12). (Muilenburg and Coffin 1956: 614).

The Servant Songs of Second Isaiah (40–55) are set in a context that (1) employs powerful positive female imagery that is taken up also in Third Isaiah, in contrast to First Isaiah where the personified woman of Jerusalem/Zion is the scorned harlot and faithless one; (2) stands in contrast to the lived reality of sixth-century BCE women, and to the prophet's attitude toward Jerusalem; (3) reminds Jerusalem/Zion of Yahweh's love and that its captivity will soon end; (4) involves imagery of marriage, of Jerusalem as bride and abandoned wife; (5) portrays Yahweh as the husband who abandons the wife, in a sixth-century BCE culture where the authority of divorce and other decision making was the husband's privilege; and (6) understands that God, as husband, has the right to divorce without being criticized by society and also uses male imagery for God in a positive light (Ackerman 1992: 166-67). The imagery of marriage and divorce is critical to how one understands servant/slave imagery in Isaiah 50, because the divine pronouncement uses the metaphor of divorce to claim there has only been a separation, not a divorce or break-up that dissolves the covenant relationship between God and Israel.

In the Hebrew Bible the term *kᵉrîtût*, 'dismissal' or 'divorce', appears only three times: Deut. 24.1, 3; Isa. 50.1; Jer 3.8. The word comes from the verbal root *karat*, 'to cut off, or down' (e.g. grapes, garments, hands, foreskins); 'to root out, eliminate, extinguish, destroy'; or 'to make' (literally, 'cut') a covenant' (Harris, Archer, Waltke 1980: I, 456-57; BDB: 503-505; Holladay 1971: 165). The motif of divorce raises questions of family dynamics and societal responses to them, parental intimacy and discord, and the whole nature of marriage and courtship. Too often, hindsight reveals that married parties were not suited to be in covenant with each other. Too often, praise of longevity in marriages fails to distinguish between covenant marriages (characterized by mutuality and caring), and marriages where partners are 'legally married', but live virtually separate lives under the same roof. These insights are important because the issues of divorce and slavery are key to listening for the possible different speaker-voices of Isaiah 50: the voice of Yahweh, the communal voice and the voice of the individual servant.

Personal and traditional presuppositions about the social, political and ethical location of the speaker-voices in Isaiah 50 shape our understanding of the text as oppressive or liberative. The interpreter's relation to issues of difference can be crucial, as in instances, for example, where a female interpreter construes the three voices of the text as all male, or all female, or mixed, in an effort to represent ancient and contemporary voices in a faithful, hopeful manner.

If the three voices are all heard as male, then one negates the voices of ancient women and discounts Second Isaiah's use of strong female imagery. If all the voices are construed as female, then one ignores the ancient patriarchal social setting and runs the risk of appearing to be not just exegetically courageous, but cavalier. Interpreting the characters, however, as either all male or all female creates interesting opportunities to break traditional gender boundaries. At the same time, dialogue about single gendered societies might give audiences the opportunity to explore the differences and gifts that a particular gender brings to society, transcending stereotypes or limiting responses to individual histories. If the voices are mixed, where Yahweh's voice is male and servant/Israel's voice is female, then there is an opportunity to talk critically about the alleged redemptive nature of suffering and about punishment as part of divine justice or restoring the covenant relationship, then and now. Such a dialogue has great significance for women in abusive relationships or congregations and groups of women where much of the authority is relegated to male leaders. If the voice of Yahweh is female and the servant/Israel (individual and communal) is male, several conversational possibilities emerge: exploring the role of motherhood; analyzing the differences and similarities between male and female leadership; and opening up the maternal side of God by comparing one's experience of the maternal with one's experience of

God. Such an exercise could be liberating or at least illuminating for those monotheists, particularly Christians, who through assent to trinitarian beliefs usually focus on the Jesus/God to the neglect of God as Creator, and God as Holy Spirit. Such an exercise might be a point of departure to expose the Christocentric reading which many give the Hebrew Bible, despite its status as a work also independent of the New Testament.

We might ask whether a Christocentric reading of Isaiah's Servant Songs, identifying Jesus as Suffering Servant, both distorts the text and requires Jesus's followers to suffer, to be victims, and forever to carry a cross despite Christ's redemptive work. Serious questions need to be raised about how an ethic of servanthood, so pervasive in US Christianity, interfaces with evangelism and self-respect. Interpreters must ask: How many faithful women in the church have experienced Jesus in a way that goes beyond survival to triumph? What is the nature of a discipleship based on the Suffering Servant model and what is its cost? Is this servant model for leadership and preaching about divine freedom to call, and human need to control? Does the image of servanthood allow one to survive by glorifying suffering instead of overcoming it? How does the experience of being a servant shape understandings of suffering and pain other than the physical? How has the heightened technology and social mobility of the 1990s affected churches and historically marginalized persons who follow the Suffering Servant model? Are persons who follow the Suffering Servant able to live out the assurance that 'we shall overcome', or have circumstances and oppression overcome them? Is there a relation between the inability to sustain this message cohesively and the present troubled state of families and increased violence in the inner cities? How can the message of Isaiah's Servant be a gift that answers Martin Luther King, Jr's question, 'Where Do We Go From Here?'

Conversations about servanthood, slavery and divorce trigger individual and communal memory, and cannot be discussed apart from lived context. The results of such conversations ultimately depend upon the interpreter's consciousness and appropriation of her or his own ethnicity, past and present familial dynamics, marital or partner status, and socio-historical and cultural heritage. For women who have inherited socio-cultural, psychological and historical oppression, reading Isaiah 50 may echo their contemporary experiences and anguish. How can a woman employed as a maid, nanny or cook experience servanthood minus servitude? How can a woman who employs a maid, nanny or cook, relate to her employed staff in an ethics of respect and fairness?

Perhaps Isaiah 50 is an opportunity for the interpreter to connect her or his reading with an awakening of silenced, oppressed voices. Perhaps the sixth-century BCE poetry of exilic life is an occasion to uncover the often-silenced, public suffering of wife and servant/slave. Perhaps pondering this text for the dispersed and dislocated is a time for developing liturgical and pastoral rites of healing to overcome the pain and stigma of divorce and the pain of those who have not yet returned to a place called home. Perhaps interpreting this text can occasion a time of change for 1990s, for women who are wives, servants, slaves, abusers or abused; for men who are brothers, sons, husbands, masters, slave-owners, or again, abusers or the abused.

Christ, the Servant/Slave of Philippians 2.6-11

The interpreter must face the fact that, like the Hebrew Bible, the New Testament not only fails to condemn slavery but uses the language of servitude to represent redemption. In the New Testament the term *doulos* can mean either 'servant' or 'slave.' For the Greek mind, a person's identity is secured in their freedom, which is the antithesis of bondage, of having no personal choice, of always being answerable to another. The New Testament use of *doulos* conforms to the Greco-Roman model of 'absolute dependence', where the servant has an absolute commitment to the total claim of the *kurios*, or lord, and is clearly grounded in the reality and existence of the *kurios*. Yet, while the *doulos* is limited and in bondage, the *doulos* is never rejected or ignored because of that slave identity and class (Kittel 1964: II, 261, 266-67).

The exegete of Phil. 2.6-11 confronts an irony, or a paradox. The christological hymn of Phil. 2.6-11 depicts Christ's majestic gesture of emptying himself for humanity; but the text likewise implies that humanity ought to be like Christ, emptying themselves, even when many believers would be hard pressed to empty themselves of anything because they are so poor. Is irony at work in the shifting roles of Jesus the Christ in Philippians 2? That is, does the pre-existent Christ 'empty' or divest himself of the divine when he comes to earth to reveal to people the nature of true humanity? Christ comes as a slave, one deemed morally inferior. But to be truly human is to be perfect, without sin; thus Christ is the only perfect human. How can an 'emptied' Christ reveal, in essence, the actual humanity that an ancient slave, possessing sin, has? Christ does not remain a slave but is later exalted. He is full, becomes empty, and then becomes full again. He experiences this cycle on behalf of humanity, who cannot duplicate the full–empty–full pattern. If the self-emptied Christ is vindicated and exalted, how can the poor also be vindicated?

Some readers focus on this legacy of Christ as redemptive, generous and hopeful. Others read this as a culturally-biased, non-liberative model of Jesus, especially for those who suffer. Some of the oppressed and the poor might have such an internal sense of destiny along with an external aggravation of patriarchal Christianity, that this hymn would make them parties to their own oppression. Many believers may experience a great gap between their 'picture' of the resurrected Christ and that of their personal reality. The juxtaposition that would allow for his emptying does not require his believers to give up so much that they will be in worse bondage after their Christ-experience than before. Paradoxically, one option is that through religious experience the self-emptying of oppressed believers allows them to empty themselves of self-pity and the reality of pain so that they can transcend their oppressed existence and move toward change. Such a scenario may also allow oppressors to see that they must empty themselves of their wealth, privilege, and status, freeing themselves to hear the marginalized in a way that does not further oppress.

Do we find the same picture of Jesus the Christ in the Gospels? How do we compare the kenotic Christ of Philippians to the Matthean Jesus, who exemplifies lived, higher righteousness and Judaism *par excellence*? How do we relate the kenotic Christ to the Lukan Jesus who embodies a salvation history where women are included and empowered, yet subordinate? How do we relate the Christ of Philippians to the secretive Messiah of Mark and to the eternal Logos of John? What about the testimony of 1 Cor. 15.3-8, regarded as the earliest New Testament material that celebrates Jesus as Lord? Does the sublimation of Christ's passion in Philippians 2 minimize the acknowledgment of suffering and the possibility of identity and transformation for the marginalized and the oppressed? The birth narratives, omitted in Philippians, Mark and John, also make an alignment with humanity, where birth is foundational. Is it possible to construct a genuinely

salvific reading by compartmentalizing Jesus events (birth, life/teach-
ings, passion) as if they were separate from the Pauline Christ-Event of
Philippians (appearance in human form which does not explicitly name
a birth, resurrection or ascension)? Following the lead of Delores
Williams in her book *Sisters of the Wilderness* (Williams 1993), it
would be helpful to emphasize the ministerial vision and lived reality of
Jesus on earth as central for an experience of transformation and
salvation.

Today's question of salvation cannot be dissociated from liberating
women and all those who are marginalized. Whether the emphasis is
upon kenosis or ministerial vision, the exegete must explore what is
emptied, what is lived and how one can transform the underlying
notions of power and the need to empower. The impact of power and
empowerment of others advances our understanding of how Jesus'
ministry informs the experience of glory and resurrection for first-century and twenty-first century believers. Can the combined paradigm of
Jesus event and Christ event as inclusive, personified love both in
human form and as the Lord of faith have value?

In assessing a Christology from below versus a Christology from
above, we must ask: How does either Christology lead to lived salvation and liberation in a way that does not reverse the possibilities and
create a new oppression? How can one develop a contemporary, balanced Christology that transcends all superior-inferior models? To
idolize the poor with a 'below Christology' or scripturally to empower
the poor in a way that they then seek to oppress others is not helpful.
The interpretation of Christ's emptying-exaltation must not rupture the
commonality between Jesus and suffering women.

If there is no common ground between Jesus and suffering women
(and other oppressed persons), then the possibility of a relatedness
between suffering women and God is lost. If the emptying alone creates
an identifying link for the sufferer, why is it that the exaltation cannot
symbolize the possibility of the sufferer's overcoming? Jacquelyn
Grant's *White Woman's Christ and Black Woman's Jesus* (Grant 1989),
in the tradition of many African-American spirituals, sees Jesus/God/
Lord as mother to the motherless, father to the fatherless, sister to the
sisterless. This is a vision of an imminent, liberating divine/human
Christ who shares an intimacy and a common ground with humanity.
An experiential, dialectical reading does not lie about suffering, yet it
offers an opportunity for solidarity, for an encounter between the

divine/human selves, individual and communal.

This christological hymn reminds us of the need to create worshipping communities that enable persons to move from denial of oppression to relatedness within a community of sufferers and their oppressors, thereby proceeding towards communal liberation. We must encounter the experience of emptiness suggested by Pheme Perkins's discussion of Philippians 2 (Perkins 1992). In Philippians, she observes, Paul gives up the privilege of Jewishness, he assumes an imminent eschaton, and perhaps most importantly, he addresses his letter to people with status and power who must empty themselves. To confront the form of God in the form of slaves requires that the privileged deal with their own complicity in institutional oppression. To create a life of solidarity between the historical oppressor and oppressed requires vision, courage and an effort by both parties to develop community free of manipulation, paternalism, condescension, dysfunctionality and entrenched dependence.

EPILOGUE

How can one create, through the interpretation of Isaiah 50 and Phil. 2.6-11, a liberating praxis for an American context whose original sin is racism? Because of the diverse socio-cultural, economic and historical forms of slavery (biblical, Greco-Roman, American), one must recognize that socio-cultural, economic and historical legacies affect how one reads these texts. Since the Bible in some instances condones slavery, it is necessary to appropriate redemptive models of servanthood critically, and to recognize that these texts are not mere historical artifacts devoid of contemporary impact. To help make these texts liberating for female domestics, maids, migrant workers and persons in other perceived 'menial jobs', where people must literally and figuratively 'empty' themselves in order to survive, we must heighten our consciousness and be willing seriously to sit with female domestics, maids and migrant workers, and perhaps, if but for a moment, walk in their shoes. Those of us who are privileged academics need to inquire about our own comfort and stability, about the nature of oppression in the ivory towers, and about how migrants and maids maintain self-esteem and sacred personhood. Such a task is critical because so many of America's children have been reared by maids and have eaten the food picked by migrants. Our readings of Isaiah 50 and Philippians 2 may have a chance of being redemptive if we never forget this fact.

BIBLIOGRAPHY

Ackerman, Susan
1992   'Isaiah', in Newsom and Ringe 1992: 161-68.
Brown, Francis, S.R. Driver and Charles A. Briggs (eds.)
1951 [1906]   *A Hebrew and English Lexicon of the Old Testament* (Oxford: Clarendon
            Press).
Grant, Jacquelyn
1989   *White Woman's Christ and Black Woman's Jesus* (Atlanta: Scholars
            Press).
Harris, R. Laird, Gleason L. Archer, Jr and Bruce K. Waltke (eds.)
1980   *Theological Wordbook of the Old Testament*, I–II (Chicago: Moody
            Press).
Holladay, William (ed.)
1971   *A Concise Hebrew and Aramaic Lexicon of the Old Testament* (Grand
            Rapids: Eerdmans).
Kittel, Gerhard (ed.)
1964–   *Theological Dictionary of the New Testament*, V (10 vols.; Grand Rapids:
            Eerdmans).
Muilenberg, James, and Henry S. Coffin
1956   'The Book of Isaiah, Chapters 40–66', in George A. Buttrick *et al.* (eds),
            The Interpreters Bible: A Commentary in Twelve Volumes (Nashville:
            Abingdon Press): 381-773.
Newsom, Carol A., and Sharon H. Ringe (eds.)
1992   *The Women's Bible Commentary* (Louisville, KY: Westminster/John
            Knox Press).
Perkins, Pheme
1992   'Phillipians', in Newsom and Ringe 1992: 343-46.
Walker, Alice
1982   *The Color Purple* (New York: Harcourt Brace Jovanovich).
Williams, Delores
1993   *Sisters of the Wilderness* (Maryknoll, NY: Orbis Books).

Epilogue

MARKING BOUNDARIES INSIDE AND OUTSIDE: THE ONGOING TASKS OF FEMINIST HERMENEUTICS

Pamela Thimmes

What boundaries were marked? What tasks do these articles reflect? In her early work, Mary Daly writes about women's 'new space' on the boundaries of patriarchal space.[1] Today, feminist hermeneutics, which has always understood itself as a liberation movement, has self-consciously carved out a 'new space' while trying to mark the boundaries of patriarchal and hegemonic systems so that these systems can no longer go unchallenged in attempts to contain, oppress or suppress. The 'new space' of feminist criticism is understood quite differently than the boundaries of patriarchal space: 'Feminist criticism must remain fluid, not fixed, so that each of us can contend with the ripples and waves of the dominant culture, diving into language to recover everything that is duplicitous and resistant and confounding.'[2]

This volume demonstrates the fluidity, agility and centrality of the twin tasks of feminist biblical hermeneutics—method and practice. In each case, it is clear the one component is incomplete without the other. In its ten years of existence, the Feminist Theological Hermeneutics of the Bible Group within the Society of Biblical Literature has dealt explicitly with the issues found in these essays—authority, difference, method, translation, exegesis of classic or mixed texts, reading strategies, commentary writing, claiming and reclaiming texts—taking seriously the cautionary advice of Adrienne Rich, 'You must write, and read, as if your life depended on it'.[3]

1. Mary Daly, *Beyond God the Father: Toward a Philosophy of Women's Liberation* (Boston: Beacon Press, 1973), pp. 40-43.

2. Alice Bach (ed.), *The Pleasure of her Text: Feminist Readings of Biblical and Historical Texts* (Philadelphia: Trinity Press, 1990), pp. ix-x.

3. Adrienne Rich, 'As if your life depended on it', in her *What Is Found*

The contributors to this volume bring advice not unlike that of Rich, so it is worthwhile, at the end of the project, to recall a few of those insights: we live in a world of difference, not binary oppositions (Tolbert); feminist readings do not sanitize or tame the horrors of texts about women (Kozar); strategies of interpretation are related to notions of the nature and consequences of biblical authority (Bird); at stake are the ethics of biblical studies in a culture that has often used (and continues to use) the Bible to support injustice and discrimination (Scholz); the so-called truth of Christianity has become the instrument of mastery, so that its ignorance of others has been embedded both in the story told and in the telling of the story (Kim); a feminist critique begins with the knowledge that feminist discourse should not 'assume in advance what the content of woman should be' (Hornsby); stepping 'inside' the text while simultaneously remaining clearly outside…these boundaries are blurred…one can never completely disappear into the language, without a trace or echo (Pippin).

As more scholarship recognizes the relationship of social location to interpretation, feminist hermeneutics finds that it has been partner to these studies from the beginning and feminist interpretations continue to examine interpretative methods, particularly with reference to gender, race and class. These *revisions* are both a critique of the scholarly business-as-usual agenda in the culture, the academy and the churches/synagogues, and a creative method of responding to the Bible as living text and tradition. Again, Adrienne Rich offers a word for the task, 'Re-vision—the act of looking back, of seeing with fresh eyes, of entering an old text from a new critical direction—is for women more than a chapter in cultural history; it is an act of survival'.[4]

As this volume demonstrates, women reading the Bible as women, along with men joining them who are sympathetic and committed to the same task, represent a diverse array of perspectives and address issues associated with the theory of interpretation from disparate standpoints: e.g. *how* one reads (interprets), *what* one reads (questions of canon), and what the reading process *does* to the reader and to the community in which a text is read (translation and authority issues). The practice of feminist hermeneutics, increasingly, recognizes that reading is a social

There: Notebooks on Poetry and Politics (New York: W.W. Norton, 1994).

4.   Adrienne Rich, 'When We Dead Awaken: Writing as Re-Vision', in Barbara Charlesworth Gelpi and Albert Gelpi (eds.), *Adrienne Rich's Poetry and Prose* (New York: W.W. Norton, 1993), p. 167.

activity, that texts have a political function, and that interpreting the Bible has implications in and an impact on both ecclesial and cultural institutions. How the synagogue and the church use and read the Bible has religious, political and cultural implications for women and for men. The issue of how one reads is further informed by *who* does the reading. The contributors to this volume (and those other voices who were in dialogue with them) struggle with these questions, and push wide the boundaries demonstrating that the questions already surveyed in the first ten years of this group need continual revisiting, sharpening and revisioning.

I titled this essay using words like 'marking boundaries', 'inside', 'outside' because these terms, I think, are central to the ongoing work and development of feminist biblical hermeneutics. As noted above, from the earliest days of the feminist movement, geographic or territorial terms were in vogue. Such usage implied that there were/are monolithic spaces that separate and create insiders and outsiders. Feminism has tried to dissemble the monolith and its attendant categories, with some success.[5] However, the wrecking crew has itself created insiders and outsiders!

From its beginnings, feminist biblical hermeneutics has been domesticated by the systems out of which it emerged—Western cultures, the academy and the churches/synagogues. This domestication has blunted the revolutionary, transformational and liberating character of the critique. That is not to say that feminist hermeneutics has had a minimal effect in academic and pastoral situations; in fact, quite the opposite is true. Nevertheless, as attention to difference turned to commitment to hearing a plurality of voices, and as postmodernism collapsed the myth of objectivity, feminist hermeneutics lost the 'edge' of its critique. Mary Ann Tolbert pointedly notes,

> Most people, then, are both disadvantaged by the culture and thus critical of it and, at the same time, also benefit from it and thus want it to prosper…Since most feminist biblical critics clearly evince a mixed-status situation, their divided interests…may encourage a more moderating approach. In addition, most feminist biblical researchers work in institutional contexts that have deeply vested concerns for the survival

5.   For a critique of these issues see, Bonnie Zimmerman, '"Confessions" of a Lesbian Feminist', in Dana Heller (ed.), *Cross Purposes: Lesbians, Feminists, and the Limits of Alliance* (Bloomington: Indiana University Press, 1997), pp. 157-68.

and growth of European/North American versions of the Christian
church and thus the capitalistic, patriarchal system that undergirds it.[6]

The continuing task of feminist biblical hermeneutics, then, requires a
new survey of the territory, maybe even a remapping of the territory—a
call to be as attentive to the subtexts as to the texts, to deal with issues
like displacement, contradiction and complicity at the edges and within,
which in turn will be implicit in methodology and interpretation.
Feminist hermeneutics prides itself in privileging women's interpretation, women's voices, but it must become attentive to the other privileges it extends. The essays in this volume agree that feminist biblical
critics assume there are no universals, and that many of the concepts
employed—such as 'woman', women's 'roles' in antiquity, ancient
cultures, and so on—are unstable. Remapping the territory affirms all
the 'instabilities' implicit in the process of interpretation, but it also
means that the partnership of method and practice must be maintained,
otherwise nothing changes and nothing gets done. Finally, remapping
also means being honest and self-conscious about the contradictions,
complicity and privilege we bring to hermeneutics, to marking the
boundaries that exclude as well as include.

6.   Mary Ann Tolbert, 'Reading for Liberation', in Fernando F. Segovia and
Mary Ann Tolbert (eds.), *Reading from this Place: Social Location and Biblical
Interpretation in the United States* (2 vols.; Minneapolis: Fortress Press, 1995), I,
pp. 266, 267.

INDEXES

INDEX OF REFERENCES

OLD TESTAMENT

Genesis

1.27	97, 213
2–3	141
3.5	33
9.18-27	229
14.1-16	23
14.10-16	25
14.19-20	66
15.8	59
17–18	56
17.19	57
18	23
18.16-33	23
18.25-26	33
19	23, 35
19.1-38	22
19.1-11	22
19.1-3	25
19.1	25
19.4-5	27
19.4	27
19.5	27
19.6-8	30
19.7	30
19.8	30
19.9-11	33
19.9	33
19.10	33
19.11	33
19.14	32
19.16	30
25.19–35.22	185

25.21	56
30.1	56
30.23	64
33.6-11	27
34	18, 185-87, 189-91, 193-97
34.2	187, 191, 193
34.3	187, 188, 192, 193
34.4	192
34.5	193
34.7	193
34.13	193
34.17	193
34.19	192
34.25-31	193
34.25	193
34.27	193
34.30	193
34.31	193
49.5-7	188, 193

Exodus

22.15-16	190
22.15	203, 205

Leviticus

15.19-22	82

Numbers

15.37-41	41

Deuteronomy

4.20	48
4.35	48
4.37-38	50
6.4-9	41
6.4-5	13, 41, 43-48
6.4	41, 46, 47
6.5	47
6.18	30
6.20-25	48
6.24	49
7.8	48
7.13	50
7.16	50
8.11-18	48
10.17-18	48
11.1	50
11.2-7	48
11.4-6	50
11.13-21	41
12.28	30
13.2-6	50
22.23-29	194
22.23-27	190
22.25-27	32
22.25	204, 205
23.1-6	50
24.1	271
24.3	271
25.1	33
29.24	48

Joshua
2 — 27
6 — 27
9.25 — 30

Judges
13 — 56
14.15 — 203
16.5 — 203
17.6 — 30
19 — 35, 36
19.1 — 30
19.7 — 27
19.24 — 30
21.25 — 30

1 Samuel
1 — 56
1.10-11 — 56

2 Samuel
7.23 — 46
10 — 28
13 — 193
13.11 — 204
13.14 — 204

1 Kings
22.20-22 — 203

2 Kings
2.17 — 27
6.20 — 33

Esther
5.6 — 25

Job
1.5 — 25

Psalms
68.5 — 235

Proverbs
16.29 — 203

Isaiah
1.10 — 22
3.16-24 — 206
3.17 — 203
6.9 — 33
39–66 — 270
40–55 — 271
42.1-4 — 270, 271
47.1-3 — 206
49.1-6 — 270, 271
50 — 20, 266, 269-74, 277
50.1-3 — 269, 271
50.1 — 271
50.4-11 — 269-71
50.8 — 33
52.13–53.12 — 270
52.13-15 — 271
53.1-9 — 271
53.10-12 — 271

Jeremiah
2.20-25 — 206
2.33-34 — 206
3.1-5 — 206
3.8 — 271
4.19-21 — 18, 199-202, 206

4.19 — 201
4.20 — 201
4.21 — 201
4.30-31 — 206
4.31 — 207
13.20-27 — 206
13.21 — 206, 207
15.8-9 — 206
20.7-13 — 203
20.7 — 18, 203, 204, 206
22.20-23 — 206
22.23 — 207
23.14 — 22
30.6 — 206

Ezekiel
16.35-42 — 206
16.49 — 22
23.9-10 — 206
23.22-35 — 206

Daniel
1.5 — 25

Hosea
2.4-5 — 206
2.11-12 — 206
2.16 — 203

Habakkuk
4.19-21 — 206

Zechariah
14.9 — 47, 48

NEW TESTAMENT

Matthew
5.11 — 108
6.24 — 230
10.32-33 — 108
10.39 — 108
11.27 — 108
20.25-28 — 113
21.9 — 111
22.15-22 — 111
22.36-40 — 147
23.11 — 113

Mark
3.33-35 — 230
8.38 — 108
8.55 — 108
9.35 — 113
10.42-45 — 210

10.43-45	113	1.57-80	59, 61	7.41-42	78
11.9-11	111	1.57-59	61	7.44-46	80
12.13-17	111	1.57	61	7.44-45	96
		1.58	61, 66	7.45	74, 80
Luke		1.59-66	61	7.46	81
1	13, 55	1.59	61	7.47-48	78
1.1-4	55	1.60	61	7.47	74, 76
1.5-80	53	1.61-62	62	7.48	77
1.5-23	63	1.62	55	7.49-50	76
1.5	55	1.63	55, 62	7.50	77
1.7	56, 58	1.77	75	8.1-3	75, 90
1.9	55	2	65	8.3	87, 88
1.13-17	57, 58	2.37	87	8.35	79
1.13	55, 57, 58, 61,	3.2-17	75	8.38-39	89
	63, 75	3.2-7	75	8.41	79
1.14	57, 61	3.7-9	107	8.44-47	79
1.15-17	57	3.16-17	107	8.48	89
1.15	57, 60, 61	4.39	87, 88	8.54	79
1.16	57	4.49	82	9.14	88
1.17	57, 58	5	74, 96	9.26	108
1.18	58	5.8	74, 79, 93	10.40	87-89
1.20	58, 61	5.10-11	75	11.27	89
1.24	63, 64	5.12-13	82	12.8-9	108
1.25	61, 63, 65, 66,	5.13	79	12.37	88
	89	5.14	89	13.13	79
1.26-35	65	5.27	75	15.2	74
1.26	64	5.30	74	17.8	88
1.27	55	5.31	75	17.16	79
1.30-33	63, 65	6.1-5	82	17.19	89
1.31	55	6.13-16	75	19.7	74
1.34	63, 89	6.19	79	19.38	111
1.35	64, 65	6.22	108	20.20-26	111
1.36	62, 64	7.14	79	22.24-27	88, 113
1.38	66, 87, 89	7.18-35	107	22.26-27	88
1.39-56	59	7.24-35	75	22.28-34	88
1.41	57, 60, 61	7.29-30	75	22.30	88
1.42-55	89	7.30	81	22.51	79
1.42	65	7.32	75, 76	23.56	89
1.43	60, 62	7.34	74	24	89
1.44	60, 61	7.36-50	14, 69, 72-74,		
1.45	65		91, 92, 95-97,	*John*	
1.46-55	65		100	4	230
1.46	66	7.36	73	5.24	241
1.47-48	65	7.37	74, 75	7.53–8.11	95
1.48	66, 87	7.38	80	12.13	111
1.51-52	66	7.39	74	13.1-17	96, 100

19.30	241			2	14, 274, 275, 277
		12.4-11	214		
Acts		12.12-31	230	2.5	115
1.25	88	12.28	209, 211	2.6-11	14, 20, 104-106, 109, 112, 114, 116, 120, 266, 269, 274, 277
2.3-4	106	13	211		
6.1	88	14.33-36	141		
6.2	88, 89	14.34-35	213		
6.4	88	15	213		
6.11	110	15.3-8	275	2.10-11	114
6.13-14	110	15.8	114	3	114
11.29	88	15.24	115	3.1-17	114
12	89	15.28	211	3.8-9	114
12.25	88			3.8	115
19.22	88	*Galatians*		4.3	111, 115
20.24	88	1.1	114	4.22	114
21.19	88	1.10	113		
		5.13-15	230	*Colossians*	
Romans				3.22-24	142
1.1	113	*Ephesians*			
1.4	109	5.22	229, 230	*1 Timothy*	
13.1-8	111			2.11-15	141
		Philippians		6.1-2	142
1 Corinthians		1.1	113		
2.6-8	115	1.13	111, 115	*1 Peter*	
6.1	111	1.27-30	114	3.1-6	141
11.2-16	141, 211, 213	1.27	114	3.18-25	142
12–14	214	1.30	111, 115	4.8-11	231

INDEX OF AUTHORS

Abu-Lughod, L. 26
Achtemeier, P.J. 109
Ackerman, J.S. 34
Ackerman, S. 271
Adam, A.K.M. 218, 219
Adam, M.B. 19
Aichele, G. 183, 197
Alexander, T.D. 22, 31
Alter, R. 22, 25, 32, 34, 63
Anderson, J.C. 53, 133, 137, 139
Antonelli, J.S. 192
Applegate, J. 15
Archer, G.L., Jr 270
Arndt, W.F. 73
Atwood, M. 20
Ausubel, F. 26

Bach, A. 70, 133, 134, 183, 184, 279
Bal, M. 126
Balch, D. 113
Balz, H. 93
Barber, B. 25
Barr, J. 145-48
Barth, F. 24
Barthes, R. 134
Barton, J. 126, 156
Bauer, A. 18, 19, 206
Baumgartner, W. 204
Bayim, N. 133, 139, 140
Bechtel, L.M. 14, 24, 26, 28, 34, 193, 194,
    282
Beckett, S. 178, 179
Bell, S. 85, 97, 99
Beneke, T. 29
Benjamin, W. 17, 165, 166, 168, 173

Benstock, S. 253, 258
Bergman, J. 46
Bernstein, B. 134
Berridge, J.M. 201, 205
Beuken, W. 182
Bhabha, H. 168, 169
Billerbeck, P. 91, 94, 96
Bird, P. 16, 128, 280
Blackmon, R.A. 84
Blank, J. 96
Block, D.I. 22
Bloom, H. 137
Blount, B.K. 182, 184
Blum, E. 192
Booth, W. 65
Borg, M. 105, 106, 108
Bottomore, T. 145
Bouque, L.B. 29
Boyarin, D. 211-13
Brawley, R.L. 86
Brenner, A. 185, 186, 199, 206, 266
Brewer, R.R. 114
Briggs, S. 120, 162
Bright, J. 200, 201
Brock, R.N. 85, 104
Brooks, S. 85
Brooten, B. 71
Brownmiller, S. 29
Brueggemann, W. 22, 23, 32, 189, 194,
    195, 201, 205
Brumberg Kraus, J. 95
Buchwald, E. 186
Bultmann, R. 107, 108, 151, 209
Butler, J. 97, 100, 199
Byung-mu, A. 112

Caird, C.B. 91, 100
Califia, P. 98
Cardenal, E. 231
Carmichael, C.M. 22
Carroll, R.P. 201, 202, 204
Cassidy, R.J. 88
Castelli, E. 170, 171
Champagne, R. 134
Chappell, D. 29
Choe, C.-U. 119
Christ, C. 171
Chung, H.K. 105
Cixous, H. 137
Clark, K.W. 237
Clines, D.J.A. 204, 218
Coats, G.W. 22, 31, 188, 189
Coffin, H.S. 271
Cohen, S.D. 71
Collins, A.Y. 127
Coote, R.B. 28, 34
Corley, K.E. 69, 80-82, 84, 85, 91, 93-95
Countryman, L.W. 145, 148
Courtivron, I. de 159
Creed, J.M. 76, 80
Crenshaw, J.L. 205
Crosman, I. 72, 154
Crüsemann, M. 212, 213
Cugoano, Q.O. 233
Culler, J. 154
Culpepper, R.A. 141
Cyril (St) 91, 100

D'Angelo, M.R. 89
Daly, M. 178, 279
Dana, H.E. 76
Danker, F.W. 54, 56-60, 62, 64, 66
Darr, K.P. 185
Davies, P.R. 189
Derrida, J. 134, 157, 163, 165, 169, 171,
    172
Diamond, A.R. 204
Dibelius, M. 107
Dijk-Hemmes, F. van 199, 206
Dodd, C.H. 181
Dodds, E.R. 26
Donaldson, J. 91, 92

Donato, E. 134
Douglas, M. 99
Dowling, R.P. 89
Duhm, B. 200, 201, 204
Dunn, J.D.G. 145, 146, 149
Dworkin, A. 85

Eagleton, M. 133, 136
Edwards, J.A.C. 19
Equiano, O. 233
Erickson, J.Q. 133, 137, 138
Exum, J.C. 126, 182-85, 206

Fant, M.B. 71
Farnham, C. 244
Fee, G.D. 112
Felder, C.H. 224, 229
Fetterley, J. 54, 136
Fewell, D. 126, 189, 197
Fischer, I. 190
Fish, S. 157
Fishbane, M. 205
Fishman, J.A. 134
Fitzmyer, J.A. 54, 55, 57, 59, 60, 62, 66, 76,
    80, 91
Fletcher, P.R. 186
Flynn, E.A. 53, 54, 72, 135
Fontaine, C. 185
Fortna, R.T. 114
Foucault, M. 32, 99, 155, 157, 220
Fowl, S.E. 218, 219
Fretheim, T.E. 187
Freud, S. 159
Freyne, S. 182
Frye, M. 77, 78, 89
Fulkerson, M.M. 232
Fuss, D. 133, 138, 139

Garber, M. 199
Gaster, T.H. 23
Gates, H.L., Jr 233, 234
Gaventa, B.R. 114
Geis, G. 29
Geis, R. 29
Gelpi, A. 280
Gelpi, B.C. 280

Gentzler, E. 167, 169
Gilkes, C.T. 20, 234, 236, 237, 242, 266
Gingrich, F.W. 73, 280
Gold, V.R. 177
Goldenberg, N. 97
Goody, J. 32
Gordon, P. 206
Graham, S.L. 20
Grant, J. 276
Greene, G. 133, 136, 249, 250, 258
Greenstein, E.L. 184
Griffin, S. 29
Gronniosaw, J. 233, 234
Gross, E. 133
Grosz, E. 97
Gunn, D.M. 189, 197, 204

Harding, S. 159
Harris, R. 270
Heschel, A.J. 204, 205
Heyob, S.K. 71
Heyward, C. 83, 84
Hirsch, E.D. 153
Hitzig, F. 204
Holladay, W.L. 200, 201, 205, 270
Holst, R. 72, 73
Horney, K. 26
Hornsby, T. 15, 280
Horos, C.V. 29
Horsley, R.A. 111, 114, 115, 117
Hsien-Chin, H. 26
Hurd, J.C. 114
Hurtardo, L.W. 113

Irigaray, L. 159, 162, 223, 227, 228
Isenberg, A. 26
Iser, W. 72

Jackson, R. 170
Jackson, R.C. 233, 234
Jacobs, C. 17, 165, 166
Jacobs, L. 42
Janzen, J.G. 46
Jea, J. 233
Jeansonne, S.P. 22, 27, 30, 32, 188

Jeremias, J. 71, 82, 91, 94
Johnson, L.T. 72, 74-76, 81, 82
Johnson, S. 153
Jones, D.L. 111

Kahn, C. 133, 136
Kaiser, B.B. 201, 202
Käsemann, E. 209
Kasl, C.D. 85
Keefe, A.A. 197, 202
Keller, E.F. 158
Kelsey, D. 143
Kenner, H. 178
Kilgallen, J.J. 75, 76
Kim, J.-h. 120
Kim, J.K. 15, 266, 280
King, M.L., Jr 273
Kirk-Duggan, C. 20
Kloppenberg, J.S. 107
Koester, H. 110
Kolodny, A. 136, 137
Kozar, J. 14, 280
Kraemer, R.S. 94
Kristeva, J. 99
Kuschel, K.-J. 109, 110

Lacan, J. 159
Lambdin, T.O. 164
Lamphere, L. 32
Lanser, S.S. 78
Lasine, S. 22, 30, 32
Lee, H.-h. 119
Lee, J.Y. 116, 117
Lee, K.-b. 119
Leff, G. 127
Lefkowitz, M.R. 71
Lenski, G.E. 25
Lerner, G. 32
Levine, A.-J. 71
Levine, S. 170
Lewin, E.D. 204
Licht, H. 93
Lifton, R.J. 24
Lockwood, P.L. 189
Lohfink, N. 46, 48

Lotman, Y.M. 134
Lucero, B.M. 197
Lukes, S. 145
Luther, M. 148
Lynd, H.M. 26

Macksey, R. 134
Magdalene, F.R. 206
Malbon, E.S. 137
Malina, B.J. 26
Man, P. de 165
Mantey, J.R. 76
Marks, E. 159
Marmorstein, A. 42
Marrant, J. 233
Marshall, I.H. 54-57, 59, 60, 62, 80, 81, 91
Martin, C.J. 69
McBride, S.D., Jr 42, 43, 46
McClintock, B. 158
McFague, S. 44, 45
McKane, W. 200, 205
McKim, D.K. 143, 145
McLaren, P.L. 170
Mead, M. 25
Meeks, W. 113
Merklein, H. 110
Meyers, C. 32
Miles, M. 98
Miller, E.C. 114
Miller, N.K. 136
Miller, P.D., Jr 44, 46
Milne, P.J. 185, 186
Moi, T. 159
Moran, W.L. 46, 47
Morgan, R. 155, 156
Morris, E.B. 118
Morton, N. 172
Mosala, I.J. 69
Muilenberg, J. 271

Nelson, J.B. 83
Newsom, C.A. 41, 54, 70
Nida, E.A. 167
Niditch, S. 28
Nielsen, E. 189
Nisbet, R. 145

Noble, P. 190
Novak, M. 244, 263
Nye, A. 159

O'Connor, K.M. 204
O'Donnell Setel, D. 41-43, 51
Ord, D.R. 28, 34
Owens, M.I. 20, 234-43

Pagels, E. 230
Pearson, B. 113
Perkins, P. 277
Peterlin, D. 114, 115
Peterman, G.W. 113, 115
Pfeiffer, R.H. 238
Phillips, G.A. 183, 197
Piers, G. 26
Pippin, T. 17, 280
Plaskow, J. 45, 96, 231
Polk, T. 202, 204
Pomeroy, S.B. 71, 84
Portefax, L. 115
Porter, R. 29
Porter, S.E. 218
Pressler, C. 14, 44, 49
Pui-lan, K. 117, 224, 231

Quesnell, Q. 88

Rabassa, G. 164, 166
Rabinow, P. 155
Rad, G. von 23, 31, 190
Radway, J.A. 152, 154
Rafael, V.L. 163, 168
Raffel, B. 167
Reid, B. 96
Reid, S.B. 183
Reumann, J. 114
Rich, A. 172, 173, 279, 280
Richardson, P. 114
Rientra, M. 232
Riezler, K. 26
Rimmon-Kennan, S. 56
Ringe, S.H. 41, 45, 54, 70, 91, 266
Roberts, A. 91, 92
Rogers, J.B. 143, 147, 149

Rosaldo, M.Z. 32
Roth, M. 187
Rowlett, L. 25
Rubin, G. 98, 100, 101
Rudolph, W. 200, 201, 204
Ruether, R. 97, 98
Ruether, R.R. 45
Russell, L. 135
Russell, L.M. 44, 45, 185

Saebo, M. 203
Said, E. 163
Sanday, P.R. 29, 32
Sanders, J.T. 86
Schaberg, J. 54, 69, 70, 78, 80, 87, 89, 93-95
Schaps, D.M. 71
Scheff, T.J. 26
Schneider, G. 93
Scholes, R. 134
Scholz, S. 18, 91, 186, 187, 280
Schottroff, L. 19, 91, 93, 208
Schüssler Fiorenza, E. 19, 69, 71, 87, 88, 91, 93, 127-29, 133, 135, 224, 225, 228, 235, 236, 242, 243
Schweickart, P.P. 53, 54, 72, 135-37
Schweitzer, A. 151, 156
Scott, B.B. 183
Sedgwick, E.K. 199
Segovia, F.F. 141, 183-85, 282
Seim, T.K. 81, 87, 91, 94-96
Shakespeare, W. 181
Sharper, P.J. 88
Sheres, I. 191, 192
Showalter, E. 133, 136-38, 140, 252, 258
Singer, M. 26
Skinner, J. 31, 32
Smith, D.E. 88, 95
Smith, M.S. 204
Smith, T.H. 182
Speiser, E.A. 22, 23, 26, 27, 32, 34
Spivak, G.C. 167, 170, 171
Spykerboer, H. 166
Stach, I. von 214
Stagg, E. 76, 82
Stagg, F. 76, 82

Sternberg, M. 189, 197
Stout, J. 218
Strack, H.L. 91, 94, 96
Strossen, N. 98
Sugirtharajah, R.S. 69, 117
Suleiman, S.R. 72, 154
Swartley, W.M. 70
Swindler, L. 76

Taber, C.R. 167
Talbert, C.H. 80
Tamez, E. 69
Tannehill, R.C. 54-56, 58-60, 62, 64-66, 74, 76, 82, 91, 100
Tapp, A.M. 32
Thimmes, P. 16, 20
Thiselton, A.C. 126
Thistlethwaite, S.B. 104
Thompson, J.A. 201, 205
Throckmorton, B.H. Jr 18
Tigay, J.H. 193
Todt, H.E. 107, 108
Tolbert, M.A. 17, 44, 53, 69, 70, 133, 134, 139, 141, 148, 183, 280-82
Tomaselli, S. 29
Tomm, W. 246, 263
Tompkins, J. 154
Tompkins, P. 72
Tomson, P. 211
Torjensen, K.J. 105
Trible, P. 22, 33, 126, 185
Trinh, M.-h.T. 121
Turner, L.A. 22, 25, 27, 31

Vawter, B. 31
Venuti, L. 166, 167
Via, J. 88
Volz, P. 200-202, 204

Wacker, M.-T. 208
Wahlberg, R.C. 74, 76, 81
Walker, A. 268
Waltke, B.K. 270
Washington, H.C. 194, 195, 206
Weber, M. 145
Weedon, C. 159

Weems, R.J. 80, 224, 231
Weinfeld, M. 46-48
Westermann, C. 22, 31
White, H. 154
White, L.M. 112, 113
Whitelam, K. 189
Whyte, M.K. 32
Williams, D. 276
Wimbush, V.L. 182
Wire, A.C. 208, 210

Witherington, B. 91, 96
Wyatt, N. 191

Yoon, N.-r. 119, 120
Yu-Lan, F. 118

Zakovitch, Y. 193
Zimmerli, W. 22
Zimmerman, B. 136, 281
Zipes, J. 164